CHINA

A Wolf in the World?

by

George Walden

P9-DMO-330

GIBSON SQUARE
London

To Sarah

First edition published in the UK by

UK   Tel: +44 (0)20 7096 1100
        Fax: +44 (0)20 7993 2214

US   Tel: +1 646 216 9813
        Fax: +1 646 216 9488

Eire Tel: +353 (0)1 657 1057

        info@gibsonsquare.com
        www.gibsonsquare.com

        ISBN 9781906142179

INDEX

ACKNOWLEDGEMENTS

The quality, reliability and liveliness of books about China—till recently an unavoidably opaque and dismal subject—have soared with the opening up of the country. I am indebted, amongst other works, to Lydia H. Liu's *The Clash of Empires: The Invention of Modern China in Modern World Making* for its accounts of Sino-British confrontations in the early years of the nineteenth century, on which I have drawn. Michael Mandelbaum's *Democracy's Good Name* was also a mine of ideas.

I have attempted to break out a little from the Anglo-American circle. Amongst the most original, fresh and forceful accounts of contemporary China are books by French authors. These include *La Chine M'Inquiète* (*China Troubles Me*) by Jean-Luc Domenach, who has lived there since 2002. Also *L'Année du Coq* (*The Year of the Cock*) by Guy Sorman, a splendidly energetic, first-hand view of the dangers of the New China to itself and to the world, as he sees them. This furnished me with insights and material on a range of subjects, notably dissidents, Taiwan and sex. *La Chine Sera-t-elle Notre Cauchemar?* (*China—Nightmare of the Future?*) by Philippe Cohen and Luc Richard is another meaty contribution based on wide-ranging first-hand experience, and I have translated a passage with the authors' consent, for which I am grateful.

China's most powerful neighbour is of course Russia, where much is now being published. For an up-to-date Russian view I am indebted to works by A.V.Lukin, Y.S. Peskov, I.A.

Malevitch, and for detail on the Sino-Russian frontier to Akihiro Ivasita, in his book *Chetire Tisyatch Kilometrov Problem* (*Four Thousand Kilometres of Problems*). These are solid works, though it may be symptomatic of our lack of interest in the implications of the New China for the future of Russia that none of them, to my knowledge, has been translated.

I am of course indebted to a number of Chinese friends, acquaintances and interlocutors, in China and abroad, for much of what I have written.

The authors of works of reference do not get the acknowledgment they deserve, so I would like to say how useful I found Graham Hutchings' work *Modern China: a Companion to a Rising Power. China's New Rulers,* edited by Andrew J. Nathan and Bruce Gilley, was also valuable. My brief remarks on Chinese opera owe something to Elizabeth Halson's book on that subject.

INTRODUCTION

'Beyond Hyde Park all is a desert. For instance, what is the true signification of that immense mass of territory and population known by the name of China to us? An inch of pasteboard on a wooden globe, of no more account than a China orange... We measure the universe by ourselves.'[1]

William Hazlitt's remark sums up the history of Western attitudes to China over centuries. From Marco Polo through the Jesuits, and from Maoists like Jean-Paul Sartre to the Western promoters of democracy in China today, in our responses to this distant, indecipherable culture our own needs and perspectives have always been to the fore.

This book is not a catalogue of our delusions about China, something that would run to many volumes and be dispiriting to write, and to read. It records the blindness, self-indulgence and moral contortions of the past only insofar as they can help clear our heads about where the new China is going. The element of subjectivity in our reactions to such a powerful culture means that each of us has his or her China, our views a mixture of imagination and prejudice tempered by knowledge and experience. My own have been formed over forty years—though not just any forty years, as it turned out.

It happens that my first engagement with the country in the mid-'60s coincided with what we can now see as the turning point of modern Chinese history: the Cultural Revolution. It was this moment of delirium, when the country behaved like a person of unsound mind bent on self-destruction, that was to lead to a radical reaction against leftism after Mao's death in 1976, and to China's transformation today. Having lived in the country for almost three years during its period of maximum turmoil at the end of the '60s, and monitored its extraordinary evolution since on many visits, for me the change in China's fortunes is starker than for most.

My involvement with China began, paradoxically, when I was a

Russian specialist. I had studied Russian at school and at Cambridge and spent a year as a British Council-sponsored postgraduate at Moscow University in 1961-2, when the Soviet Union under Khrushchev enjoyed a limited thaw. After that I worked in the Foreign Office as a Soviet expert. By then China and Russia, the giants of the world communist movement, were showing signs of estrangement. People sensed a tectonic shift in international affairs and somebody in the FCO appears to have decided that we needed people who were acquainted with both countries and cultures. So it was that in early 1965 the Russian specialist was dispatched to learn Mandarin Chinese on an intensive two year course in Hong Kong.

The Cultural Revolution broke out half way through my course, and I just had time to finish before the violence and disorder spilled over onto the streets of the Colony. There were bombs and murderous riots, and incidents along the frontier played on British fears about invasion. When an emergency was declared I was appointed Assistant Political Adviser to the Governor, a position that involved me in my first dealings with Chinese communists. Suspected by mainland militants of having gone soft after long residence in the Colony, the local Party leaders were attempting to refurbish their revolutionary credentials by working up a climate of sedition, in which many were to be killed.

After a nerve-testing period during which the British stood firm, it became clear that for all its dire threats in support of the rioters the Chinese government (or at least the less demented part of it, represented in our case, we had reason to believe, by the Prime Minister Zhou Enlai), did not intend to take the Colony over. The economic cost to China would have been too great, not to speak of the signal such a move might have sent to Taiwan, and the pre-emptive response it might have provoked.

There followed secret talks with local communist leaders. Ostensibly their purpose was to arrange for an exchange of prison visits (we had arrested hundreds of rioters and bombers and the Chinese had picked up the Reuters correspondent in Beijing, Anthony Grey, as a hostage). In fact the talks were also about measures to control the crisis. The negotiations were two a side, with my boss Anthony Elliot, the Political Adviser, leading for us and myself as assistant. To ensure secrecy and to save the communists' face they were conducted in a private back room of a restaurant in the Wanchai district run by mainland sympathizers.

I do not know what the personal demeanor of the local communist bosses we dealt with had been before the riots. But now, with their giant Mao badges, venomous manner and palpable resentments against the British, these were deeply unpleasant people. The three years I was subsequently to spend in Beijing during the Cultural Revolution, and the brutalities and inanities I witnessed, added to my distaste for the Mao regime.

It would be absurd to pretend that our views of a country are not influenced by first contacts. My two years in Hong Kong had been enthralling, and I had made many Chinese friends. On the mainland I was confronted by people who, though ethnically identical, appeared to come from a different civilization, behaving as if they had been stripped of every positive faculty the Chinese have to offer. Of course there had been variations in the political atmosphere since Mao had come to power in 1949. All I can say is that in the communist China I saw there was scant sign of the resourcefulness, eagerness to learn and adapt, productive energy, courtesy, delicacy and aesthetic sensibility for which the Chinese can be renowned. Instead there was mass credulity, brutality, chauvinism, ugliness, mendacity, a gang mentality, violence.

One of the themes I shall pursue in this book is the causative connection between the failure of the Cultural Revolution and the China we see today. In this post-communist age it is perhaps necessary to recall briefly just what the Cultural Revolution was about. The most concise description I have seen is by Graham Hutchings, a sinologist and foreign correspondent:

The 'Great Proletarian Cultural Revolution', a cataclysmic movement launched by Mao Zedong, was not particularly proletarian and was about culture largely in the sense that it sought to destroy much of what existed. But it was truly revolutionary because it toppled many of Mao's comrades and destroyed the institutional basis of Communist Party rule. It also marked a departure from the norms of civilized behaviour, producing cruelty and oppression on an horrific scale. Millions of Chinese suffered; many behaved pitifully and disgracefully. Nearly forty years after it broke out, the movement continues to stain the Party and nation that gave birth to it.[2]

The roots of the movement lay in a paradox. By the mid-'60s China was beginning to recover from the famine and disasters produced by the Great Leap Forward of 1958. But the recovery was happening because economic pragmatism (and especially material incentives to workers and peasants) were gradually taking the place of ideology, despite endless campaigns designed to reinvigorate Maoist thinking. At the same time Mao himself was haunted by the progress of 'goulash communism' in the Soviet Union. This was the strategy of securing stability and popular support by going easy on dogma and indoctrination and concentrating on raising living standards. Goulash came into it because of the policy of semi-appeasement adopted by Khrushchev following the bloody anti-communist uprising in Hungary in 1956.

The paradox is that Mao saw that the country was recovering—and quickly resolved to send this recovery into reverse. In 1966 the aim of the seventy year old Chairman was to prevent the dilution of his revolutionary gains and a return of the 'bourgeoisie' by a frontal attack on what he saw as 'rightist' members of his own Party. To accomplish this he exploited his quasi-divine status to unleash the 'masses' onto Party and Government personnel. The greatest and bloodiest of all purges in the history of the international communist movement was to be carried out not behind the scenes, but on the streets. In reality of course 'the masses' were manipulated by Mao's leftist lieutenants in the Party, such as Lin Biao, the army boss, Chen Boda his ideological chief, and his own fearsome wife Jiang Qing.

It was because he wanted not only a change of personnel but a re-radicalization of the Party that Mao's assault began in the cultural domain, with an attack on a play, *The Dismissal of Hai Rui* by Wu Han. Hai Rui was a model official of the Ming dynasty who openly criticized the Emperor. The implied analogy was with the former defence minister, Peng Dehuai, who had courageously questioned Mao's policies during the Great Leap Forward.

The main targets of the revolution were Liu Shaoqi and Deng Xiaoping. Formerly Liu was being groomed as Mao's successor; now he was denounced as a capitalist traitor. Publicly humiliated and physically tormented, he was imprisoned and died in 1969. Deng, who held what Mao saw as intolerably pragmatist economic views, was persecuted and imprisoned. Fortunately for China he survived to accomplish in practice what Mao had rhetorically accused him of doing: leading a counter-revolution that paved the way for a return of market economics, albeit under Party control.

One of the deadliest aspects of the revolution was that by attacking the Party and government apparatus itself, it created a kind of official anarchism. In areas remote from Beijing especially, this was used to legitimize the violent settling of grievances by bureaucratic, personal or ethnic enemies. The results included everything from the lynching of individuals to local armed conflicts. In one place (Guangxi province) there were reports of instances of a resurgence of cannibalism. The revolution also played on nationalist emotions to produce a climate of hysterical chauvinism and paranoia towards both the capitalist and socialist camps, in which Mao's sole allies were in the end the small, ugly, leftover Stalinist dictatorships of Albania and North Korea. In effect it was China versus the world.

The Cultural Revolution not only produced a lamentable impression on those who witnessed it close to; it left a residue of scepticism about the nature of Chinese power and the malleability of the Chinese people. Watching the mass parades, or seeing the ready response to anti-foreign propaganda—sullen hostility was the best we could hope for in streets, shops or restaurants—could only reinforce the impression that Mao had achieved his collectivist goal, and that under his rule the Chinese nation had congealed into a single homogenous mass.

It is not easy to shake off the memory of the semi-crazed faces and chants of Maoist marchers, the transformation of millions of human beings into malignant-eyed robots. Had I not had experience of overseas Chinese it would have been hard to escape the conclusion that the individual had no meaning in this culture. Outside North Korea it was difficult to imagine an entire people behaving in such a zombie manner, of the human personality being reduced to nothing.

The functionaries we dealt with were the worst. I was later to spend more years dealing with communist bureaucrats in Soviet Russia, an

unappealing human type, though as fanatics, liars, chauvinists, bullies
and paranoid fantasists they had nothing on some of their Chinese
comrades of the time.

And yet there was a comic side. Were the results for the Chinese not
so tragic it would be easy to write off much of the Cultural Revolution
as burlesque propaganda. One example. I am the possessor of a wax
mango, bought in Beijing in 1968, whose origin is as surreal as its design:
beautifully modelled, it could be mistaken for the genuine thing except
that, the Chinese being unfamiliar with mangoes at the time, pips rattle
when you shake it.

The reason I bought it was that 1968 was the height of Mao
Zedong's personality cult, and after a series of weird occurrences the
mango had become his symbol. In August of that year the Foreign
Minister of Pakistan, one of the few countries maintaining civil relations
with China, visited Beijing and presented Mao with several boxes of
mangoes. Mao asked his bodyguard to distribute them to workers who
had recently occupied the Qing Hua University campus, in an attempt to
unify warring Maoist factions. Students were killing and maiming one
another with home made spears and guns; I saw a demonstration in
front of the Public Security Bureau in which a dead student was being
carried on a block of ice.

When the workers left the campus a mango was presented to each of
their factories in recognition of their efforts. Since Mao's refusal to eat
them was seen as a personal sacrifice to the proletariat, attempts were
made to preserve the sanctified fruits as relics by placing them in
formaldehyde and displaying them as shrines. Workers filed past,
bowing. At the Beijing Textile Factory the fruit rotted beneath a wax
coating. It was peeled and boiled and workers filed by to drink a
spoonful of the water.

Similar scenes occurred throughout China as facsimile mangoes
toured the country in 'Mango Trucks'. As well as being treated as a
sacred relic there was popular interest in what a mango looked like. In a
town in Sichuan province Dr Han, a dentist, was heard to remark that
the fruit was nothing special, and resembled a sweet potato. He was
arrested as a counter-revolutionary and paraded through the streets on
the back of a lorry before being taken outside the town and killed with

a single shot to the head.[3]

My memories of that China have mellowed in the course of many visits since, as a diplomat, an MP, an education minister, a journalist, a writer and a tourist. But they have not wholly disappeared. My view of China has not been poisoned by what I saw, though my experiences make me alert to any echoes of that era in the country's current behaviour. Just as I marvel at the contrast between the smiling, snappily-dressed, confident-looking Chinese women on the streets of Beijing today, and the hate-filled harridans of forty years ago, so I confess to a tremor of recognition when I hear Chinese politicians in suits and ties slipping into chauvinist rhetoric or threatening language towards dissidents or Tibetans.

In this book I nevertheless endeavour to approach the future in an even-minded way. As the question-mark suggests, the title does not prejudge the issue, and the word wolf is used in a particular way. It was inspired by a best-selling Chinese novel, *Wolf Totem* by Jiang Rong. He is a democrat whose message nevertheless appears to be that the Chinese must become less sheep-like and rather more wolfish, in the sense of ceasing to behave like faceless masses and of asserting themselves fearlessly in the world.

This book begins by looking back at the excesses of the Cultural Revolution, and at the illusions of many people about it. Partly this is because I happened to be there, though mainly because, as we are rapidly coming to see, it was a milestone not just in Chinese but—as modern China goes global—world history. The paths they took were different, but the China we see today sprang from the catastrophe of the Cultural Revolution as surely as modern Europe was shaped by the defeat of Hitler. And just as China can never be a society based on justice until the truth about Mao Zedong has been fully told and acknowledged, the West will never know what to expect from the new China until we understand the roots of our mistakes about the old. It is time to look at China as she is, not as we wish or fancy her to be, even for the best of reasons. Only then will we be prepared for her irruption into the world.

Having seen China at her worst makes me more than usually alert to the possible dangers ahead. Will a country evolving in a positive direction revert under domestic stress to nationalism and reaction? Or will wealth and international status make China a more contented power? Such questions, it hardly needs to be said, are of global import. Yet how are we to know which way things will go? Nothing on the scale of what is happening in China has happened in the history of humanity. All the more reason to be prepared for every eventuality. I am by no means prophesying war. What I am sure of is that if we decline to learn the lessons of the past, notably about our own misperceptions of China and its civilization, how they arose and why they still persist, the chances of conflict in some form will be increased.

THREE YEARS THAT CHANGED THE WORLD

1

'Remember old bitterness.'
Mao Zedong

In Shanghai recently, alone in the street for a few minutes while my wife was in shop, I was propositioned. In today's China this is no big deal, nor is the service reserved for foreigners. Hotels used by ordinary Chinese swarm with prostitutes, not to speak of clubs and bars. I mention the incident because, to a veteran of the Cultural Revolution whose first image of China was one of virulent chauvinism and a pathological Puritanism, the idea of a pretty young woman approaching you in the street with a smile was still a little surreal. Not far from the Bund, the old colonial quarter facing the river, three girls were at work under an arcade, and such is the force of custom that for a second the sight of them in a Chinese street made you feel priggish. Till you remembered that, regrettable as it was to see women selling themselves in public, here was a country that catered, like any other, for human fallibility.

At least they looked friendly, these young whores, chattering and laughing and smoking away. Forty years earlier the sight of a long-nosed imperialist brazenly walking their streets risked putting women their age in a state of ideological frenzy. They would follow me with disgusted eyes, maybe spit some venomous slogan as I passed. Now, instead of being balled out as an imperialist or revisionist swine (sometimes the Red Guards mistook you for a Russian), at three-thirty in the afternoon I was cheerfully accosted. Minutes later a police car appeared, and the girls scampered off.

Who were the women who stared at me with hostile faces forty years ago, and who were the hookers grinning and cajoling me now? Socially speaking they were probably the same people, from similar rural backgrounds. In the late '60s young people from the provinces wandered the country 'making revolution', which is to say sight-seeing, marching in demonstrations, loafing about, smashing up old temples, taking part in lynchings and 'struggle meetings', or beating up people whom someone had taken into their heads to denounce as anti-Maoist.

But in those days the traffic between town and village was two-way. While crusading provincials crowded the cities to no purpose, 'bourgeois' students and cadres were dispatched from town to deepest countryside to sanitize their thinking by humping night-soil or cleaning out pigsties. Seeing little future in that, most of them escaped back to the towns as soon as the political situation allowed. Mao had his despot's reasons for re-familiarizing townees with peasant life, of which they had a horror, but a stint in a godforsaken, poverty-stricken village in the middle of nowhere usually meant that their horror grew. The only lasting benefit appears to have been to literature, where the tribulations of rusticated intellectuals, and occasionally claims of increased wisdom through contact with the peasantry, are frequent themes.

I have seen the Red Guards compared in the West to adolescent pop fans on the rampage, but it wasn't music that had got them going, nor was it drink or drugs. It was hate: hate, and the nihilism of violence. Years later, when people who had participated in all this viciousness and cruelty at such a young age were asked in a survey why they had done it, only a few replied that it was out ideological passion and devotion to Mao, or because they were forced to. Most said they beat people up because it was all right to do so, and because they enjoyed it.[1]

Another pastime for youngsters on their revolutionary *hajj* was gawking at Red Guard posters pasted on walls around the city ferociously denouncing someone or other. At the time it was important for foreign missions to know who was for the chop, as an indication of which way the revolution was tending, and I spent a lot of time standing amongst them, ten deep sometimes before an especially juicy or informative series. Many were ruddy-faced teenagers who had been sleeping rough and didn't smell too good.

As I quickly discovered as we peered at the latest bulletins slashed in black paint on pink paper, by no means all of the youngsters from the provinces could read. (This was before the Cultural Revolution took a brutally chauvinist turn; people let me copy out posters because they still assumed that the handful of foreigners in the capital were Albanian comrades or other 'friends of China'.) Fortunately my Chinese course in Hong Kong had included training in recognizing the cursive script and 'grass writing' which can collapse stately, square-jawed Chinese characters into a scarcely legible shorthand squiggle. All that apparently pointless effort now paid dividends: my proudest moments were when, seeing that I was a few years older than him, a young bumpkin would point to a phrase and say 'What does that mean, comrade?' I would explain that it meant cut off Deng Xiaoping's stinking revisionist head, or some such, and his face would dissolve into a vacant, faraway look as he exclaimed, as though in deep comprehension, 'ahh...'

But that was then. Today the raw-looking, poorly educated men and women who can be seen exiting from mainline railway terminals with their slender baggage are in town for more pragmatic reasons: they are coming for work, and in some cases, survival. The girls hawking themselves in Shanghai were in all probability three in a tide of an estimated 200,000,000—a sixth of the Chinese population and nearly four times that of Britain—who have abandoned the countryside and roam the towns in search of jobs. The males amongst these *gongmin*— itinerant workers—find it easier to be taken on, mainly in the booming construction industry, even if the pay is a paltry £15 a week.

For women it can be harder: many who can't find jobs in the factories or service sector gravitate into girly bars or prostitution. Others end up there after abandoning the struggle to live on the derisory wages unskilled women can be paid. Stories of how indigent young peasant mothers go to towns, leaving children with grandparents, and after failing to find work resort to prostitution to send back remittances for their education, while disguising the source of the money, are part of the true-life Victorian melodrama produced by the greatest displacement of population history has seen.

After all those years of enforced self-control sex has become a major industry. As in the rest of the world, the primary use of the Internet in China is for sex or games, something the regime may deplore but does little to discourage. Absorption in pornography and the proliferation of prostitution may be unedifying and against Chinese traditions of public chastity, yet from the regime's viewpoint it is preferable to an unhealthy interest in politics. As readers of the mammoth seventeenth century novel *Dream of the Red Chamber* know (the original has 4000 pages and a plot involving 400 characters) the country has a healthy erotic tradition, though sexual prudishness predated the communist revolution. There would be more evidence of the extravagance and sophistication of Chinese erotica extant today had not the Emperor Kangxi (1655-1723), a mixture of aesthete and Puritan, destroyed whatever traces he could find.

Historically sex in China, as in Britain, has its hypocritical side. While chasteness was prescribed for ordinary people, the Chinese upper classes, as ever, felt themselves exempt, and in communist times Mao Zedong exerted himself in the maintenance of this tradition. (According to one of his doctors his preference appears to have been for virgins.) As the Chinese saying goes, the rich can burn down houses while the poor are not even allowed to light lamps.

During the Cultural Revolution official Puritanism reached a zealous peak. Posters denounced alleged anti-Maoists for, amongst other things, 'yellow' (indecent) practices, which so far as it might be true at all meant a partiality for harmless novels. Just as we worry about the mental balance of Saudi youths brought up on a God-struck, sex-free diet, it was hardly fanciful to see in the fanaticism and ferocity of the Red Guards a reflection of their frustration in other fields. Kissing their girlfriends or boyfriends (had they been allowed to have them, or to kiss in public) would have been a more natural, and more productive, way to spend their time.

In one way however the regime inadvertently encouraged sexual excess. During a visit I made in the '80s to China as Minister for Higher Education, the Chinese Education Minister explained to me that he was obliged to run two schools in one building because the population explosion had left him with fifty million more children to handle. When I raised an eyebrow he looked surprised in turn: 'You were here during the Cultural Revolution. You saw the closed factories and the people 'making revolution'. What do you think they were doing when they weren't marching about? Playing cards and sleeping with their wives.' In this period at least Mao's puritanical revolution seems to have had the same results as an extended brown-out in New York City.

Even after the Cultural Revolution was over a measure of sexual repression continued. In the '80s an announcement on a prison notice board in Sichuan province described the crime of a new prisoner:

> Lu, male, 25 years. Held private parties and danced cheek to cheek in the dark, forcefully hugging his female dance partners and touching their breasts. Seduced a total of six young women and choreographed a sexually titillating dance that spread like wildfire and caused serious levels of Spiritual Pollution. Execution imminent.[2]

Today Chinese sexual habits are evolving, fast, in a libertarian direction. Anti-vice laws have become far more lax. In Chinese hotels notices prohibit prostitution, betting and drugs, but many are hives of all three, with an endless supply of inexpensive *mingong* girls volunteering, or being driven, to sell themselves. This reversal of Maoist primness seems unlikely to be motivated by an attachment to individual liberties. The flourishing of prostitution in China—Hong Kong can seem tame by contrast—is remarkable and explained by many factors. First there is the abrupt release from much of the former system of control and surveillance of people's daily lives. Then there is the desperation of *mingong* girls. One-child families, a policy which leads to a shortage of women as girls are aborted, also feed demand. And finally there is the moral vacuum the collapse of Maoism brought in its wake, and the cynical pursuit of profits it has helped induce.

The doyen of Chinese sexologists (the discipline, though expanding, scarcely exists) Pan Xuming has investigated the phenomenon. His results support the theory of official tolerance bordering on connivance. Technically prostitution is outlawed, yet fines are so modest they act less as a deterrent than as a means of monitoring the trade, like a pimp's payoff. Corruption amongst Party and government officials and the police is rife, to the point where even the different levels of demand are semi-officially regulated: concubines for Taiwanese entrepreneurs, high-class call girls for Americans, Europeans and Japanese, and peasant girls for itinerant workers.

Then there are the students who, short of funds to pay for their courses, are ready to sleep with up-market clients. The phenomenon is not unknown in the West, but in China it is redolent of a new amorality.

As one girl told Pan sardonically: 'I am contributing to national development without consuming oil, which is rare in China, and without contributing to our pollution problem.'[3]

There are limits to the Chinese Communist Party's broadmindedness. An article in *The People's Daily* in 2005 took solemn exception to the news that 95 per cent of cadres found guilty of corruption had mistresses. It was pleased to announce that in one town the local government had taken the initiative in establishing a register of extra-marital relationships. '*Always more creative in the struggle against corruption*', ran the headline that will have ruined many a top cadre's day.

*

The girls seeking my custom in Shanghai were dressed as you would expect: in the high-skirt, low neckline combination in fashion amongst fast young women their age across the capitals of the world. Of their make-up there is no need to speak: let's say their faces were another splash of colour in an already cheerfully garish city, with its flashy commercialism and its firmament of phosphorescence in the adverts arcading the streets at night. The contrast with the dour old days of the late '60s is so stark as to lead you to wonder how this can be the same country, the same people? In Maoists times it used to be fashionable for Westerners to praise China for its asceticism, by comparison with the decadent West. Except on propaganda posters I do not recall any signs of ordinary Chinese glorying in the poverty of their lives—by contrast with their well-fed, smartly clothed Hong Kong brothers and sisters they seemed pretty morose to me—but then for Western admirers of a Spartan existence for the Chinese (if not for themselves) the feelings of those with no choice but to endure it were of little account.

The reason Beijing was the most dismal big city in the world at the time (discounting Pyongyang in North Korea) was not just the hard-pinched lives of its citizens, or its soul-curdling Stalinist buildings emblazoned with slavish slogans ('*Study Chairman Mao's writings, follow his teachings and act according to his instructions*' said one quoting Lin Piao, his defence minister and closest comrade-in-arms, later to die in an attempt to flee the country). What really depressed the place was the uniform way people dressed, and in particular its studiously uglified women. One of the greatest conurbations in the world teemed with frumps and scarecrows of all ages, classes and conditions. In the unisex miserabilism of the time colour and form were equally absent. Women's clothes were in regimental dark blue or khaki, and the only colour you saw on millions of sallow, disgruntled faces was when the winter cold rouged their cheeks.

Like everything else in their lives fashion was dictated by the Chinese Communist Party (CCP), and at the time the fashion for women, so rigorously self-policed I do not recall seeing any deviation, was to look as unfeminine as they possibly could. Skirts, frocks, blouses or jumpers, tolerated before, were out. For women the options were the same as for men: short jacket (quilted in winter) and trousers (baggy all year round) in matching blue or khaki.

In Cultural Revolutionary China, where class insignia were as taboo as the display of secondary sexual characteristics, being a fully uniformed member of 'the masses' had its advantages. On the daughters of non-proletarian families likely to be harassed or worse if they stood out in the crowd, the style-free apparel was a handy disguise: a woman dressed in a drab and dirty plebeian suit of thick blue cotton could not so easily be identified as a bourgeois renegade, a Chiang Kai shek agent, an imperialist spy or a capitalist turtle's egg.

When the revolution began in 1966 girls in Beijing who didn't already wear regulation outfits climbed into them, chopped off their plaits and tied up the stubs in brown elastic bands. Suitably de-sexed (in padded winter, everyone looked like Michelin men) they donned their khaki caps, strapped on their *hong wei bing* (Red Guard) armbands, and marched about chanting their love for the Chairman and death to his enemies, like shrieking harpies. Often the only way of telling them from the men was that, while both could behave like political hysterics, the women screamed their slogans and abuse in a higher octave. This helped give the impression that, when it came to Mao mania, the women could be the worst. The subsequent claim that many were merely taking a rare opportunity to vent anger against a male-dominated world is by definition not subject to proof.

One of the ripostes made by Maoist sympathizers in the West to those who believe the Chairman was a bloody tyrant is that the Chinese people genuinely loved their leader. In many cases this was incontrovertibly true. The near orgasmic states I witnessed in men and women's eyes and detected in their voices as they screeched their worship for the Great Helmsman were not necessarily feigned, yet their sincerity proves nothing. Many a Russian cried when Stalin died, just as in the Second World War many a German fought to the last in defence of the Führer. This tells us little about the loveable qualities of these despots, or their achievements, though much about the human condition.

It is strange that we continue to be surprised by such behaviour. Love of slavery is nothing new. Already in the sixteenth century Etienne de la Boétie told us in his *Discourse on Voluntary Servitude* how people can come to bask in their bondage, though it was Montesquieu who in the early eighteenth century put it in terms most applicable to Mao's austere rule:

> The less we can satisfy our individual passions, the more we give ourselves up to passions of a general order. Why do monks so love their order? Their love comes from the same thing that makes this order intolerable to them. Their rule deprives them of everything upon which ordinary passions rest. What remains, therefore, is the passion for the very rule that afflicts them.[4]

Deprived of normal outlets for their emotions, sexuality and ambitions the Chinese under Mao lived a monkish life, though few monks have endured what they suffered. For the twenty-seven years of his rule they were plagued by purges, a militarized existence, the most intense indoctrination the world has seen, hunger and avoidable deaths that ran into the tens of millions. Yet many continued to revere the Great Helmsman.

The Cultural Revolution was more than another campaign aimed at turning a billion people into mechanized instruments of his will: it was an attempt to render them immune to the revisionist virus that was gaining ground in Soviet Russia once and for all by stamping out the human personality altogether, to empty their heads and hearts of everything except Mao Zedong's Thought. Amongst other affronts and indignities this involved abolishing their family and sexual affections, which on a mundane level meant stripping them of all grace or distinction, however humble.

But whatever the historical conditioning Confucianism has wrought in them, and their popular image in the outside world, and whatever Mao Zedong wanted to make of them, the Chinese are not mindless automata. So it was that young mothers, denied the right to wear even the simplest clothes, such as blouses, drew the line at uglifying their children. Although meanly dressed by our consumerist standards, small infants could sometimes be spotted in prettified smocks or bonnets. Even some of the Michelin women found ways to give themselves a certain allure. It isn't so much your clothes, we all know, it's the way you wear them, and as the revolution advanced there were girls who contrived to impart to their militarized get-up a certain modish swagger.

For this they had a model at the top: Mao's wife Jiang Qing, former actress and leader of the ultra-leftist Gang of Four. Once I had a glimpse of her on the podium at a rally, looking stagily combative in army cape and kepi, for all the world like a Chinese Vanessa Redgrave playing a revolutionary heroine. (It was Jiang Qing who was later to seek to establish a 'national costume' for women, consisting of a collarless top and three-quarter length pleated skirt, after feeling under-dressed following a meeting with Imelda Marcos in 1974. She appears, after all, to have been a creature of fashion.)

Then, at the end of the three worst years of revolution, came a moment when you sensed an unspoken feeling spreading (who dared say it, or think it?) that the entire vicious, destructive farce had reached an apogee of senselessness and run its course. Perturbed by economic losses, and even more by their isolation in the world—exposed in the near-war with Soviet Russia in Spring 1969—the Party began to emphasize in subtly coded propaganda the need to pay attention to production as well as to 'making revolution'. Simultaneously the radio, TV and public loudspeakers became marginally less manic. Though nothing was said about a formal end to the mayhem, people began to hope that the worst was over.

The first sure sign I remember that the revolution was on the wane was in the appearance of women. Inhabitants of totalitarian countries—

especially communist China with its history of violent campaigns interspersed with calm—become good at sniffing the wind. So it was that the zombified women of Beijing somehow decided the time had come to reassert their feminism by degrees. A sudden brightening of their clothes would have been perilously premature, and a resort to makeup out of the question. Instead the girls did what they could where you would most expect it: in their hair. Chopped-off plaits or tresses do not re-grow overnight, and it would be going too far to prettify themselves with combs or decoration. But the women found a way. Almost overnight the heavy brown bands on the plait stubs disappeared and were replaced by lighter, different coloured elastic.

That was the beginning. After a while even more of the khaki caps they affected began to be worn at a rakish angle, or be dispensed with altogether to reveal longer hair. Meanwhile military-style belts imperceptibly tightened. A month or so later here and there blouses began to reappear. Final proof of the country's re-sexualisation came when a colleague at the British Mission reported seeing a chalk outline of a woman—nothing more—on a pathway in a park. After years of unhealthy repression the Chinese male had made it back to cave-man level.

It was to take time for daubs of rouge to appear on virtuously pallid cheeks, let alone lipstick, and it was 1975 before it was possible to wear a skirt. But China is a country of infinite nuance, hair-styles have a talismanic value, and once they began changing other things began changing too, though it was only in 1976, the year that Mao Zedong died, that the ten ruinous years the Cultural Revolution had lasted came to a final end.

The reason Mao Zedong had launched it was to temper the nation's socialist soul, to the point where the 1949 communist revolution could only go endlessly forward, never back. A glance at any large city in China today and at the mores of its citizens is enough to reveal both the totality of his failure and the strength of the reaction. In a people the Chairman had sought utterly to dehumanize humanity is back with a vengeance.

*

On another of my visits to Beijing not long ago four young Chinese stopped me in the street. Instinctively I was on my guard: being accosted by a group their age during the Cultural Revolution usually meant trouble. Their purpose would have been to remonstrate, forcibly, about some piece of presumed disrespect towards China or Chairman Mao, to accuse me of being an imperialist spy because I had been reading a wall poster, or of genocidal impulses towards the Chinese people after some wobbly cyclist had brushed against my car. However trivial the incident it would often balloon into a set-piece confrontation between East and West. As they screamed abuse I would seek to confound them by manufacturing a quotation from the Chairman to the effect that foreigners who are guests of the Chinese Government should be treated politely.

Invoking the great name sometimes worked, and you could slip away. At others it didn't. When detained by 'the masses' the firsts thing you learned was to stand up for yourself. As a twenty-seven year old I quite enjoyed the slanging matches between 'the Chinese people' and her Majesty's Second Secretary at what remained of the British Mission in Beijing, burned down by Maoist yobs like these in August 1967. Physically you were on your own, but despite the fists brandished within inches of your face and the ugly, xenophobic expressions, by and large they stopped short of beating you up. Their aim was usually to humiliate rather than lynch you, and you felt a strong compulsion to deny them the satisfaction. Face is no Chinese monopoly.

As the confrontation continued hundreds of poisoned-eyed gawkers would assemble around us. The Chinese in the late '60s needed little encouragement to display animosity towards foreigners, though the Party ensured they got plenty. The exchanges would continue, with hostile contributions from the crowd, till interrupted by a policeman. On his mettle to showcase his revolutionary ardour, the scarcely uniformed officer (he would be dressed in khaki drab) would insist I apologize to the Chinese nation for whatever it was I had done (the apology was more important than the offence). I would refuse, but protestations of innocence would not affect the outcome. Like the annals of the Court of Beijing, which recorded the British eighteenth century envoy Lord Macartney as kowtowing to the Qianlong Emperor when he hadn't, simply because it was unthinkable that he shouldn't, the policeman would find words to imply that I had humbly confessed my guilt. For communists as for imperial China there are facts, and there are superior truths that transcend them.

I could have challenged his verdict and prolonged the confrontation, but bored after an hour or more of operatics, I would shake my head and let it pass. If kicking a lone foreigner around like a tin can in the streets made the masses feel good, bully for the masses; the British had kicked the Chinese around enough in the past. As I made for my car the policeman would hasten to disperse the swelling crowd; authority was beginning to grow nervous of spontaneous gatherings.

Thirty years later the youths and girls who waylaid me (there were two of each) showed no ill intent. In fact I was struck by the friendliness of their expressions. The writer Pankaj Mishra has said that on the faces of the older generation of Chinese, who have lived through wars, revolution, and Mao, 'a cruel history has written a kind of grace.'[5] Such faces are everywhere to be seen in today's China, a point of calm amidst the acquisitive frenzy.

The faces of the younger generation, whose parents must talk to them about the Cultural Revolution as ours did to us about the war, have a distinctive expression too, which is new in recent Chinese history. They may not have seen Mao at his worst or lived under him at all. Instead they have experienced a surge of prosperity and the rapid opening-up of their country, and the optimism is palpable. It was there in the youngsters who had stopped me. There was an eagerness about them, an exuberant, freshly un-caged look you see on many Chinese urban faces today.

All they wanted, it turned out, was to talk English. To show I knew something of the country, as we chatted I slipped in a few Chinese phrases. They asked when I had lived there, I told them during the Cultural Revolution, and away they went. It wasn't Mao who'd done it, said one of the girls, speaking Mandarin now and addressing the others: it was bad people misinterpreting his commands. Well there must have been an awful lot of bad people around one of the boys said, grinning, though with a trace of nervousness. Freedom of speech in China is greater than at any time for over half a century, but has not reached the point of publicly questioning the bona fides of the Chairman, even though statues and posters of him are rare. His name is synonymous with the recent history of the country, and if the Communist Party rejected him totally their legitimacy, such as it is, would collapse.

As they argued between themselves I refrained from interpolating my view. These were educated youngsters, and sometime in their lives they would read Jung Chang's *Mao: The Unknown Story* (I had noticed her bestseller *Wild Swans* in Chinese bookshops, though the Mao biography is banned), and their last illusions about him and his era would be shattered.[6] One day it will be necessary, as a Frenchman has written, for ordinary Chinese 'to take old photos out of cupboards, and let the dead speak. Dead from what? Dead for what?' When it happens the result could be that the moral wasteland the Cultural Revolution left in its wake will be greater than before, but like Nazism and post-war Germany, or racism in South Africa, there can be no future without recognition of the past.

Still, meeting those youngsters and others like them left you with an up beat feeling. There had been none of that forty years ago. The best you could hope for then was that the country would stop lashing itself into a lethal and destructive frenzy, and revert to grim normality.

*

Another time on the same trip, snatching a quick lunch in a cheap restaurant in downtown Shanghai, as the kitchen door flew open and closed I saw a group of people arguing. I couldn't understand their Shanghai dialect, but it was an unpleasant scene, in which two or three of them seemed to be browbeating a fourth, frightened-looking fellow, small and entirely bald, who looked like the cook. The tiny, aproned man seemed at bay before the suited figures as they yelled away. Again the sight triggered memories of the '60s.

The worst incident I recollect of that time is not one of the lynchings that would occur in the centre of the city, for no discernible reason, or of Red Guard victims being paraded through the streets on lorries like tumbrels, manhandled as they went, or the vicious slogans mouthed by a degraded people. It is of a group of children playing in the dust. At first I failed to understand their game. Dirty-nosed urchins with glowing cheeks and lively faces, they were from a poor quarter of the capital. It was spring 1969, and the reason I had gone to the winding *hutongs* (lanes) where they lived was to check out aerial intelligence we had received from the Americans that the Chinese were building a network of shelters and tunnels, Vietnam style, against a possible attack by Russia.

Odd as it seems, as we shall see there was a link between the urchins' game and the war psychosis that was building up. Only one thing is more vicious than a civil conflict, and that is one between proletarian brothers. Tensions with Moscow had been high ever since the launch of the Cultural Revolution. 'The New Disciples of Goebbels' was a typical headline on one of the many anti-Soviet articles in *The People's Daily*, and *Pravda* was hitting back in style. To outsiders it all appeared to be so much ideological steam—but then the lid blew off.

Suddenly there were military clashes between Soviet troops and the People's Liberation Army on Damansky Island (Zhenbaodao to the Chinese), a long-disputed part of the Sino-Soviet border on the Ussuri river. Now the tensions rose to an unprecedented pitch. Against all international expectation the frontier between the two great socialist brothers, the longest in the world, had erupted. Hastily-produced patriotic films giving the Chinese version of the incident inflamed the mood further: I went to one, but not wanting to be mistaken for a Russian as the audience worked itself into hysterics and glances my way increased, was forced to forgo the finale.

A Russo-Chinese war! The very possibility was an extraordinary thought. As we know from newly released documents, it came closer than many believed at the time. What had happened was that Chinese forces had been authorized to mount an ambush aimed at preventing real or imagined Soviet incursions along a contentious stretch of the frontier. According to Russian military reports 61 Soviet soldiers had died and some of their corpses had been mutilated. Soviet officials were in the habit of lying, even to themselves, so about the mutilation we cannot be sure. What we know for certain is that the Russians hit back smartly, and in force. Their superior artillery pounded the Chinese so hard that, in the words of Robert Gates, CIA director at the time, from American satellite pictures the Chinese side of the river bank was pockmarked like a moonscape.

All this came as a shock to the handful of Western diplomats still in Beijing at the time. The consensus had been that, whilst Mao was behaving in an unrestrained manner against his domestic opponents as he saw them—and he saw them everywhere—externally he would be prudent. For all the British 'provocation' in arresting 'Chinese compatriots' in the communist-organized riots in Hong Kong in 1967, he had not swept into the Colony as he could so easily have done. Nor, apart from ratcheting up the propaganda, had he done anything to worry the Americans overmuch in the Straits of Taiwan. Yet there he was militarily provoking the Russians. Our little circle of analysts and observers would have been even more astonished to learn that the confrontation had swiftly acquired a nuclear dimension. The Russian reinforcements that came promptly to the scene, we now know, were armed with tactical nuclear weapons.

And that was not all. 'How would the United States react if the Soviets solved one nuclear proliferation problem by attacking China's nuclear weapon facilities?' The question was put over lunch to a senior American intelligence official by Boris Davydov, a GRU (military intelligence) representative in the Soviet Embassy in Washington. The installations in question were in Lop Nor in China's North Western Xinjiang province, handily close to the Soviet frontier. It was Nikita Khrushchev—one of the biggest villains in the Chinese anti-revisionist canon—who had somewhat thoughtlessly supplied Mao with a nuclear capability under an agreement signed in 1957. At the time the Soviet leader had been threatened by domestic hardliners and needed Mao's help to bolster his position in the international communist movement. Two years later, as the dispute with China intensified, he withdrew Soviet technical personnel.

There were doubts about how far the Soviet probe was authorized, but Henry Kissinger (rightly, as it transpired) took it seriously. For all the instant attractions of having China's fairly recent nuclear potential eliminated (she had exploded her first device in 1964) he and President Nixon concluded that the risks of escalating nuclear exchanges far outweighed the gains, and declined to give Moscow the nod. 'We deplore the idea of a Soviet strike against Chinese nuclear facilities or any other

major Soviet military action', American diplomats were instructed to
respond to any probing of their position. 'A strike against Chinese
nuclear facilities would be a threat to peace'. Nixon's agreement to turn
a blind eye to Soviet action would also have been a threat to his
rapprochement with China two years later.

In the face of the overwhelming Soviet response Mao eventually
backed down, leaving some of his Politburo members concerned about
his handling of the crisis, and many a Russian general, one suspects,
dismayed by the loss of a chance to hit China where it would hurt most.
It was time to give the Mao regime a reality check and from what we
have learned since the Soviet military had been more than ready to
administer it. Mao had boasted that nuclear weapons were nothing more
than a paper tiger, but the risk of seeing his own tiger go up in flames
was no doubt one of the factors that persuaded him to back off.

*

It was at the height of the confrontation that Spring of 1969 that I had
gone to my slum in search of on-the-ground confirmation that
preparations against possible Soviet bombing of the Chinese capital
were indeed underway. The reports turned out to be true, though the
shelters I saw were highly improvised. In one place I spotted ten year old
children dragging stones from the nearby remains of the Ming-dynasty
City wall that Mao had cavalierly ordered to be demolished into their
houses for use as roofs on underground shelters in the centre of the
courtyards.

Not knowing how real the risk of a Soviet attack had become, still
less of the nuclear dimension, to me the whole thing seemed a little
theatrical, a Chinese attempt to whip up neurosis about a foreign invader
as a way of keeping up Maoist vigilance against revisionist 'traitors'.
Even more surreal, I discovered on my way back to the main road, was
the game the street children I had seen on the way here were playing. A
weedy-looking boy, of the kind that gets picked on, was grovelling in the
dirt, crying bitterly while the others shrieked at him. One of them kicked
him from time to time, desultorily. I was about to intervene—God
knows what they would have made of a six foot foreigner telling them

off—when I heard one of the girls screaming with childish malevolence at the prone, sobbing figure *women yao pi ping ni* (we're going to criticize you).

It was then that I understood: the urchins in the mud were imitating a 'struggle meeting'. In themselves such sessions were nothing new. Since Mao's early days as a revolutionary leader in Yenan there had been self-criticism meetings, psychologically tough affairs, though nothing compared with what was to come with the launch of the Cultural Revolution. Criticism meetings had now become *ad hoc* inquisitions where the victim was not just balled out, but physically 'struggled.'

The purpose was to interrogate and draw confessions from 'counter-revolutionaries', 'capitalist roaders', or merely those of insufficient faith. In reality they relied on fear and violence to force usually innocent people into confessions of imaginary sins, often as a means to settle personal scores. Lucky victims got off with a verbal assault and a beating. Others died in the collective hysteria such meetings could inspire, or by subsequent suicide. (I discuss Western reactions to this phenomenon in a postscript to this book.)

'Struggle meetings' and the fascistic behaviour they represented (I use the term in the sense of state-backed group violence against individuals) were at the heart of the Cultural Revolution, as Mao sought to browbeat into submission anyone tempted by Russian-style revisionism (i.e. an easier life), and to that extent were a factor in the Sino-Soviet conflict. The entire country had to be cajoled or if necessary physically bullied into toeing the line.

We were not allowed to attend them, but mimeographed images spread by the Red Guards of PLO soldiers with a boot on the neck of some unfortunate victim spread-eagled before the masses at struggle meetings held in the stadiums of the city came our way. Even our Soviet diplomatic colleagues in Beijing, hard men and not a few of them KGB China specialists, were appalled at what was happening. Talking to them one got some idea of the reports they must have been sending back to Moscow at the time of their confrontation on the frontier: that China was in a state of mass dementia and capable of anything.

*

There is an unacknowledged rule in life that a residue of affection exists for whatever you have been a part of, in my case the cruel and sordid events in late '60s China. For me at least these were adventurous times. I have an agreeable memory of setting out on my poster-reading, scene-observing round in my heavy-duty overcoat and fur hat on icy days, when the air seemed as bracing as the tingling political atmosphere. In the Beijing climate the sharpness and clarity of the skies and the dryness of any wind gave you an energizing shot of static electricity as you reached for the handle of your car.

Today my immediate image of Beijing is of a city under a lowering cloud of pollution. There is something eerie about the absence of sun in a cloudless summer sky, like a picture by the surrealist painter, Magritte. Instead an ash-grey pall covers everything. The ingredients are factory effluent, the smoke of antiquated coal power stations, car exhaust, and the dust of building construction. The poisoned compound they produce goes for your throat and puts out the sun. Once in a while you discern a moon-like disk skulking behind the dirty smog, and hope for a break-through, but a minute later it is gone.

Once you start focusing on pollution in China it begins to colour everything you see and do, such as taking a taxi. For a Westerner they are cheap and their drivers by and large honest. A meter produces a receipt for the average £1.50 fare, and there can be awkwardness on both sides about tipping: to offer one might seem condescending, to accept it demeaning, and there is no sign of resentment if you don't. Now that people in China are free to talk to you—it is a dismal fact that during three years in China in the '60s I never had a single civilized conversation with a Chinese, and neither could any other foreigner at the time—a chat with the driver normally ensues. When asked how I learnt Chinese and I have said my piece about the Cultural Revolution the younger drivers can scarcely believe it, while the older ones shake their heads in silent despair, or recount some tragedy or absurdity that happened to them or their family.

There is plenty of time to reminisce darkly (though Mao's name is never mentioned) because, more often than not, you are stuck in a jam and the cab is going nowhere. In summer you let down the window to release the heat, only to feel the fume-infested air doing still more terrible damage to your throat, its stink made worse by the low-quality petrol. In the '60s the petrol stank too, but there were hardly any cars to speak of, and at most we would occasionally be troubled by a burst of flying sand from the Gobi desert in the North. Now that desert is expanding by about 950 square miles a year there will be more. A third of all urban dwellers in China, I read, breathe air so toxic it is the equivalent of two packs of cigarettes a day. And the Chinese are already the world's greatest smokers.

Though Shanghai can be an improvement on the capital, on an average day the Huangpo river resembles the smog-veiled Thames of the 1870s painted by Whistler or Monet, minus the romantic glow. And if ever there was a busy river, this is it. Squadrons of ghostly barges glide silently through the yellowed water day and night, carrying aggregate, steel piping, timber, joists or other materials for the erection of yet more skyscrapers in a city whose outskirts already resemble some giant porcupine.

These tight and slightly threatening clusters of high-rises recall a line in the memoirs of Li Hongzhang, China's first foreign minister. On his first visit to New York towards the end of the nineteenth century he surveyed the skyscrapers thoughtfully, before remarking that he was in favour: their stupendous height would make them excellent places from which to pour boiling oil on enemies below. The fact that the memoirs turned out to be forged scarcely diminishes the poignancy of the observation: a good deal of Shanghai was smashed to pieces by the Japanese, and now that some of the more alarmist observers of China are predicting an eventual break-up of the country and conflict between provinces it is conceivable there could one day be more strife in the city.

'It's important to make Chinese people not blatantly imitate Western consumer habits so as not to repeat the mistakes made by the industrial development of the West over the last 300 years' said Pan Yue, deputy boss of the State Environmental Protection Administration a few years ago. To nil effect it seems. Car-wise the blatancy of the imitation is striking. It has taken China's speeded-up version of the industrial revolution only thirty years to catch up with the transport calamities we have been gestating for about a hundred. In 1994 there were a mere million vehicles in China, in 2004 16 million, today millions more. At this rate she will have 170 million private cars on the road by 2020. Most years I can be found fuming in traffic in either London, Moscow, Paris or New York, but outside Mexico City I have rarely seen jams like they make them in China, and they haven't even started. So much for not repeating our mistakes.

But there are differing views about how far they should try. 'China is in the process of industrialization for economic growth to meet the basic needs of the people and to fight against poverty. I just wonder whether it's fair to ask developing countries like China to take on binding targets,' said a Chinese spokesman at the Bali international climate conference a few years ago. The fleets of peddle-pushers I used to steer clear of when driving around Beijing would I suspect agree with that: for four out of every five Chinese customers, the car they drive is their first.

It is extraordinary to think that the climatic effects of China's transfer from two wheels to four are already global. When next I sit in a jam in Los Angeles I can persuade myself that the pall over the city is not entirely my and America's doing; an increasing proportion of California's fine particulate pollution now comes from Chinese cars. Coal used to be a bigger problem, but as some cities went over to natural gas heating in the '90s cars took over the pollution baton, and are racing for the prize of the main source of dirty air in China's cities. Wait till they have a one-child, two-car culture.

Meanwhile coal contamination is not going away. A giant pipeline due to export Russian gas down from the North, delayed for a while as the Chinese haggled over the price, is now on stream, but the costs of Russian oil and gas extraction are rising. Coal, on the other hand, remains plentiful and cheap, chiefly because of the negligible production costs compared with other countries. Miners' lives appear negligible too. 80 per cent of Chinese energy is produced by coal-burning power stations large and small, in a country where demand for electricity is rising at 15 per cent annually. In theory the large state-run mines should benefit, with improvements in the salaries and living conditions of workers, and in their safety conditions. But this does not happen.

Casualty figures are atrocious. Ten times more miners are killed in China per million tons of coal extracted than in India, thirty times more than in South Africa, and a hundred times more than in America. Conditions in private mines can be worse, and the number of fatalities overall is colossal: some 6000 miners killed in accidents in 2004 alone. (The figure for workplace accidents as a whole in China in 2005 was an incredible 127,000.) As well as economizing on safety, bad employers make further savings by ignoring government edicts to curb emissions. So while miners face horrific dangers deep in the earth, above ground their families breathe in contaminated air from some polluting local electricity station. No wonder miners, according to a friend who has toured coal-producing areas, sometimes refer to the Mao era as the good old days, and keep a picture of the Chairman.

Like so much else in today's China we read statistics about pollution with widening eyes, but the reality is beyond imagination. In Beijing the water table is going down a metre a year. Yet flamboyant water follies (a vast artificial lake and a fountain 134 metres high), not to speak of 20,000 acres of water-guzzling golf courses in the Beijing area, were constructed for the Olympics. While the fountains played and the golf courses glowed green in the Potemkin Beijing of the Games, farmers on the outskirts of the city were rationed in their consumption. The cynicism of the planners smacks of the *ancien régime*. While the people led a joyless existence the Chairman ate more than his fill and commandeered many a young woman for his pleasure—all the while preaching the chaste, frugal life.

It is not clear who is going to supply water to this thirsty megalopolis in the future, a city of about two million people in 1948 that is soon to be three times the size of London. It certainly won't be the wells and underground aquifers from which it currently sucks up 80 per cent of its supplies. There are plans for huge pipes and viaducts to bring water up from the south of the country, an extraordinarily expensive process whose effects on jealous inter-province relationships could be troublesome.

Where there is water it is increasingly unusable. China's great rivers seem cursed by man-made interference. In 1967 it wasn't just the dams that were beginning to cause problems, it was decomposing human bodies. In that year the Pearl River was contaminated by the corpses of victims of the Cultural Revolution. We know this because refugees said so, and because at one point trussed and headless torsos floated south into Hong Kong harbor. Unprintable pictures of workmen in masks fishing them from the water with boathooks, I recall, were reproduced in Hong Kong Chinese tabloids, sending a shudder through the Colony. Now it is discharges of every description that are doing the damage. Will China's rivers ever run clean again? Today the Pearl river and many another have a soupy appearance, fouled by waste water or industrial effluent. Half of China's waterways are so badly affected they can no longer be used for irrigation, let alone drinking water.

Then there are the fish. The food in China is better, more plentiful and varied than I have ever seen it. The number of restaurants has increased massively, and for all our cult of the chef the refinements they offer make Western cuisine look limited and unimaginative. I do not only mean the black toads you select from tanks, or the steamed live crickets served in tureens whose tops, for obvious reasons, must be swiftly replaced. As an amateur of the crab, in Shanghai I was recommended a specialist restaurant where I was served a highly varied five-course meal composed entirely of that crustacean.

But the pollution bug won't let you alone, and as you ponder the bloated menus sometimes you wonder about sources of supply. At a time when China has become the biggest exporter of fishery products in the world, marine water, as well as freshwater, has become horribly polluted. Hugely expanded coastal cities spill half their wastewater directly into the sea, and the number and extent of coastal fish die-offs have risen dramatically. So Chinese fishermen venture further, with the result that in the China Sea many species face complete extinction.

To suggest that China does not have a care for what she is doing is wrong. Concern for the environment is reflected in Chinese philosophy. Traditionally the 'five elements' which form the essences of nature (the equivalent of the four elements of Greek philosophy) are Air, Fire, Water, Wood and Metal. They are associated with astrology (e.g. water=Mercury, Mars=fire, Venus=copper), whose 'Great Plan' is included in the *Shu Ching*, or *Book of History*. And there it is written for modernity to see that climate change is directly related to the moral conduct of the people.

What traditional-minded Chinese will make of that today can only be imagined. Air and water are contaminated, and metal (especially copper) is in short supply, as are domestic sources of wood. Fire, on the other hand, has a bright future as the globe warms and many a forest burns. One way and another it seems as though China's astrological essences are out of joint.

But this is not the old China, when people did what they were told and kept quiet, even in their own families, no matter how disastrous or bizarre the Party line. In the late '50s the entire country hurried to obey the Chairman's whim to eliminate the country's sparrows because of the grain they ate. People were required to go about banging cymbals or gongs to force the birds to stay in the air till they weakened and died. The result was a severe disruption of the ecological balance—sparrows eat insects harmful to grain—and an eventual request to the Soviet Union, conveyed in a Top Secret telegram, for 200,000 replacement birds.

That was then. Now local victims of pollution from state-directed dam-building or chemical plants, who would never have dared raise a murmur of objection in Mao's day, have begun to demand their environmental rights. Non-governmental organizations—an oxymoron in the China of the past—with a green agenda are amongst the most active in the country. Another gleam of hope is that more research into clean coal production is carried out in China than in any other country.

But what is to be done about the driving force behind China's ecological problems—its people? Amongst the blights the Chairman inflicted on his country is one that is easily overlooked: its swollen population. As part of his strategic plan to boost the economy and make China militarily invincible by virtue of numbers (at one point he pronounced himself indifferent to the loss of half his people in a nuclear attack), he denounced birth control as 'bloodless genocide' and encouraged his over-populated, underfed nation to have as many progeny as possible. Again the nation did what it was told, and the rise was so vertiginous that in 1979, three years after Mao's death, the government was forced to swing the other way, with a one-child policy introduced in cities.

The effects on the status of children is troubling to behold. In the old days small children were the reverse of pampered. There was no shortage of them, and the disciplined poverty that ruled their parents' lives rubbed off on them. Today the change is striking. One of the most revealing images of the new China is of a father and mother strolling around parks or squares with a single, clearly over-indulged young child in tow, complete with mobile, soft drink, snazzy clothes, a fistful of toys, a whining voice and a spoilt expression.

Yet this could change. Now that the middle classes are expanding, better-off people are prepared to pay the fine for non-compliance with the one-child policy in order to have a son as well as a daughter, or simply two children. And the extra hands could be needed. Incredible as it seems the World Bank has predicted that the labour market in China was beginning to contract, and that there could be shortages within four years. Already there were many unfilled jobs in four provinces— 2,500,000 of them in Guangzhou alone, where foreign firms have taken to grumbling that they are forced to pay an average of £130 a month, including food and lodging.[8] Union activism in 2009-10 will have obliged them to pay more.

A new baby boom could help put more hands to the national economic pump, taking the population of almost 1,400,000,000 beyond one and a half billion, getting on for a quarter of the world's population. The new tens of millions will of course need flats and water and heating and cars. So the circle turns.

*

In his wonderfully imaginative book *Six Memos for a New Millennium* the Italian writer Italo Calvino set down what he thought would be the defining qualities of the new age: lightness, quickness, multiplicity, exactitude, visibility, consistency. On the first five counts the new China fits the bill. What could be lighter or swifter than her irresistible advance? Till recently there was a shambling side to the country. Propaganda images of heroically productive peasants and selfless workers were a far cry from the truth. That is why they needed the propaganda.

In reality, except during fevered campaigns, workers drifted about overmanned state enterprises with no sense of direction and little to do.

(Where such enterprises still exist, they still do.) While the regime goaded and cajoled, Party and government officials by the million and bureaucrats by the legion sipped at ever-present mugs of tea, smoked, and took their time. In shops and restaurants indolent and irascible personnel took pleasure in making the public wait.

Now, with incentives restored, the country is alight. Everyone—even bureaucrats—is impatient. As in Hong Kong, where office workers can be seen trotting to the ferry, China has speeded up. A specialized computer component ordered in Los Angeles one day arrives from a mechanized warehouse in Shenzhen two days later. Restaurant meals are served by quick-witted, willing staff, and taxi drivers are perilously pushy. The country wants flats, shops, offices, jobs, wealth and international clout, and is disinclined to let sentiment or inertia stand in its way.

Beyond political melt-down the one thing that could stop China in her tracks is the crisis over pollution. A symbol of what may be to come struck me on my last visit. A young man was buzzing noisily along the street. In the past he would have travelled by bicycle and be dressed in proletarian drab. Now he revved away at his Vespa, in sunglasses and stylish clothes. The life of many a young man in the West has become freer and easier too in recent decades, but in terms of the suddenness of his liberation and prosperity there can be no comparison with this.

In a single generation every aspect of the young man's life will have been changed, most notably the music: instead of hymns to the revolution like *The East Is Red* blaring from loudspeakers in streets and workplaces every hour of the day, *Love Me Honey Honey Love Me* or equivalent will be running through his head. And rather than his presence being forcibly required at a factory or office self-confession meeting to round off his day he will be free to spend his evenings drinking and dancing in one of many new louche locales.

The only way his life will have changed for the worse compared with his father's might be his heightened exposure to serious illness, such as cancers or emphysema. That is why instead of a crash helmet he wears, over the shades, a massive visor to deflect the dust, while the remainder of his face is swathed in a mask, against the filth and the fumes. The young roustabout has the limbs and clothes of a dandy and the head of an alien—a weird yet wholly unselfconscious sight. Unless dramatic progress is made in the battle against the poisoned atmosphere he lives in everyone will go about like that soon. Which will be no way to live.

For most of the twentieth century China suffered external aggression and civil war, then a totalitarian regime bringing purges and starvation as the price for order. Now she faces ecological pestilence. Will a country blighted by almost a hundred years of history be crushed, just as she emerges from the wreckage and pulls herself together, by this new catastrophe? I don't think so. The wonder of the modern Chinese world is not so much her industrial productivity as the revival of a spiritually moribund people. Looking at them forty years ago, an undifferentiated mass immersed in economic and moral squalor, a billion lifeless puppets mouthing ventriloquized slogans or raising clenched fists when the Party yanked the strings, there seemed only one direction the country and its people could go.

One of humanity's most radiantly creative civilizations seemed destined to be washed up on the shores of history like some giant shoal of dead-eyed fish. Its resurrection within a matter of decades into a dynamic and increasingly diversified society is a triumph of human nature. That is what gives hope that with determination and ingenuity they can triumph, not over nature, as Mao wanted to do, but over what they have done to it.

The country's handling of the earthquakes of May 2008 and the new impetus to national openness they appear to have provided are more grounds for hope. Seeing the country coming alive generates a natural urge to put the past out of mind so far as you can and to look to the kind of future the Chinese are creating for themselves—and for us. Yet before we can hope to guess where the country is ultimately heading we must begin by acknowledging how and why we so often got China wrong in the past.

2

'China offers an enchanting picture of what the whole world might become, if the laws of that Empire were to become the laws of all nations! Go to Peking! Gaze upon the mightiest of mortals! He is the true and perfect image of Heaven!'

Pierre Poivre, explorer of South East Asia, 1769

'Paul Theroux said to me that China was not so much like school, as I had suggested to him, but like the Boy Scouts, and Mao was the Chief Scout.'

Stephen Spender[1]

We should not be surprised at the difficulty we have in taking a cool, objective look at China, even today. The strain of mythology that has persisted in our view of the country since the earliest contacts will be hard to shake off. In a way we have never really taken China or its people seriously. Instead we have treated the country as a playground for our impressions, a place where the laws of logic ceased to operate and the critical intelligence fell into abeyance. China for us has always been a country of tall tales and misty sayings. From the heavily embroidered reportage of Marco Polo to fascination with the impenetrable aphorisms in Mao's *Little Red Book,* every generation has had its inscrutable and alluring East, a mysterious, inaccessible land that was a ready-made receptacle for our dreams and nightmares.

A twelfth century myth, the first of many, had it that China was the secret domain of the Christian sage Prester (preacher) John. He was thought to be an Eastern potentate, an ideal prince ruling an earthly paradise. In the letter he is said to have sent to European powers in 1165 which gained him mythological status, he described himself as 'lord of lords' and 'king of the Indies'. Considering himself divine, he addressed the rulers of the Western world as inferiors, and rumours of his identity over the years went from Persian king to Genghis Khan, and so to China.

The land he ruled was thought to be one of milk and honey, but also peace and justice, with no strife, no crime, no vice and no poor. The coincidence of this myth with the image of Mao's China in the eyes of its admirers eight centuries later is more than casual. In their praise for the simplicity, egalitarianism and purity of personal relations they claimed to have discovered in the land of Prester Mao, in contrast to our own sinful decadence and capitalist rapacity, Western visitors like the Italian writer Alberto Moravia were the latest in a long line of escapist mythologists.

Earlier we had Voltaire's excited image of the country as a place where rationalistic government was practiced in the welcome absence of pestilential priests. The Frenchman kept a portrait of Confucius in his study, much as a later generation of radicals would have a poster of Chairman Mao. What tended to be overlooked, in the eighteenth as in the twentieth century, was that the China so unreservedly admired in the West was ruled by despots who, for the purposes of their admirers, were transfigured into benign autocrats. It is easy to see how Voltaire saw things as he did. For much of the eighteenth century China flourished, and Jesuits amongst others had sent back glowing accounts. Here was a country administered by scholar officials selected for their literary qualifications and their wisdom. In other words, men much like himself. What could be more civilized, more virtuous, and more suitable for imitation?

The Chinese system of promotion in particular caught the Enlightenment imagination. Instead of being ruled by the elevation of favourites, in China a meritocratic elite held sway. An examination system had been established as early as 206 BC, and under the Tang dynasty (618-917 AD) began to be used to select government officials. The strenuousness of the procedures was legendary: during a nine-day written examination candidates frequently lived in a small cell with no room to sleep, but this was a small price to pay for the prospect of a secure and prosperous future. In terms of social promotion such procedures seemed far in advance of Europe, and were later to help inspire change for the better in Britain, when posts in the senior Civil Service were belatedly made subject to competition. In this at least the West learned something from China.

But like everything about the country, eighteenth century notions were highly impressionistic and subject to later change. The examination system seen by Voltaire as progressive is now thought to have played a part in the country's decay. The competitive approach was socially worthy, but what mattered was not the form but the content of the exams, which concentrated on the classics. Instilling Confucian virtues of duty, submission, obedience and respect for tradition did little to encourage the creative spirit, but much to underpin an autocratic empire. The parallel with the Maoist era of political indoctrination is clear enough.

In formal terms the examinations were artificial in the extreme, requiring abstruse and pointless skills. The 'eight-legged essay', so called because it was divided into eight parts, was the best example. Style alone was considered, and sentences had to be written in four and six characters alternately. The essay was only finally abolished in 1898. (There was a loose parallel with Britain, in the sense that until not all that long ago young men who had composed Latin verse at public school and at Oxbridge were deemed the best qualified to run the country, or empire, including parts of China.)

The arbitrary aspect of Voltaire's approach to China is highlighted by the fact that Montesquieu, ideologically not so distant from the sage of Ferney, took a directly contrary view. For the purposes of his book *L'Esprit des Lois (The Spirit of the Law)* he needed a colourful model of despotic government, and China, much in the news in his day, could be written up as exactly what he wanted. So it was that Voltaire's country of enlightened emperors became for him an obscurantist culture ruled by vicious autocrats. Contact with the real China being so fitful, and reliable information hard to come by, there was little to support or contradict whatever view you decided to take of it (a situation that was to be replicated in the Maoist era). On England, a country he knew something about and actually visited, Voltaire was less doctrinaire and more perceptive.

*

Unsurprisingly, the most sober voices on China often belonged to those who spent longest in the country. Usually they were nineteenth-century diplomats, military men, businessmen, scholars, journalists or missionaries. 'In no other country is education so prized, so honoured, so utilised, and so rewarded' wrote Sir Robert Hart, Director of Maritime Customs, helping to explain why in our own day Chinese immigrant pupils in Britain score higher in GCSE examinations than children of any other ethnicity, and why there are some ten times more Chinese than other nationalities in British private schools. As for their attitudes to authority, Sir Robert decided, they had been 'poured into and shaped by a mould of duty.' A dutifulness which, we might reflect, however admirable in the classroom, also appears to have prepared them for the rigours of life in a totalitarian state.

On their attitudes to the outer world, Hart was less complimentary. 'Conceited' is his word for the Chinese as a nation. Contacts with them, in his view, can never be natural: 'However friendly individuals may have appeared or been, general intercourse has all along been simply tolerated and never welcome.'[2] In exculpation of the Chinese one might say that the Western armed intrusion into China, the source of Hart's presence in the country and of his authority over Chinese people, was rarely welcome either. Yet there is little point in pretending that we do not know what he meant.

I myself have never felt truly welcome in China, not just in the crazy, chauvinist '60s but on many a visit since. Courtesy, helpfulness and efficiency can now be the norm, but that is something different. To this day the impression remains that, while foreigners are tolerated far more than they were three decades ago, and are far more deeply engaged in the country alongside Chinese in the arts or business, in contacts with authority in any of its many guises they are rarely given to feel that they are truly welcome. There is such a thing as an official Chinese expression, and its gaze on foreigners is rarely benign. It consists of a kind of arrogance mixed with resentment lightly glazed with politeness. Beneath it is not too fanciful to discern the memory of the humiliations the Chinese suffered at Western hands over centuries and a determination to compensate for the affront.

You see it on the face of soldiers, bureaucrats, diplomats, government leaders and minor officials. On Chinese businessmen it can be there too, though it is generally overlaid, naturally enough, with an acquisitive alertness. Something not dissimilar can characterize the expressions of ordinary Chinese. This is no subjective impression I have acquired: confirmation of the prevalence of an underlying frostiness towards the foreigner has come in the official recognition that something must be done to correct it. Visitors to the Olympic Games must have been interested to learn that the Beijing authorities had given instructions for Chinese to cultivate individual foreigners, the better to immerse them in an aura of friendliness. The artificiality of the procedure carries its own message.

Clearly attitudes change from generation to generation, and can be more or less pronounced, though the ingredients remain the same. Having met many official faces over several decades, in fair political weather and foul, I am left with a sense of awe before Chinese powers of adaptation. It can be disconcerting to see educated people, very like the ones who wore Mao suits and spat slogans at you when they were government officials, reincarnated in shirts and ties, beaming and doing management speak. You are reminded of the Empress Dowager at the turn of the twentieth century encouraging the Boxer insurgents to blockade and bombard Western embassies one day, and inviting heads of mission to tea the next.

Whether all this is seen as evidence of a two faced attitude, or as the wearing of separate faces for different occasions, scarcely matters. In a country where being 'Daoist in private and Confucian in public' (which translates loosely as leading an individualistic but outwardly dutiful life) is a national trait we should beware of reading too much into external behaviour. What can safely be said is that we are finally beginning to see more of the Daoist side of China, and that the change is welcome.

*

The arbitrariness of Western views of China meant that opinions could fluctuate rapidly. In the eighteenth century Europeans marvelled at reports that such civilized people existed so far away. In the nineteen hundreds, when the country was forcibly opened up, the race of men and system of government that a century before had been held up as a model for the West came to look less ideal when encountered at closer quarters. Feeling against the Chinese was especially strong when they had the effrontery to resist imperial domination. At this point the genteel *chinoiserie* of a century before could give way to coarse derision:

A Chanson for Canton

JOHN CHINAMAN a rogue is born,
The laws of truth he holds in scorn;
About as great a brute as can
Encumber the earth is JOHN CHINAMAN.
Sing Yeh, my cruel JOHN CHINAMAN;
Sing Yeo, my stubborn JOHN CHINAMAN;
Not COBDEN himself can take off the ban
By humanity laid in JOHN CHINAMAN.

With their little pig eyes and their large pig-tails,
And their diet of rats, dogs, slugs and snails,
All seems to be game to the pan
Of that nasty feeder, JOHN CHINAMAN,
Sing lie-tee, my sly JOHN CHINAMAN,
No fightee, my coward JOHN CHINAMAN:
JOHN BULL has a chance—let him, if he can,
Somewhat open the eyes *of JOHN CHINAMAN*.

One of the striking things about this racist lampoon, published in *Punch* magazine in 1858 at the time Britain was imposing the Treaty of Tianjin on China, obliging a defeated country to exchange ambassadors, permit travel and open up ports, is how little we recognize the caricature it presents today. The feelings of contempt that inspired it have largely disappeared, not to speak of the risible notion of the Chinese as a 'nasty feeder.' Whereas anti-black or anti-Muslim prejudice continues to be widespread in Western societies, except in the minds of a few right-wing American politicians (and not a few Russians), sinophobia is today a rare condition. This has something to do with our more delicate sensibilities over racial stereotypes, but the improvement in the Chinese image is also related to experience.

The experience can be both first-hand and remote. The rapid evolution of the Chinese economy and the growing freedom to travel and take part in international events are compensating for the negative popular perception of the Chinese under communism as faceless automata, the sort of people whom you would never want to meet even if you could. Meanwhile the picture of the overseas Chinese community, in America, Canada, Australia or Europe remains one of diligence, modesty, respectability, and a legendary devotion to education and to commerce. Aside from the activities of Triad gangs in Toronto and elsewhere, amongst immigrant communities the Chinese are perceived as the one least likely to cause trouble, even when they make little or no attempt at assimilation, and from whom we have most to learn. They are, to put it simply, the kind of people you would most like your children to go to school with.

*

China has always belonged to a separate realm of the Western imagination, and the contrast with Russia is instructive. In Soviet times, even when they had gone there with an open mind, journalists, diplomats, writers or businessmen came away with a distaste for the administration that could spill over into dislike of the country itself, and sometimes of its people. In this they were echoing the example of Alphonse de Custine, the French marquis who went to Russia in the eighteen thirties with the intention of using its Tsarist government as a model of enlightened autocracy, but whose famous account of his stay in *Lettres de la Russie* concluded that the regime was rotten to the core and the Russians congenital liars. In China, even under Mao, many a foreigner managed to preserve their romantic notions about the country in a way that was far more rare in the Soviet case. I never met anyone who had lived in Moscow and came home a Russophile, still less a Soviet communist. There is precious little orientalist mystique about Russia.

The list of twentieth century figures who found China a convenient outlet for their prejudices, dreams or passions is too long to recite, but a random selection gives the flavour. The novelist Alberto Moravia went there at the onset of the Cultural Revolution, of which he declared himself a supporter on the basis that Mao was ridding the country of the weight of the culture of the past, whose burden, as in Italy, had become unbearable. Unlike Italy, however, wrote the author of the *Woman of Rome*, China was not corrupted by 'excremental' consumerism: 'In other words, for me China today is a Utopia that has been achieved, perhaps involuntarily, perhaps by chance, it makes no difference.'[3] If a major writer had spoken that way of the Soviet or Nazi dictatorships he would never have been allowed to forget it. Yet few of Moravia's readers will know of these remarks today, or feel concerned at their irresponsibility, yet another reminder of how frequently China and the Chinese have been treated as a plaything of the Western mind.

The humorous side of such declarations is what strikes us today: while proclaiming the universal application of the Chairman's message Moravia failed to explain how Italians, of all people, were to be disciplined in the Maoist mode. Later, in the '70s, with the country still crippled by Mao's legacy, Tony Benn came back beaming from a ministerial visit, to assure us that 'we have a lot to learn from China.' A few years later David Hockney also went there, returning with some whimsical doodles, embarrassing when compared to Chinese masters of watercolour techniques, and even more whimsical views. Though his conclusions were less parochial than those of his travel companion, the poet Stephen Spender, whose remark about Mao's regime being 'like school' is quoted at the heading of this chapter.

It is entertaining to see how, in their reactions to China, Western countries so often conformed to stereotype. Ignoring realities, Jean-Paul Sartre saw it as a quarry for bloodless French abstractions about the New Model Man. Moravia allowed himself to play for a fashionable moment with the frivolous notion of China and Italy doing away with their respective pasts. Then comes Spender's suggestion, with that lifelong fixation on prefects and dormitories and matrons peculiar to his race and social caste, that what Clive James was more accurately to call Mao's 'abattoir of a state' reminded him of nothing so much as an English boarding school. After all, you could almost hear him adding to appreciative giggles, the slightest defiance of authority and they beat you there too.

Before them others had adopted a make-believe China as their own. Amongst them was the scientist Joseph Needham, venerated to this day for his ten-volume *Science and Civilization in China*. He was one of a generation of socialists and religious believers who were convinced that communism and Christianity could be reconciled without difficulty (a thesis famously refuted by a wit who declared that in fact they were opposites, since Christianity preached 'What's mine is thine', whereas with communism it was the other way round.) Needham's thesis was that the West had underrated China's historic contribution to science and engineering. This was undeniably the case, though his record as an uncritical defender of the regime—more than a little ingenuous when it came to politics, he was Chairman of the Society for Anglo-Chinese Understanding, a communist front organization—will always leave a question mark over the objectivity of technical judgements about science on which laymen must rely.

In particular he distinguished himself (as did Sartre) as a supporter of the 'germ warfare' campaign waged by China against America during the Korean conflict in 1952. A six-strong international scientific commission visited China and decided that bacteriological warfare by the Americans had indeed taken place. The commission in question appears to have had a high quotient of fellow-travellers, of whom Needham was one. In 1998 revelations from Russian archives confirmed what the Americans had been saying for years: that the scientists had allowed themselves to be duped. To this day sympathizers struggle to rescue Needham's reputation by seeking to prove that there was something in the allegations, and current hostility to America in Europe softens their task. Yet all the evidence suggests that the original Chinese/North Korean charges were a communist exercise in disinformation so gross that, as we have now learned from the archives, even the KGB were driven to beseech its Chinese perpetrators to go easy in propagating it.

C.P. Snow's flirtation with Soviet Russia is another example of the vulnerability of scientists to the wiles of communist regimes. As a young Russian speaker it was once my job to interpret for him at a dinner with Soviet officials to which he had been invited, and I recall my temptation to substitute something irreverent in place of his gross and oily flattery of his hosts and of Soviet achievements.

There is no reason why scientists should not have political views about this or that country, even when experience suggests they can be more exposed than others to the lure of more rationally organized societies. Though less of a fellow traveller than Needham, Snow is a useful example of how mistaken it can be to expect from men of science an objective evaluation of the 'scientific' Marxist experiment, and of their tendency to forget that the experiment was being carried out on human beings.

*

Anglo-Saxons had their myths and neuroses, and their debilitating guilt about colonialism, but in the manufacture of a hallucinatory China they were amateurs compared to the French. Voltaire had provided the precedent, and in the twentieth century it was Jean-Paul Sartre who led the pack. The French philosopher outdid other admirers of China by openly proclaiming himself a Maoist. He was seconded by his wife Simone de Beauvoir, who proclaimed after her single visit in the '50s that 'New China's Constitution renders impossible the concentration of power in one man's hands.'

As always in such cases her views told us more about herself than China. The source of her indifference to the truth (further demonstrated in her book *The Long March*) can be traced partly to her belief that there should be a closer union between philosophy and literature. Existentialist thinking, she was convinced, expressed itself sometimes in theoretical treatises and at others in fiction. On China she appears to have combined the two, and nothing in her writing suggests that she had the remotest qualms. On feminism, a subject she knew and cared about, she had more worthwhile things to say.

The fact that Sartre too took few pains to acquaint himself with the country (he went there only once, for a formal occasion) did not prevent him lecturing the world about its wonders. (America, a country he execrated but was free to visit, seemed to attract him more.) The only logic in his position as a Maoist who disdained contact with China was that knowing scarcely anything about it brought him closer to the object of his veneration, in the sense that the Chairman himself had seen nothing of life outside China beyond Moscow. So it was that two willfully blind men, the oriental dictator and his Western acolyte, remained in ignorance of each other's country, yet found much on which to agree.

In curling his lip at a world he had never set eyes on, Mao was continuing a venerable Chinese tradition: Chinese emperors too felt no compulsion to travel, or even to send envoys to discover the facts about Westerners who, like their neighbours, were treated with an absence of curiosity mixed with monumental condescension. The Chairman's lack of experience of foreign countries did not inhibit him from pronouncing on the past, present and future of a world of which he had no direct knowledge before awestruck Western statesmen whose own lives were spent criss-crossing the globe. Similarly, Sartre felt no qualms about using as a model for the perfection of the human condition a country he had barely seen, and made little effort to study.

Mao's indifference to the facts about the world outside China is of course part of a long tradition. There remains no convincing theory as to why the extraordinary voyages of discovery the Chinese eunuch admiral and explorer Zheng He made in the early fifteenth century to the East Coast of Africa amongst other places were discontinued on orders from the Chinese authorities, and never resumed by later generations. The ships were not lacking: Zheng He's central command vessels were three times the size of Nelson's Victory, and his armada immense. We know that it was the young Emperor Zhu Zhanji who forbade further exploration in the 1430s, partly through jealousy of Zhang He's renown, partly because he felt that the Middle Kingdom had nothing to learn from the outside world. The question is why later emperors never allowed China, with her proven naval abilities, to follow up these early successes.

The French, too, can be reluctant to change their ways, and while condemning Sartre's totalitarian sympathies his biographer Bernard-Henri Lévy nevertheless made an attempt to excuse them.[4] In allowing himself to become carried away with the Maoist experiment the philosopher was driven, Lévy pleads, not by mere rationality but by a passion to change the world:

Why have so many great minds said so many stupid things about the 'new man' in Cuba, or China, or the USSR? Because, at the wellspring of stupidity is passion... Because, at the source of the most sophisticated ideological choices, before the great follies, identified or not, which allow us to say of intellectuals that they made a 'mistake', we find simple feelings, which are like the breeze-blocks of their constructions and which they share with non-intellectuals on exactly the same level as the ineradicable feeling that we are seeing a sun as big as our fist. This, then, is the attraction of the new man... Why shouldn't the intellectual yield, like anyone, to this fascination with youth?

Lévy can be a brilliant writer (the same book contains wonderful passages on Sartre's relationship with the French writer Louis-Ferdinand Céline) but China has a way of bringing out the worst in people, and his exercise in exoneration is an example of the higher silliness that can afflict unusually intelligent men and women. What it comes down to is that, in their political judgements and behaviour, intellectuals can be absolved from all considerations of rationality, proportion, experience and commonsense, and hence of humanity. What matters is not China or the Chinese, Lévy is ultimately saying, but the way you feel about them.

What he fails to realize is that every sort of excess on all sides of the China question—from support for the Chairman's purification through slaughter in pursuit of the 'new man', to the countervailing urge on the extreme American Right to protect 'Western man' against the coming scourge from the East—can be validated in his own terms. All it needs is passion. And should a passion for the new and for youth happen to take the form of an unhealthy enthusiasm for the blond Teuton in his alluring uniform, with his iron discipline not totally dissimilar to that of the new Maoist man, why should the intellectual not yield to fascination with him also, as not a few reactionary French writers in the 1930s did? It cannot be objected that Sartre's passions were in a humanitarian cause, whereas the feelings of Nazi fellow travellers were racist, since both were intrinsically totalitarian, and ipso facto inhuman.

The '70s were a hey-day of French sinolatry, and in retrospect a large slice of the French intelligentsia has a lot to be ashamed of. For me once again personal memories are involved. For the middle five years of that decade, after a year at the École Nationale d'Administration (ENA), I was working at our Embassy in Paris as its specialist in French political affairs. At ENA, amongst the coming *grands fromages* of France, I found absurdly inflated notions of the importance of the Franco-Chinese relationship, such as it was, but when I began work at the Embassy there was worse to come.

One of my most vivid memories is of an evening spent at a party in a smart Left Bank apartment, where I listened with what I hope was every appearance of seriousness to the elegant fatuities about China of a group of fashionable radical thinkers. One of them (I seem to recall that it was the sociologist Edgar Morin) wore immaculate new jeans in which artificial holes had been made and sedulously patched, as if in tribute to the austerity of notional Chinese comrades. And naturally we ate in the luxurious apartment sitting on the carpet.

Writers of the statute of Roland Barthes and Jacques Lacan visited China and came back bubbling with enthusiasm, having seen nothing untoward. Maria-Antonietta Macciocchi, a China expert active in France and Italy, pronounced that after three years of disorder the Cultural Revolution would usher in a thousand years of happiness. Less sober members than Bernard-Henri Lévy of France's *nouveaux philosophes*, an eclectic group of young free-thinkers influential at the time, trumped her by describing Mao as Jesus Christ reborn and his Little Red Book as a new edition of the scriptures.

The celebrated writer Julia Kristeva also did the China run, returning with some strange impressions. As so often her claim that she personally had witnessed no violence was used to suggest that no violence had existed. But it was her book *Des Chinoises* (*About Chinese Women*) that illustrated the extent to which the Chinese played the role of puppets on the French social and political stage. It concerned two woman workers who lived together. The fact that the husband of one was not around (it is not clear whether this was because he was under arrest) was for them a liberation, allowing them freedom to become spare-time artists in the evening. On the basis of this somewhat contrived scenario Kristeva claimed that women were more liberated in Maoist China than in Europe.

For all the callowness of the conception and the absurdity of the conclusion Kristeva too is a highly intelligent woman. It is easy to dismiss her as yet another French intellectual cynic, but something worse than cynicism is at work. For writers like her, and for Sartre and de Beauvoir, China was a mental colony, where Western ideas could be played out heedless of the true lives of the inhabitants. The fantasies of French thinkers about modern China were the intellectual equivalent of the nineteenth century imperialist exploitation they so righteously denounced. Nor were their political *jeux d'esprit* harmless. By validating Maoist cruelty and oppression such people did their bit in creating an international climate of tolerance towards one of the most odious regimes in history.

*

With the rise of a freer, more prosperous China, the change in French attitudes has been radical. *Le Monde*, for years a vehicle for fashionable leftist thinking, is today playing a new tune on China, and its reception of the French translation of the biography of Mao by Jung Chang and Jon Halliday, *Mao: The Unknown Story*, was symptomatic of the change. The first line of a glowing review it carried by a former Maoist intellectual referred to the Chairman as *une ordure* (scum). Elsewhere in France the book was equally enthusiastically reviewed, more so in fact than in Britain.

Gone is revolutionary romanticism à la Malraux. Today's capitalistic Chinese Communist Party (CCP) has left the dwindling band of French Maoists in the position of jilted lovers. It was certainly time for a *prise de conscience* in a country with such a record of self-indulgence and delusion. The problem is that the shift in attitudes has frequently worked not just against Mao, but China. The biggest paradox of all in a country where they have never been lacking is that, as millions of Chinese have finally come a enjoy a higher measure of freedom and prosperity, the atmosphere in France has turned against them. Put bluntly the logic behind this change appears to be that the French have come down to earth with a bump. Whereas Maoist China served as an enthralling political and intellectual toy, a freer, thriving China carries no ideological glamour and is a threat to French jobs.

As in everything else in France the change of atmosphere on China has its anti-American dimension. Left-wing opinion is henceforth at liberty to ally itself with the protectionist Right in denouncing the nefarious effects for the French economy of China's adherence to the American creed of neo-liberalism and the global free market. Previously China's self-isolation ensured that she had virtually no international presence, and so no impact on French reality. Now that she is hyperactive in the world, the country that once fuelled Gallic mind-games has become an economic Moloch threatening everything that France stands for, notably employment protection and resistance to outsourcing. (The French term *délocalisation*, with its suggestion of loss of roots, is more emotive than the matter-of-fact English). Suddenly it is not just the reviled American Wal-Mart doing much of its outsourcing in China, it is the French chain Carrefour too, and France is appalled.

If America is the country of what the French like to call 'jungle capitalism', what words will suffice for insufficiently regulated, manically go-getting China? 'The monstrous coupling of communism and neo-liberalism' is the suggestion of two French writers, Philippe Cohen and Luc Richard.[5] Richard is a young journalist and writer I met in Beijing. A Chinese-speaker who by his energy and ingenuity has penetrated deeper into the rural heart of China than anyone I know, his travels have ranged from Inner Mongolia to Canton and from Xinjiang to Fujian, and his descriptions of what he has seen are both humanly vivid and economically literate. In the atmosphere of thirty years ago, who knows, like so many educated Frenchmen Richard might have been ideologically sympathetic to China. Today he is a fierce critic of a country whose exploitation of its people by profit-crazed employers and rejection of the rules of international competition he believes will one day wreak great damage not only in France but throughout the West.

While Anglo-Saxons reconcile themselves to seeing China at the centre of the global market, Richard is one of those Frenchmen declining to accept the seemingly inevitable. For them China has embarked on a long-term programme of domination by illicit economic means. At the time of the Great Leap Forward in 1958 it was Mao Zedong's boast that within fifteen years China would overtake Britain; now it is Western bankers who propagandize on her behalf, promising us that by 2030 China will be the largest economy in the world, the subtext being 'and nothing is going to stop her.' As the recession bit, the West began relying on the economies of emerging countries, and in the first instance China, to take the place of America in pushing world growth – an historic transfer of functions.

This headlong advance is crucially dependent on a labour force paid from ten to thirty times less than their American or European equivalents. When journalists marveled at the miraculous speed of China's preparations for the Olympic Games or Expo 2010 in Shanghai they rarely stopped to ask how the hundreds of thousands of workers had been recruited. Nor do many trouble to investigate working hours, pay levels, safety provision or the standard of on-site lodging they are frequently obliged to endure. (I have see it, and it is primitive.)

'Sino-beatitude' is the term French critics like Richard have coined for this lack of curiosity about the uncomfortable truths behind the country's take-off, in their view an echo of the indulgence shown by many towards communist China in the Maoist era. Richard and his fellow critics have a point. In the past the West played down the cost of Chinese communism in terms of the crushing of the human personality, not to speak of human life. Now, in our enthusiasm for cheap prices, we ignore the cost of our consumerism to the living conditions of hundreds of millions of Chinese, not to speak of the threat to the employment and living standards of workers in the West.

The French of course have a national axe to grind, but hearing China praised as a model of neo-liberalism is enough to make you feel warmer towards French neo-protectionists. At the opening of the French cultural centre in Beijing some years ago the French Minister of Culture at the time had the poor taste to remark that it would never have been ready on time if China, like France, had a thirty-five hour week. This is of course the case, but it is to be hoped that not too many of the Chinese workers, who habitually labour for more than twice that number of hours, were listening.

In his book Richard tells a poignant tale of the fate of a group of *mingong* he once encountered:

> In 2005 in the industrial zone of Pinghu, a provincial town, a group of girls and lads were sitting at the edge of the road shouting and laughing. At first glance you might take them for youngsters on a group holiday waiting for a bus. They're between fifteen and twenty years of age. The girls are squatting on their bags, holding orange ice lollies. They wear tight jeans and sandals with enhanced height. The boys, of whom there are fewer, drag their feet in the dirt and throw us amused glances.
>
> It turned out they were not holidaying school kids but *mingong* who had just walked out of the textile factory where they'd been working. They came here three months ago. It had taken them all that time to get the measure of the impossible situation they had been put in: more than twelve hours work a day; no statutory day off; and worst of all, no salary, or almost none. In three months they have received in all 100 yuan (ten pounds today). So they've had enough. The day before they had got together in one of the dormitories where they sometimes sleep two to a bed. They decided to throw everything up and go back to the province of Anhui where they came from.
>
> Fiddling with a mobile bedecked with trinkets a sixteen year old girl told me: 'Our work days began at seven o'clock till eleven thirty, with two breaks of half an hour each. By the time we had washed ourselves and our clothes it was one in the morning. So we only had five hours sleep before starting again. In those conditions it's better to go back and help our parents work the fields.'
>
> A murmur runs through the group when a little round man dressed in a jacket walks through it looking steadfastly ahead of himself and into the factory. 'The boss' one of them says softly. They almost seem sorry for him. 'Leaving like that made him lose face, and he was quite kind to us' said a fifteen year old boy. They were more against the supervisors who they said swindled them out of money. But how can you claim your rights when you haven't signed a contract? Because obviously there was no

contract, no health insurance, or pension rights. So they have no hope of getting their back pay. When we mention the word 'trade union' they look at us with wide eyes. They've never heard the word, and don't know what it means.

So there they are, at the side of the road. Why not knock on the door of the factory opposite? There's no lack of work round here. 'Impossible, we don't know anyone there.' It was a teacher in a technical school who had got them jobs in the place they'd just left. A fellow with a moustache approaches from across the street: 'Hey, you youngsters, I'll take you on for 500 yuan a month. OK?' They shake their heads. 'It stinks. Once is enough. Tomorrow we'll be with our parents.'

For France the Sino-European textile war of 2005 crystallized the problem. That was the year a transitional phase began of a World Trade Organization agreement to open up textile markets that was to last until 2008. Chinese exporters, poised for an assault, jumped the gun and piled in at once with an increase of 500 per cent in pullovers exported to Europe that year and of 450 per cent in trousers. The British, more resigned than the French, were only mildly interested in the resultant crisis. Had it not been for the fact that the new European Trade Commissioner was Peter Mandelson, a controversial figure with whom the media enjoy to sport, there would have been less coverage than there was.

In France it was a different matter. A furious conflict erupted between French retailers and the Brussels Commission, who were fighting a rearguard war in the battle to curtail the flood of T-shirts, pants and brassieres. When French clothing distributors—an incomparably more powerful lobby than the textile industry—discovered that large quantities of Chinese imports were locked in bond on the orders of the Commission, a hue and cry was got up, in which the prospect of millions of Europeans shivering for many months—or still worse being forced to go through winter in last year's clothes—was raised.

'Quotas won't keep consumers warm this winter' was a favourite slogan of the distributors. Job losses in the French textile industry notwithstanding, public opinion moved in behind them. And there is the wider message of this somewhat farcical episode. It is enough to see the ravenous faces scouring any clothing department store for bargains in Paris, London or New York to understand what is happening: the Western public are hooked on their cheap manna from China, and to hell with the implications for the Chinese who make them, or for their own countrymen who could lose their jobs. Beside a dirt-cheap pair or shoes or jeans none of this matters. Nor do concerns about the soaring Chinese contribution to the problem of global warming inhibit Western consumers from snapping up its low-priced fridges, TVs and toys.

Throughout the crisis, it is worth recalling, the Chinese played hardball. Sometimes they had a point, though a remark by a Chinese trade minister that it took 800 million Chinese shirts to buy an Airbus was less telling than it sounds. We see what he means, but importing the Airbus does not throw Chinese out of work, and it is not manufactured by sweated labour. When they are more powerful than today and become more aware of the contradictions between workers and consumers in the West, in trade negotiations with the EEC and America they will play it even tougher. The Chinese reaction to the recent scandal over potentially dangerous paint used on Chinese-made toys may be a portent of what is to come. While undertaking to investigate, the authorities also suddenly discovered hitherto unremarked defects in Chinese imports of American soya. More hardball.

While there may be some temporary reduction due to the credit crisis, the torrent of Chinese imports to Europe has scarcely begun. The image of endless container ships transporting consumer goods cumbrously from East to West became outdated some years ago, as the first direct freight trains from Beijing to Hamburg via Mongolia, Russia, Belarus and Poland knocked 22 days off transportation times. The first train carried a cargo of clothes, electrical goods and bathroom tiles. In the future there is reason to believe that more sophisticated items will follow. The idea that China is doomed to remain a manufacturer of mass-produced, sub-quality goods copied from foreign models, while the West maintains its technological lead into the indefinite future is a consoling fiction. The British, slow off the mark as ever, are currently considering laying down high speed railway lines. For these they will require some sixty advanced locomotives, but they will not be manufactured here. Using technology mainly developed in Europe the Chinese are reporting to be offering the trains at half the price they would cost on the Continent.

Europe's problems with Chinese imports have a centuries-long history. Already in the seventeen hundreds the Jesuits reckoned that in the Shanghai area alone there were '200,000 weavers of calicoes', a stupendous number of workmen by contemporary European standards. Before long the results began to be felt as exports climbed inexorably till a million pieces were being shipped to Britain and America by the beginning of the nineteenth century. Another century and cotton manufactures were 44 per cent of China exports. Only our spinning machines had allowed us to continue to compete at all, but with that advantage long gone, and the gates of China opened, the employment implications have been huge. Between 1990 and 1997 the number of French textile workers was halved.

Western dependency on cheap products will grow, especially now that we need to keep interest rates down in the face of a credit crunch. For the French to lose much of their textile industry in the process is bad enough, but in the longer term their vineyards could be threatened as well. All the talk at present is of new-rich Chinese snapping up Chateau Lafite Rothschild at stupendous prices and drinking it with a shot of Coca Cola, but we have got things the wrong way round. Currently the French are seeking to make up for competition from New World producers by conquering the Chinese market, and the outlook seemed promising: ten years ago Chinese consumption was 100 million litres a year; by 2010 it was 800 million. A mouth-watering rate of advance, it will be thought, but the French face three problems.

The first is that the Americans are currently the biggest exporters of wine to China. The second that the Chinese are developing their own vineyards. And whereas France has the most highly regulated production in the world, the Chinese have the least: in Beijing you can buy a 1999 claret from a vineyard that did not exist until five years later.[6] Chinese wine is rough, but it will improve. An acquaintance who is a winegrower with thirteen choice hectares in Burgundy told me of a visit he had made to a prospective vineyard in China at their request. His hosts explained that they planned to plant some twenty thousand hectares. 'But who will drink all this wine?' my friend asked. 'You will' came the reply.

No doubt Chinese wine, calibrated to appeal to every taste, will be retailing before too long at unrepeatable prices. The reaction of French winegrowers towards China will I suspect be more robust than that of the intellectuals of the '70s. (A quarter of the *bars-tabacs* where the latter tend to congregate, incidentally, have been acquired by Chinese interests.) And should the winegrowers of the Languedoc become unruly and demand action President Sarkozy will know where to turn: like the (recently deposed) Australian Prime Minister Kevin Rudd, the President's foreign affairs adviser, Jean David Levitte, is a China specialist. Another sign of the times.

*

Excessive tolerance towards Mao's domestic policies was not confined to France, or to the Left. The former British Prime Minister Sir Edward Heath, a vain man keen to be seen as an interlocutor of the Chairman and his successors, was an example of a politician eager to take the Chinese line when he reasonably could. His attempted exculpation of the Chinese leadership over Tiananmen will be remembered alongside the later observation by the Mayor of London, Ken Livingstone, that the killings could be compared to the London poll tax riots under Mrs Thatcher.

The Canadian Prime Minister, Pierre Trudeau, was another whose complimentary remarks about one of the most repressive regimes the world has seen can be read in his book *Two Innocents in Red China*. Written after a visit in 1960, it remained silent on the question of the famine that was raging at the time, a piece of discretion that helped earn Trudeau the coveted title of a 'friend of China'. While the French were not alone in their ingratiating stance towards Beijing they were never to be outdone. 'A beacon for humanity' President Giscard d'Estaing called Mao when he died, a judgment that, even allowing for the demands of etiquette, seems a little flowery for a man personally responsible for the death of more of his countrymen than the entire population of France.

To politicians of all parties one of the most attractive aspects of Chinese society, on the mainland or abroad, was its discipline. In the '80s, when debate in Britain was raging about Victorian values and Tory politicians were looking for positive models for the lower orders to follow, in private senior Conservatives were speaking in envious tones of Asian values and what could be done to implant them here. The idea that Confucian patterns of behaviour could be grafted onto the multi-ethnic underclass of Birmingham or Manchester harks back to Voltaire's illusions. The irony of the notion that the British should conduct themselves more in the manner of one of their former colonial peoples is especially rich.

In thinking this way these Conservatives were displaying a mindset that had something in common with admirers of Chinese communism on the Left. Just as Tony Benn had nothing to say about the absence of political freedom in China before, during or after his visits, so Conservative converts to Asian values were unconcerned by the lack of personal liberty in the Chinese family structure. The reason Marxists and Tories can find themselves envying 'the Asian way of life' can be explained in a single word: order. The discipline of the patriarchal family recommended itself to Conservative patricians, and the orderly organization of production impressed Tony Benn (a patrician himself, as it happens). In their respective left-wing and right-wing Nirvanas workers would show themselves to be dutiful and submissive towards the demands of the state, and children to those of the family.

While the Right flirted with Asian values, as in France the Left was to become more judgemental about the new China than the old. All at once people who had closed their eyes to decades of abuses by the Mao regime became stringent critics of the country. It is consistent with the West's erratic stances that at a time when China's human rights record has improved greatly (though from an abysmal base) its former sympathizers should have grown more censorious.

Certainly there is repression in China, most recently dramatized by her astonishingly inept behaviour over the award of a Nobel prize to the dissident journalist Liu Xiaobo, though nothing resembling what was happening thirty or forty years ago. Indeed it is often because of the improvement in personal freedoms, for example access to the Internet, that we are aware of cases of persecution at all. In the past tens of millions of Chinese suffered in global silence.

In some cases this new-found concern for Chinese freedoms may be genuine. In others it must inspire suspicion. For many on the Left the current Chinese regime has lost most of its socialist credentials and all of its romantic appeal. A neo-capitalist order in Beijing provides few incentives to be tolerant about human rights abuses, and every reason to demonstrate a new vigilance. The cynicism is unappealing, but in the case of China, not without precedent: one of the lessons of the past is that when China has ceased to serve our purpose we judge it by a different standard. Of one thing we can be sure: that if the totalitarian-inclined Sartre were to visit China today he would return saying the country had become a hell on earth where people could be put in prison merely for expressing their thoughts.

The application of a tougher standard on human rights to an improving situation is also noticeable in the conduct of governments. There is no record of President Nixon pressing Chairman Mao on personal freedoms during their meetings in 1972. Today however most Western leaders make a point of raising the issue on their visits to his far less oppressive successors, knowing they will be held to account by the media, the opposition and public opinion on their return.

It is good that it is being done, though the morality is confusing. To travel to China today without insisting publicly on democratic advance is seen, as the British Prime Minister Gordon Brown was to discover in his trip early in 2008, as kowtowing to a nasty regime for sordid commercial reasons. To go there thirty-five years ago, when the hand of oppression was so heavy that the notion of dissidence did not exist, and to say nothing for fear of annoying your hosts, even though the commercial stake at the time was relatively insignificant, was seen as a diplomatic triumph.

*

Ingratiation with the Mao regime was not exclusive to film stars, intellectuals and politicians. A strange deference, not far short of reverence, could afflict even seasoned diplomats where China was concerned. I have heard otherwise hard-nosed functionaries speak of China's leader as of some awesome Eastern potentate, beyond human scale. Like the Chinese, Westerners were encouraged to see themselves as sunflowers turning to the sun in the form of the Chairman's smiling face, a favourite motif on Mao posters at the time, and unlike the robust Lord Macartney two centuries earlier a surprising number humbly accepted their semi-tributary status.

Though my British colleagues in Beijing at the time did not suffer from this mindset (I was aware of no Chinese equivalent of the Foreign Office Arabist lobby) I noticed it in other diplomats, French and Scandinavian especially. With the French it formed part of the Malraux tradition of an airily aesthetic rather than a soberly pragmatic attitude to China. With neutralist Scandinavians, eager for a sense of purpose, things went further. At the height of the Cultural Revolution, when the violence and disorder were visible on the streets, Mao's behaviour increasingly irrational and several Western missions under siege, senior diplomats from these countries were resourceful in inventing excuses for what was happening, claiming that the chaos was not as bad as it seemed, or seeking to absolve the Chairman from responsibility.

Occasionally they would be rewarded with an interview with a Chinese Foreign Office minister or senior official, or—much less often—Zhou Enlai himself. (Western diplomats did not see Mao). Such meetings would occur on the rare occasions the Chinese Prime Minister thought it worth conveying something to the diplomatic corps, using neutral countries as intermediaries. Meanwhile requests by Western missions to call on Chinese ministers and officials were frequently declined or ignored. This preference for holding foreigners at bay, a throwback to an earlier, isolationist tradition, must of course be seen against a background of Western colonial incursions, when to give way to normal diplomatic intercourse was seen as tantamount to throwing open the entire country to the rapacious foreigner.

The myth of the 'middle kingdom' behind this mindset persisted in a new form: the delusion that the China of the late '60s was the centre of world revolution. The reluctance of the Chinese to receive Western representatives at all was redolent of Emperor Qianlong's reply when asked to consent to a British embassy: 'Europe consists of many other nations besides your own. If each and all demanded to be represented at our court, how could we possibly consent? The thing is utterly impracticable.'

The equivalent of the Chinese Foreign Ministry in his time was called 'The Department for Tributary States', and something of that title's flavour remained in the disdainful way the Chinese under Mao managed such foreign contacts as they deigned to have. In negotiating with Chinese communists I noted a similar tendency towards condescension. If after many frustrating hours of stonewalling they were obliged to shift their position in the face of undeniable facts, the concession was invariably phrased in a top down, contemptuous manner: 'In order to meet your difficulty...' The difficulty wasn't usually ours: because the regime made it all but impossible to reconcile reality and ideology, it was theirs.

Even when they were putting on a show of reason Chinese officialdom managed to behave in an uncivil fashion. Not that it mattered: the recipient of the positive gesture was usually too awed to analyze why the Chinese had decided to make use of him or her, or to feel resentment at cavalier treatment. At one point in the late '60s a Scandinavian Ambassador was summoned, at indecently short notice, to see Zhou Enlai. We were a tiny community, and I recall the glaze of pleasure in his eyes when he was debriefing colleagues after being accorded his half-hour in the deputy imperial presence.

So bedazzled was the poor man by this privilege that, despite the urging of fellow heads of mission, he had omitted to speak up during his interview in defence of the diplomatic community and to protest against the wholesale flouting of the Geneva Convention by both the Red Guards and the Chinese Foreign Ministry. Maybe he had forgotten. Or perhaps he was afraid. Watching the ingratiating behaviour of some Westerners in the Chinese presence today, sometimes I get the same feeling.

*

In a field where everything conspires to promote misunderstanding, one of the least rewarding ways of looking at China is through the prism of orientalism. The tendency to invest everything Eastern with an occult glamour was there from the beginning, each generation convinced that it was prying open China's mysteries anew. Neither French Maoists nor President Nixon would have been pleased to be told that the oracular status they conferred on the Chairman's pronouncements was part of a long tradition of eagerness to lend an ear to the gnomic utterances of wise men of the East.

Now that the term orientalism has been purloined by the late Edward Said to suggest something rather different, it is worth getting the meaning straight. His book *Orientalism* was based on the notion that in its approach to the East, the West was the 'self' and the Orient 'the other'. The argument that European and American images of the Orient have tended to reflect their own prejudices and preconceptions rather than the reality of life in the countries concerned seems irrefutable. Said's purpose however was to show that Europe and the US were and remain guilty of deprecating, racist and colonialist attitudes and behaviour, notably towards the peoples of the Middle East. Be that as it may. The largest and most populous country in the Orient is China. It is strange therefore that Said did not stretch his theory that far East, though perhaps there were reasons.

The most obvious difficulty in extending his strictures to the Western treatment of China in the past and today is that, while there has been plenty of Western deprecation of its customs and values, in the eighteenth century it tended to be the other way round: far from scorning Chinese habits and customs, the West idealized them. Reducing the image of China to a country of ultra-refined décor and delicatesse, *chinoiserie* could also be said to have been a form of condescension, but as we have seen with Voltaire and others, it is one that went along with a positive appreciation of aspects of Chinese government, society and culture.

A second problem with Said's concept of 'orientalism' when applied to China is that, while the overall Western view of its civilization has indeed been *de haut en bas*, the Chinese returned the compliment. To adapt Said's formula, in early relations between Europe and the Chinese each was the 'self' and each was 'the other'. In its treatment of the Western 'other' as barbarians whose culture and industrial ingenuity held nothing of interest to them, and as people who owed allegiance to the Middle Kingdom, Chinese arrogance and deprecation outdid that of the West.

'The English barbarians are an insignificant and detestable race' said a nineteenth century censor's memorial to the Emperor. Detestable is fine, but insignificant? The British never said that of China. The same censor assured the emperor that English soldiers were buttoned up so tight that once they fell they could never get up again (a precursor of communist propaganda cartoons of ludicrously over-equipped American troops being killed by lightly armed guerrillas.)

'The apathy with respect to foreign things generally', wrote a British interpreter, Thomas Meadows, in 1847, 'even in the higher and in the Chinese sense of the word educated classes, and that when they meet a foreigner who understands their own language, is to a European quite astonishing. They very seldom ask questions, still more seldom is the information they seek after of the kind that tends to enlighten their minds on the state of foreign nations.'

In its ignorance and obscurantism, the image the Oriental 'self' constructed of the Occidental 'other' surpassed the imperialistic arrogance we were later to visit on China. Neither attitude was attractive: the difference was that, being militarily and technologically backward compared with the West when the two civilizations collided in the nineteenth century, China was in no position to impose its view. Yet nor was she in any hurry to learn. Such were her autarkic instincts that while Western explorers, writers, scholars and missionaries began studying China intensively in the nineteen hundreds, not just for commercial reasons, it was not until the second half of the century that the Chinese deigned to interest themselves in what had hit them, and to enquire with any degree of rigour into Western languages, engineering and science.

All this may help explain why Said made no serious attempt to extend his definition beyond the Middle East and India. A theory of orientalism from which the most populous country in the East was excluded would seem a strange beast. The least one can say is that this giant hole in his argument does not appear to have damaged his campus popularity. In the minds of a generation of students amongst whom it has become gospel, it is doubtless assumed that his theory is global, as theories are meant to be.

The Said thesis can however be said to apply to China in a sense its author would not have welcomed. The weakness of his argument that Westerners were concerned merely with the gratification of their aims and convictions is that it applies to Western support for Chinese communism too. For what is the disregard for the suffering of the victims of Mao's rule by his sympathizers in the West, if not a form of contempt for 'the other'?

The truth is that in minds driven by partisan political passions the Chinese 'other' had ceased to be human and become an ideological cipher. On many a Western campus Left-wing idealism, bourgeois self-hatred, historical guilt, cultural self-abasement and academic careerism took precedence over any consideration for the freedom and wellbeing of individual Chinese. Seen in this light the indulgence of people like Said himself towards the regime becomes a classic case of orientalism, in his own definition of the word.

The fact that educated, informed and financially comfortable Westerners could declare themselves Maoists is a sign not just of blinkered ideological vision but of a certain patrician insouciance. The disciplined, puritanical, ascetic, egalitarian and bloody life of permanent revolution in China was never for the French, Italian and American intellectuals, writers, philosophers and film stars who enthused about it: it was for the 'others'.

*

Western commentators, writers, academics and politicians who got Mao's China wrong had an excuse of sorts: the paucity of information made available by the regime they championed, and its casualness with the truth. In totalitarian as in imperial China words, rather than reality, were what mattered. Under imperial government scholarship was prized, the writing of ideograms could take the form of a ceremony, and calligraphy was an art that could have quasi-mystical powers. Towards the end of the ultra-sophisticated Ming Dynasty (1368-1644) things reached the point where writing was more highly rated than painting, which commanded lesser prices than a well-turned piece of calligraphy.

There are ways and ways to write Chinese characters. They can be lightly and airily sketched, or wielded like a bludgeon. Ideograms are a far more substantial mode of communication than our 26 letters: you cannot hit someone over the head with a word in Latin script, but with a character, you can. The tradition of using them as a form of punishment was revived in the Red Guard practice of pinning denunciatory posters to their jet-planed victims, and displaying their names upside down and crossed out—a terrible humiliation as well as an inconvenience to those like myself anxious to spot which 'bourgeois power-holder' was being hounded through the streets that day.

The communists also preserved from the past a fastidiousness about language—when it suited. I recall the unfeigned shock on the face of a Foreign Ministry official when we referred bluntly to the Red Guard attack on the British Mission which resulted in its demolition by fire. The aim of the interview was to discuss arrangements for its reconstruction, a process made difficult by the Chinese resort to elaborate circumlocutions to avoid admitting that it had been burnt down. The semi-approbatory phrase 'the actions of the masses' was the closest we got.

More tiresome were Maoist incantations. One of my least pleasant memories of Beijing in the late '60s is of trying to get to sleep while Red Guards beat drums and cymbals accompanied by the endless chanting of slogans beneath the imperialists' windows. (Once I was driven to retaliating by playing Wagner at them from an open window, extra loud). Because of the language structure sloganeering, especially in the form of so-called four character phrases, comes easily to the Chinese. Any four words that fell from the Chairman's lips could be swept up reverently and fashioned into a sententious maxim for hundreds of millions of obedient mouths to recite. The operatic element in Chinese rhetoric, always strong, was also a boon to Mao's propaganda machine. Its Marxist-Leninist prose excelled even that of the Russians in its venom, some of it so excessive as to be comic: 'The Yugoslav revisionist Tito has dropped his fig-leaf and exposed his ugly features.'

Disputes centering around words and language had frequently been at the core of China's fraught relations with the West. Dr Johnson declined to admit that China was a civilized country at all because of its failure to evolve an alphabet. As Foreign Secretary Palmerston objected to the use of the word 'petitions' to describe communications with the Chinese authorities, as Chinese custom required, for the excellent reason that it smacked of fiefdom. Translations too could be sensitive territory. It was a dispute about the rendering into English of a single character that was to cause the first blood to be spilt between Britain and China.

That character was *yi*, meaning loosely 'barbarian', and as early as 1832 it had caused a skirmish. Hugh Hamilton Lindsay, a supercargo (merchant captain) of the British East India Company dropped anchor off Shanghai and petitioned the local magistrate to open up the area to foreign trade. The petition was turned down and Lindsay instructed to be on his way to Canton. The ship's journal recorded:

> We reasoned our [Chinese] friends out of the use of the epithet yi, 'barbarians', which they apply to all strangers indiscriminately. The idea of cunning and treachery is always attached to this name when uttered by the Chinese. As foreigners trading to China have hitherto patiently borne such an appellation, they have been treated as barbarians. It was highly necessary to object to this epithet and to show from its use in Chinese writings that the term conveyed reproach. From this time they abstained from the use of it and called us foreigners, or Englishmen.

The mutuality of incomprehension and suspicion between East and West is neatly illustrated by the fact that the later English slang for foreigners, Wop—wily oriental person—also conveys 'the idea of cunning and treachery.' In this instance the Chinese magistrate in question, an admiral, had sought to justify the word by claiming that he was merely using a common form of address for foreigners which had no pejorative associations, and said the English were overreacting. But face was involved, this time on the English side, and Lindsay refused to obey the Chinese order to sail until the word was removed from the order. The Chinese admiral finally agreed, substituting the word 'merchant.'

Blood-letting over the term was to occur two years later when Lord Napier arrived as Britain's first official trade representative. He went to

Canton, but in his arrogance made the mistake of sailing into the port without clearing his trip with the Chinese. In subsequent exchanges with the Chinese Governor-General, his title of Chief Superintendent of British Trade in China was rendered by the less sonorous *yimu*, translated as 'barbarian eye'. Napier responded by calling the Chinese a 'presumptuous savage', reminding him that the King of England 'rules over an extent of territory in the four corners of the world more comprehensive in space, and infinitely more in power, than the whole empire of China.' Summoning two sloops to his aid he then joined battle. In the engagement British sailors were killed, as well as Chinese, and in the same year, worn down by dealings with China, Napier himself died.

So sensitive was the *yi* word that a ban on its official use was included in the Treaty of Tianjin after the Opium Wars. There is even a link between the quarrel over *yi* and the acquisition of Hong Kong: the English loss of life and the death of Napier were used as a spur to conflict by English merchants and colonisers who favoured teaching the Chinese a lesson, and this eventually led to the first Opium War of 1848. The showdown would have come anyway, but it is poignant to think that a single word could well have been one of the grains of sand that led to the clash between two jealous empires.

During Lord Macartney's visit in the late eighteenth century the confrontation over status had taken the form of whether or not his Lordship should kowtow. This time it was a question of language, but the issue was the same. There are scholars who argue that the British were being both prickly and provocative in rendering *yi* as barbarian, but being prickly was the point. That single troublesome translation went to the core of everything that was to occur between China and the West, not just in subsequent decades, it could be argued, but ever since. 'Who are the barbarians?' is a theme that never went away. Still today it is there beneath the surface whenever there are acerbic exchanges about Western democracy and Chinese authoritarianism. To take Western lessons in government would mean to accept a relationship between teacher and pupil, which is not one to which modern China aspires.

It is pointless to take sides as to who was right about *yi*, since words change their flavour. According to the 1963 edition of the bible of

Chinese dictionaries, Mathews, published by Harvard University, however, the English had reason to take offence. *Yí* is still said to designate 'barbarous tribes on the east, often used for any foreigner.' The Chinese of course had excuses. Many of their early experiences of Europeans had been unpropitious. Amongst the first were Portuguese traders and adventurers in the mid-sixteenth century who robbed, murdered and carried off women and children into slavery. And there is no denying that the Opium Wars—provoked by our insistence on the right to sell drugs to Chinese—were themselves barbarous in their cynicism. It was the letter to Queen Victoria from the Governor of Canton, Commissioner Lin Zexu, complaining of the trade that was truly civilized:

> It is said that the smoking of opium is forbidden in your country, the proof that you are clearly aware of its harm. Since you do not permit opium to harm your own country, you should not allow it to be passed on to other countries, certainly not the Central States! Of all the products the Central States exports to foreign countries there is not a single item that is not beneficial to the people: they are beneficial when consumed, beneficial when used, and beneficial when re-sold. All are beneficial. Has any article from the Central States done any harm to foreign countries?'

If only Lin's letter had reached Queen Victoria—an improbable defender of dope-smoking and a consumer of China's main exports of tea, silk and porcelain—and she had been obliged to respond, but somehow it appears to have been mislaid. And if only the British press had been aware of this episode when it frothed against China's arrest and execution of Akmal Shaikh, a British citizen, in 2009 for acting as a drugs mule.

It was after the Opium Wars that the expression 'foreign devil' became more current. The best we can say is that Chinese xenophobia was from the start based on experience as well as prejudice, though in a country which regarded itself as the centre of the world, those prejudices came easily.

If the English had been called barbarians by an African country rather than China they might have laughed it off ('who are you calling barbarian?'), but the Chinese were, if not a military rival, a rival civilization. It says little for our serenity at the height of empire that we allowed ourselves to be so provoked, though I have to add that the Chinese have made a fine art of humiliation, which can be exercised to terrible effect. I have seen the self-esteem of distinguished soldiers and diplomats irreparably damaged by bruising encounters with Chinese demonstrators or officials. I also recall the viciously mocking faces of the dozen or so guards who held captive the Reuter's correspondent, Anthony Grey, after he had been put under house arrest in retaliation for the jailing of communist rioters in Hong Kong. Between them they almost drove him to suicide.

According to a distinguished Chinese-American scholar, Lydia H. Liu, Western resentment against the Chinese refusal to see them as equals was still alive in England 150 years later. She argues that by acquiring the purloined throne of the Qianlong emperor in 1922 the Victoria and Albert Museum in London was 'settling an old score with a dead Qing emperor.' The imperial chair had found its way to Britain indirectly. Looted during the occupation of the eight powers during the Boxer revolt at the beginning of the twentieth century, it turned up in London some twenty years later in the possession of a White Russian émigré and former Tsarist Ambassador, who let it go for £2,250. The Queen was notified about so prominent an acquisition, prompting Ms Liu to observe: 'With hindsight her endorsement may well be read as a direct assertion of the sovereign right of the British crown vis-à-vis that of the Chinese state.'

I am unacquainted with the Museum's motives, or with the Queen's sentiments at the time, but I doubt it. In all probability the acquisition of the throne was an act whose prime movers were academics like Ms Liu herself. I do not exclude some incidental satisfaction, probably expressed in the light-minded, jovial form favoured in royal circles, at the fact that the emperor who had wanted George III's diplomatic representative to grovel before his throne had forfeited it to his grand-daughter's museum, though no more than that. But then the scholar in question is a semiologist, for whom nothing happens by chance and everything is a token of something else, an attitude that makes it difficult to explain the meaning of the word 'curio.'

*

The fact that the Chinese tongue is so resistant to study and interpretation makes it one more barrier, yet another Chinese wall. Even today it sometimes seems that everything is done to keep the Chinese language hermetic, and catch you out. When it comes to China nothing, not even the most modern system of transposition into English, is what it appears. Simple sounds are rendered in such a way as to make it impossible for the average intelligent Westerner to pronounce them correctly. Some examples: Chou as in Zhou Enlai is in Chinese pronounced Joe. Tian (heaven), as in Tiananmen (Gate of Heavenly Peace) is pronounced 'tien'. The Emperor Qianlong is pronounced Chienlung. Xi is pronounced '*hsi*', etc.

At one stage China sought to forbid its people from teaching its language to foreigners at all, with the result that an already opaque tongue became technically a state secret. The logical extension of China's preference for isolation and exclusion was to have no foreigners in the country at all, and in the late '60s she almost achieved that happy state. Until then a trickle of visitors had been allowed in, especially if they could be relied upon to write in flattering terms about the country. Then, from late 1966, almost no one went to China, or—given the turmoil—sought to go. When I worked in Beijing there were very few Westerners or foreigners of any kind. Because so many countries did not recognize communist China till later even the diplomatic corps was unnaturally depleted. The US, Germany, Italy, Spain and Japan had no presence, leaving only the French and ourselves of the larger Western powers. Business visits had pretty much dried up. There were only three or four Western correspondents at any time, none of whom were Chinese speakers.

This is no trivial observation. What it meant was that during a turning point in China's history—and in retrospect global history—no more than a dozen or so Western observers were able to register and report what was going on. Even they were unable to travel beyond Beijing, Shanghai and Tianjin. Nor were there any 'Chinese contacts' from whom diplomats or journalists could glean impressions or information; except for a handful of gruff, buttoned-up foreign ministry officials the ban on socializing with foreigners was complete, and no one would dare break it.

The tenuousness of our links can be seen by the fact that one of our sources of knowledge on the Party's thinking was a brief document circulated to Party cadres called *tsan kao xiao xi—Reference Information*. Not a word of it was of Chinese origin. It consisted of judiciously culled extracts from the foreign press. A hangover from the 'let a hundred flowers bloom' period of 1956, it had originally been set up as a newspaper by the head of the Xinhua news agency. Confined to officials after the post-'56 clampdown, its purpose now was to avoid managers and cadres operating in a total international void, given that the communist press carried virtually no factual foreign news. It was while I was there that the Americans sent Neil Armstrong to the moon, a feat that went unreported in the Chinese media. *Reference Information* carried a brief report.

It's production must have been an exercise in scholasticism in itself. The delicacy of the task facing the Chinese compilers—a step too far and they would open themselves to charges of circulating anti-Chinese propaganda—was matched only by the arbitrariness of our interpretations. But then for us this was reliable stuff. What the leadership wanted their officials to know and what they persisted in hiding from them was for us intelligence of a kind. In retrospect it is outlandish to think of mundane articles in *The Times* or *The Washington Post* being studiously selected and censured, then laboriously translated into Chinese by government hacks, only to be translated back and critically de-constructed by hapless functionaries such as myself.

Strange times, which we must hope will not recur. One of the undoubted advances of contemporary China is that, within limits, for the first time in nearly half a century we are free to go there, to talk and to listen, and to travel.

3

'My capital is the hub and centre about which all quarters of the globe revolve.'
The Qianlong Emperor to King George III

Had they known that the Russians had fielded tactical nuclear weapons on the Chinese frontier in 1969 it would be pleasant to believe that the British government would have given a thought to the safety of our mission. The Americans, on the other hand, had no reason for concern about the fate of their nationals in those tumultuous times. Apart from a Korean War era prisoner detained by the communists ever since (he was released before President Nixon's visit) and a couple of US Maoists resident in China, the astonishing fact is that not only was there no American Mission in Beijing: in a country of over a billion people there was not a single US citizen, in the normal use of the term.

This fact alone tells us everything about China and the US at the time. Estrangement was mutual and thorough. On the American side successive administrations were to blame for sealing themselves off to the extent that they did, by their failure to recognize the legitimacy of the regime or to contrive any permanent high-level dialogue with it. The only contacts were fitful meetings between the Chinese and American representatives in Warsaw, which though useful as a channel, resolved little or nothing. In behaving in this way the US not only cut itself off from China's leaders and their thinking; it deprived itself of a practical basis for its policy.

Treating the most populous country in the world like Cuba—a place you could quarantine while you waited for the regime to change—was not serious. For reasons of both principle and practice the British had recognized the government the 1949 revolution had brought to power almost at once: the communists satisfied our criteria of controlling the majority of their territory, and we could never have continued to run Hong Kong without dealing with the administration face to face.

The Americans disapproved of our stance, but they were lucky the British were in there from the first. Being for many years the only large Western country represented in Beijing made Washington dependent on us for first-hand information. Foreign policy made in the absence of any chance to look the other fellow in the eye, or, to the extent you are able, to smell out the constraints he is operating under on his own turf, can lead to dangerous simplicities evolved from emotive abstractions, and for many years that was the effect on American policy-making.

There were many reasons to be alarmed by the establishment of a nationalistic totalitarian dictatorship sworn to help foment international revolution wherever it could, a policy the Russians themselves were later to denounce as a Trotskyist deviation, and China's role in the launch and prosecution of the Korean War did nothing to calm apprehensions. But for many years cool analysis never had a chance. Ignorance about what was happening in China on the ground, over-reliance on second-hand reports or on loaded intelligence from Taiwan could result in an atmosphere of semi-hysteria towards the communist regime. Maoist sympathizers in the West clung to their vision of China in defiance of the facts. American fears and fantasies about the regime turned the country into a greater bogey than Mao contrived to be. For twenty-three years between the 1949 revolution and Nixon's visit in 1972 mutual isolation precluded new thinking.

*

America had its own line on China from the first. As an anti-imperialist power its record in nineteenth century China is in general more defensible, and certainly less rapacious, than that of Europe. All the more reason for her bitter disappointment when communism triumphed in 1949. Her attitude to China had always owed much to the missionary spirit, and from the start of her contacts her finger-wagging inclinations were on display. Being less involved than the British in the China trade (the Cantonese called them 'second-chop Englishmen') meant that Americans were less anxious to acquire the facilities or territory to conduct it. This left them free to moralize, which they did with fervour, both as an evangelical culture and as a diplomatic power.

Preacher or President, salesman or academic, diplomat or human rights
advocate, America has always known what the Chinese needed and has
never hesitated to tell them.

One of its earliest envoys was a Dr Parker, a divine who was six times
Chargé d'Affaires in Beijing in the middle of the nineteenth century. In
1856 he drew up a manifesto for the country in which he reduced the
Chinese equivalent of President Wilson's fourteen points to four.

1   The residence in Beijing of three envoys from the US, Britain
and France, and the dispatch of Chinese representatives to
Washington, London and Paris.
2   The unlimited extension of the trade of the three nations to the
whole of the Chinese Empire.
3   Freedom of religious belief for all Chinese subjects.
4   Reform of the Chinese courts of justice.

It is symptomatic of a certain continuity in American attitudes, and of
the Chinese capacity for resistance, that Parker's four points pretty much
embody American policy to the country to this day. Translated into
modern parlance they mean a China fully open to the world, the free
market, human rights, and a legal system based on Western principles.

America's high-minded stance irked Europeans at the time as much
as it can now: the French, Germans and Italians are still less likely to nag
China about democracy and human rights than the Anglo-Americans.
Then as now there were accusations of American hypocrisy in
combining a prissy moral tone with unscrupulous commercial self-
interest, and evidence to support them. Though America played no
direct part in the shameful import of opium, it was later to be alleged
that some 20 per cent of the trade was in fact in US hands, and that
special agents had been commissioned in India to promote it.

Since the communist victory America's hypocrisy and sanctimony
have shown themselves on all political sides. Isolation from China meant
that both the liberal Left and the Yellow Peril Right were free to invent
their own China, and they did. On one hand was the conviction that the
regime was the very devil with whom America must never sup; on the
other a breast-beating approach, laden with Puritan self-reproach, whose

rose-tinted vision of Maoism underplayed the toughness of the regime such people rightly insisted America should deal with. What was scarce (though it existed) was what America so badly needed: a cool-headed, unemotional perspective.

It was a quality that could be particularly lacking on campus. Absence of political and official contact with China from which professionals could learn gave disproportionate weight to the academic community. Closer ties in America between government and universities on foreign policy-making than exist in Europe can be an advantage, though less so when neither side knows at first hand what they are talking about, and have a tendency to fall back on political or intellectual prejudice in elaborating policy. In academia there were distinguished, well-informed figures, but younger scholars were as bereft as Washington of direct experience, though never short of opinions about how relations should be conducted.

Then there is the emotional factor—an aspect of what might be called the China differential. It is natural that specialists should become involved with their specialism—why else would they choose one culture rather than another?—but with China something else was and is going on. Great civilizations exercise a lunar pull on the intellect and feelings of those who study them, and the seductive power of China needs no explanation. The very process of studying a notoriously impermeable language and culture can instill a sense of mission: with such laboriously accumulated knowledge students of China can come to feel they have acquired not only a technical facility but a priest-like vocation. The danger is of seeing themselves as transcending their role as interpreters of a culture to become moral arbiters between East and West.

For a long time there was a sense in which the China debate in America was not about China at all, but an endless internal political and ideological wrangle of which China happened to be the subject. There were and remain different camps and personalities, and many impressive individuals, but it is a fair guess that the majority of sinologists in America believe that Western policies towards China have been misconceived for centuries: a defensible view, it seems to me, provided it does not spill over into the kind of compensatory indulgence towards China rife amongst what more sober American analysts refer to as 'panda huggers'.

Such was America's distance from events at the crucial juncture in China's history in the '60s that anyone with direct experience of this semi-mythological country became an important intelligence source. When, lowly Second Secretary as I was, the CIA asked to de-brief me on the way back to London for a spell of home leave, and I sat in a room in Washington answering questions from a dozen or more China specialists, I was conscious that for all their intellectual qualities and expertise few had ever set foot on the mainland, or laid eyes on a real Chinese communist. There were sober folk, but I also sensed a weakness for extravagant theories.

A favourite at the time was the so-called 'descending spiral.' According to this view Mao's new adventure, in which politics would supplant economics ('Red not expert'), would drive China into a tailspin, a vortex of poverty and starvation from which it could not possibly recover. Clearly the economy was suffering as factories closed to allow workers to march about 'making revolution', or beating up bosses and intellectuals, yet if the theorists had the smell of the place in their nostrils they would have known of the Chinese ability to operate on two levels.

The damage to the country was huge, but important personnel such as nuclear scientists were spared the rigours of struggle meetings and confessions, and essential services (e.g. public transport and many restaurants) somehow continued to function throughout the turmoil. And while public edifices such as temple sculptures were indeed knocked about in Cromwellian fashion during the campaign to 'smash the four olds' (old culture, old habits, old customs, and the old habits of the exploiting classes) the regime was careful to close major museums and galleries, so as to prevent wholesale Red Guard iconoclasm and the destruction of China's past.

Another way the US misunderstood China (though here she was not alone) was in her attitude to the Sino-Soviet alliance. So fundamental did this seem to the unity of the international communist movement, and so vital to its ability to appeal to the Left in both developing and developed countries, that for the Americans (and for us) it was impossible to imagine that the fraternal parties would ever allow it to be seriously weakened. Ideological squabbles were inevitable, but a break seemed inconceivable. In its reluctance to accept what was happening before its eyes the West was to a surprising extent taken in by communist propaganda against 'bourgeois nationalism' and in favour of 'unbreakable eternal brotherhood' between socialist peoples. We appear to have accepted at face value the claim that communism had indeed produced a new breed of men, for whom proletarian internationalism overrode the archaic voices of race and nation. In the event the divorce between the communist giants, when it came in the early Sixties, had ugly racial as well as abstruse ideological elements.

Still there were those who refused to take the stark evidence of a split seriously. So reluctant were they to recognize their own good fortune that a thesis put forward by right-wing anti-communists in the early '60s that the Sino-Soviet dispute was a fraud, a snare and a delusion cooked up by the Russian and Chinese disinformation services to persuade the West to drop its guard, was given serious credence. This fantasy, promoted amongst others by the Soviet KGB defector and conspiracy theorist Anatoly Golitsyn, was taken up by senior people in the CIA, such as James Jesus Angleton, head of the counter-intelligence branch.

I myself had first become sensitized to how momentous the dispute might become when working on Russia and China in the Foreign Office in the early '60s. What struck me was the racial element. Like others I was tracking the doctrinal bickering visible in public statements and in the Soviet and Chinese press, and in intelligence reports. What finally persuaded me that this was something profound was however an article in an obscure Soviet learned journal vehemently attacking Genghis Khan, in a way designed to make clear that the author had in mind a more contemporary scourge from the East. As for the whole business being a delusion, when I was later mistaken for a Russian and stoned by Red Guards besieging the Russian Embassy in Beijing after a visit there in 1967, their hostility seemed genuine enough to me.

Self-imposed ignorance about China left the field free not just to the vaporings of Yellow Peril-ists, but to credulity of all descriptions. The reaction to America's anti-China policy, when it came under Nixon, was wildly in the other direction, with the President in a state of euphoria about his meeting Mao and hanging on the Chairman's every word. The result could be high-toned farce: 'The Chairman's writings have moved a nation and changed the world' said the rabid anti-communist of a decade earlier during his visit to Beijing. Did he have in mind *The Thoughts of Mao Zedong,* whose infliction as gospel on the Chinese people had certainly changed their country massively, and for the worse. 'Your book, *Six Crises,* is not a bad book' replied the Chairman, in tones of condescension reminiscent of the Qing emperor's treatment of Western envoys two centuries before.

It is fitting that a meeting so replete with operatic aspects should in fact have given rise to one—*Nixon in China.* Inevitably China was once again romanticized, this time in the person of Zhou Enlai, the new Wise Man from the East. The Prime Minister, nicely described by Jonathan Fenby as 'Mao's urbane servitor', emerges from the opera as global statesman and the conscience of nations. It seems unlikely that the opera's composer, John Adams, or the librettist, Alice Goodman, or many of the audience were concerned with the facts about Zhou.

Had they enquired more closely into their hero's background they would have learned that the forte of Mao's ever-faithful executive lay in smart retreat from exposed positions, followed by abject self-criticism for taking the pragmatist road. It has become common to assert that Zhou moderated Mao's excesses. In some foreign policy instances he no doubt did, but in the domestic field there are questions. Where is the evidence that Zhou succeeded in 'moderating' the Great Leap Forward and the Cultural Revolution to any serious extent? And how conceivable is it that, in these key instances, Mao's policies could have been more excessive than they were? Frank Dikötter's recent book *Mao's Great Famine* contains powerful evidence to suggest that Chou played a central executive role in the biggest man-made catastrophe the world has seen, in which 40-50 million people died. Listening to the Zhou in the opera singing 'How much of what we did was good?' is ironic in the circumstances.

It is also worth recalling what he is recorded as saying of Liu Shaoqi, a leading moderate and principal victim of the Cultural Revolution, when his life was at stake: 'This one can be executed' said Zhou of his colleague of more than forty years. (The Prime Minister did not get his way: Liu was kept in solitary confinement, deprived of medicines and fed just enough to keep him alive, as Mao used him as a living target in his campaign.) For what it is worth Zhou's widow, Deng Yingqao, was one of those who resisted reform after the death of Mao. Later it was his adopted son, the widely disliked Li Peng, Prime Minister from 1987-98, who was the leading proponent of using force against the students in Tiananmen Square.

Willful ignorance about the scale and authors of the Great Leap continues to this day, and is not confined to Americans, opera composers or librettists. Responding to a BBC Reith lecturer (Jonathan Spence on Confucius) a few years ago the Archbishop of Canterbury, Rowan Williams, spoke wistfully of a Chinese Communist Party that before the Cultural Revolution had in his view 'guaranteed everyone's welfare', a position that in today's China was under threat from growing inequalities. During the Great Leap the 'guarantee' ran out for tens of millions, leaving them equally dead.

*

In an ideal world it would be the function of academia to avoid the emotion generated by politicians and stick to the facts on China, insofar as they could be known. An objective approach was however explicitly ruled out by American liberal scholars in the '60s. The fact that they were reacting against the anti-China lobby in Washington and the Vietnamese imbroglio may be some excuse, though it only made their sense of righteousness the more vehement:

> The tragic events of the last few years have made us realize that the scholar has a duty to do more than analyze material and act as a technical expert for those who make decisions. He must take a rational and moral position on issues.[1]

'Rational' is fine, but in a Puritanical culture 'moral positions' can easily become moralistic, and moralizing by Chinese scholars could frequently defy reason. If what was meant involved letting a hundred flowers bloom in the sinologists' garden, that too would have been fine, but it most certainly did not: the only position deemed rational and moral was that of the authors, and the upshot was that a dangerous measure of conformism in the field was achieved.

Now that China is more open to the world, myth-making will become harder. Yet an evangelizing temperament, infused with historical guilt and ethnic romanticism can still be evident in assessments by American scholars anxious to see the best in the country, and to champion her against doom-laden books like *The Coming War with China*. All this can lead to a puritanical tendency towards extremes. It is easy to come away from the American debate with the impression that war or a democratic idyll are the only alternatives on offer. Where China is concerned, in America the apocalypse or the millennium are rarely absent.

Again, we have been here before. Along with a quasi-mystical attitude towards the country went an assumption of Maoist infallibility, not only amongst the regime's sympathizers but experts, writers and commentators of all descriptions. Nor was this tendency confined to sinologists of the rose-spectacled variety: even anti-communists could entertain a baleful belief in the devilish resourcefulness of the Chairman. What was seen by dispassionate observers as a gross blunder by the CCP in Chinese domestic or foreign policy was to them a potential master-stroke, whose brilliant cunning only the future would show.

Mao's domestic disasters are too numerous and too obvious to catalogue. Internationally his biggest blunder was to expose himself to an attack by Russia. His arrogance and obduracy in putting ideology before practical politics resulted in China facing an incalculable threat from a neighbour many times more powerful than herself at a time when—for the same reasons—she was isolated and alone. Yet the outcome was later to be seen by those in thrall to the Chairman's magic as a diplomatic coup of incomparable magnitude. It was after this perilous confrontation, from which Mao had been forced ignominiously to withdraw, that the Chinese decided that the threat from Moscow required some strategic reinsurance. Around the same time, for reasons partly to do with Vietnam and Russia, President Nixon and Henry Kissinger were thinking of a rapprochement with China. For once Sino-American interests coincided, and there followed Nixon's visit.

In the excited coverage the event still occasions it is rarely mentioned that Mao's 'coup' in agreeing to normalize links with the US was in truth the result of a massive miscalculation. Awe for the Chairman led many to overlook the simple facts of the situation. The chief sacrilege of the Soviet revisionists in China's eyes was their readiness to downplay revolution and pursue normal relations with the United States. As a result of his behaviour towards Moscow the Great Helmsman was now obliged to do exactly that.

After the Cuba crisis of 1962 China had criticized Khrushchev for adventurism in installing nuclear weapons on the island, and for capitulationism in pulling them out. Mao's conduct on the Ussuri river in 1969, together with his general goading of the Russians, was open to precisely the same criticism. His narrow escape from Russian military punishment was a key factor in forcing him to wind down the most virulent phase of the Cultural Revolution with nothing but massive economic and international damage to show.

Though we still do not know the whole truth about the episode, it has been argued that the reversal of policy towards Washington may have been one of the factors that drove Mao's chosen successor, Marshal Lin Biao, to flee to the Soviet Union (his plane crashed in Mongolia and he was killed.)[2] This seems doubtful on many grounds. Others have said that it was Lin Biao himself who was hot-headed enough to have provoked the Russians on the frontier. Yet even if that were true the responsibility for the overheated atmosphere at the time (not to speak of the appointment of a distinctly unimpressive and oddly neurotic soldier as his 'closest comrade in arms') is Mao's alone.

The normalization of Chinese-American relations after decades of dangerous estrangement was clearly to be welcomed. Yet to applaud the event as a tribute to Mao's strategic genius is exoticism pure and simple. The way Mao switched horses overnight, we are told, demonstrated his infinite resourcefulness (the 'wily oriental ' again), yet a true master of strategy and tactics does not put himself in a situation where such resourcefulness is so desperately required. When Zhou Enlai confirmed that the Chinese were ready to receive the American president publicly in Beijing the White House correctly believed that it was fear of a Russo-American accommodation that was driving China. 'They're scared of the Russians. That's got to be it' Nixon told Kissinger, who himself believed that the Chinese saw the visit as a deterrent to a Soviet attack.[3]

Later the Chinese even began to worry lest their cozying up to Beijing should provoke Moscow into a pre-emptive strike on China to eliminate a threat on two fronts. Claims that Mao's genius consisted in his ability to turn on a sixpence and convert his military reversal into a foreign policy triumph which put Russia on the defensive are equally difficult to credit. Obviously a China that had opened a window to Washington was in a better position than before, but that was because she had ceased behaving like an international leper, and had begun running down the Cultural Revolution.

For all the high-flown prose we read on the epoch-making nature of the summit, it was an event of secondary importance. The crucial point is that, in terms of Mao's domestic agenda, the defeat was total. It was not the Nixon-Mao meeting that changed the course of history and brought about China's integration into the world, it was the reaction against his monumental folly at home. The purpose of the sacrifices he had imposed had been to purify the country. Now his crusade was halted and China was being drawn into the very system of grubby compromise Mao abhorred. And this was only the beginning. Beyond lay—exactly as he had feared—a betrayal of the Chinese revolution and a retreat from almost everything he stood for, whose thoroughness was provoked largely by the irrational, irresponsible and ultimately obtuse policies of the Wise man from the East.

*

In reviewing US attitudes to China populist factors cannot be omitted. America is a diverse society in which extravagant views and behaviour are not unknown, so it is no surprise to find a span of opinion that portrayed Mao in every possible light. For some he was the icon of a highly unspecific world revolution; for others, the living incarnation of Dr Fu Manchu. For the first group decency and moderation in their attitudes to one of the world's most pitiless dictators were for the birds. The Mao-badge craze was suggestive in this regard. A penchant for Nazi insignia tends to designate neo-Nazi sympathies; at the very least it is seen as distasteful. Yet few saw the use of the symbols of a man who had brought about the death of so many of his countrymen as a fashion item or political toy as in any way reprehensible. Like a fancy dress shop catering for a pampered clientele, you borrowed from China what you thought would show you off to advantage.

Following her father's rapprochement with China, Julie, grown-up daughter of Richard Nixon, met the Chairman in Beijing in 1975 wearing a Mao badge. The Chairman was thrilled. (A parallel with Unity Mitford's infatuation with Hitler suggests itself, but doesn't apply, insofar as Julie didn't have the excuse of being a Maoist. She was just having fun.) Like Cameron Diaz, whose decision to sport a bag with a red star and a Mao slogan on a trip to Peru 30 years later, a country where an insurgency led by the Maoist group Shining Path in the '80s and early '90s had left 70,000 dead, the President's daughter was also following fashion. In reporting the Peruvian incident it is noteworthy that the media did not claim that Diaz was showing insensitivity towards the Chinese victims of the Chairman, only towards Peruvians.

To say that it is a mistake to take such behaviour seriously misses the point: what Mao kitsch and Mao fads show is that we do not take China or the Chinese seriously. Beyond the Warholian 'irony' lies an ultimate indifference. An indifference that, now that China is at large again in the world, we shall no longer be able to afford.

*

After centuries of Western fantasies about China it is natural to look sceptically at new attempts to change our understanding of the country and its history. Debates about China's past frequently concern its failures or achievements, and it is true that the levels of civilization achieved by China in the late Ming period and the middle/late Qing dynasty have often been underestimated in the West. The latest bout of revisionism, however, appears designed to persuade us that, until the end of the eighteenth century, in significant respects China and Europe were not just on a level, but that China was often ahead.

A leading exponent of the new view is Peter C. Perdue, an MIT professor. His thesis is that:

1. In late imperial [ie eighteenth century] China, in technology and economic productivity there were no significant differences between China and Western Europe up to the year 1800.

2. In demography and family structure many of China's social practices showed marked similarities to Western Europe. Chinese families did not breed heedlessly, creating a Malthusian situation.

3. In commercial activity, literacy, urbanization or religious doctrines, in both societies there were attitudes and institutions favouring and opposing growth and technological change.

4. There have always been different paths to economic modernity. The one taken by England was merely one of them. The Chinese were especially good at a mixed system, involving state intervention, eg a highly organized grain distribution system, canal construction, the relief of poverty, and land settlement on the frontier.

5.From this it follows that Malthus, Marx and Weber were wrong to base so much of their analysis of capitalism on cultural differences between East and West, and the superiority of the latter.

In taking this line Professor Perdue is arguing against the commonly accepted notion of Chinese mummification and European dynamism in the industrial revolution. Later in that period Chinese economic and social energies did indeed slacken, he admits, after the Empire had finally defeated the tribes threatening them in the North, and a fall in discipline opened the way to corruption and oppression. Hence the flaccid state of the nation when it came under Western assault.

To an extent this view is not new. Large claims have been made for China in the eighteenth century by American China scholars before. Amongst the more startling evaluations underwritten by authoritative figures in China studies was the following:

No country granted its people such durable peace; no country had so high a standard of living; none could match China's constitutional stability; none had comparable art and literature… Life was pleasant, for intellectuals as well as for most of the common people.[4]

These extraordinary statements are not from the mouth of some maverick sinologue. They come from a prestigious and wide-selling publication: *Introduction to Imperial China*, edited by Franz Schurman and Orville Schell. The aim of such extravagant compliments—to give China its historical due—is noble, but the claims on her behalf are unpersuasive. No European country with art and literature comparable to that of eighteenth century China? It is not through any feeling of Eurocentrism that many will find this implausible. Leaving aside Diderot and the Encyclopaedists, which is to leave aside a lot, could not life in the eighteenth-century England of Hume and Burke and Dr Johnson and Sir Isaac Newton and the chemist Joseph Priestley be as pleasant and as cultivated as in China, as well as scientifically and intellectually much in advance? And—unlike China—did not intellectual life in London and Paris at the time encompass a lively interest in distant cultures, and (except for Dr Johnson and his hang-up about alphabets in China), a readiness to see merit in them?

Praise for China's 'constitutional stability' seems equally nonsensical: where individual freedoms are not an issue and the powers of the son of Heaven without limit a measure of stability is guaranteed. One might as well commend Russia for enjoying centuries of stability under a succession of autocratic Tsars. And unlike Catherine the Great, for all his literary merits (his memoirs are a marvel) the Emperor Kangxi (1661-1722) does not qualify as an enlightened despot. Having escaped the influence of his regent thanks to an uncle, he later had him put to death without trial, before killing his six sons in the same way. Suspecting his own son of homosexual dalliances he had three cooks and serving boys murdered. Later, when an adviser suggested that the son, Yin-jeng, be rehabilitated, Kangxi ordered that he be beheaded and his father put to the lingering death afterward. Then he relented, and merely made the father watch while the son was publicly beheaded. Some constitution, some stability.

In the first four decades of Qianlong's reign later in the century the emperor's arbitrary powers reached new heights, though by and large he used them wisely. Public works were undertaken on a large scale, the population grew and the arts flourished, the emperor himself being an essayist, poet and artist. Towards the end of the century however corruption grew and decline set in. There is no doubt that this was something of a Chinese Elizabethan era (minus the voyages of exploration), but if we are in the risky business of comparing civilizations we must surely have regard to the fate of individuals and human progress in its broadest sense.

The claims advanced for China as the most civilized country in the world quoted above were made in 1967, in the middle of the Cultural Revolution, at the same moment (and in the same book) that scholars were enjoined to adopt a 'moral' stance. What is the morality, one wonders, of applying different yardsticks to different cultures? It is strange how China specialists, frequently hyper-sensitive on the history of human rights in their own countries, such as freedom of expression, the condition of women or constitutional advance, become markedly less demanding when engaged in boosting the reputation of the East against Europe or the United States. There would seem scant comparison, for example, between the all-powerful Qianlong and the constitutional monarchy of George III. For all its relative progress and economic and cultural accomplishments one country remained a semi-obscurantist despotism closed to the world while the other was in the vanguard, not just of science, but of modern government and human freedoms.

Perdue takes this idealizing trend further. His research into Chinese technological and organizational advances in the eighteenth century are fascinating, but its import is weakened by overstatement, especially as regards the reasons for China's slippage behind the West at the time of the later industrial revolution. He appears not to believe that this revolution began in Britain as the product of the scientific Zeitgeist, individual freedoms or an entrepreneurial caste of mind. Instead he suggests it was a lucky accident, in particular the discovery of coal close to manufacturing centres. The stark improbability of this explanation puts us on our guard. Eyebrows rise further when he endorses the notion that the reason the Chinese did not develop the steam engine was because they had no use for it.[5] (As Western economies stutter and China forges ahead we are going to hear more of this. Ian Morris, of Stanford University, takes Perdues's theme further in his recent scientist tome *Why The East Rules—For Now.*)

At times Perdue can seem keener to attack European self-regard than to elucidate Chinese history. It is reasonable to puncture overweening Western self-esteem, though not if the purpose is merely to brush up the image of other peoples:

> China was at least equal, if not the superior to Europe, in many measures of economic productivity, popular welfare, and social equality…

The more Perdue ratchets up his claims for the achievements of late imperial China the more we begin to doubt the objective spirit of his enquiry. Individual examples he provides of China's precocity can be persuasive. Arrangements for the centrally organized relief of famine through government activity in the grain market seem to have been particularly advanced, though even here we should avoid being excessively overawed by China's sophisticated economics and enlightened state intervention: in seventeenth century Boston (later the seat of Perdue's MIT) the American Puritans were already discussing Keynesian public investments to stimulate the economy, one of which was a bridge over the Charles river. Like *Imperial China* thirty years before, with its ingratiating tone towards China, the impression Perdue conveys is that, compared to the China of the time, Europe of the eighteenth century was an inferior civilization, not just in some of its economic mechanics, but in the round. This is not a matter of opinion, it is manifestly untrue.

While boosting the achievements of the China of the time he is anxious to defend it against charges of introversion. When the Qing emperor met Lord Macartney, he writes, and told him that his empire 'possessed all things in prolific abundance and lacked no product within its borders', he was not expressing a deep-rooted Chinese sense of xenophobia, but boasting of a very recent achievement, i.e. ending the long threat to his country from the Central Asian steppe. Perhaps, though I doubt it. The Emperor Qianlong's 'decree' to the George III is hardly lacking in chauvinistic touches:

> I have perused your memorial. The earnest terms in which it is

couched reveal a respectful humility on your part, which is highly praiseworthy.... My capital is the hub and centre about which all quarters of the globe revolve... I do not forget the lonely remoteness of your island, cut off from the world by intervening wastes of sea... Our dynasty, swaying the myriad races of the globe, extends the same benevolence towards all.

A moment when China's economy and prestige are rising from the Maoist ashes is an excellent time to question inherited assumptions about the country and its history, and Perdue invites us to take a fresh view of the state of China on the eve of the Western assault. To do so, he appears to believe, will help rid us of cultural preconceptions about the invention of the modern world. In my mind he raises the possibility of a China trundling its way towards its own version of modernity when Western intervention threw it off course, a China that today, after two hundred years of colonialism and Marxist communism, both of them foreign afflictions, is finally renewing with its history. The idea is tantalizing, and could provide clues about how the New China may develop. Yet worries about the author's motives will not go away.

There is no need for us to take sides in a debate which seems to a troubling extent moralistically driven. The risk is one of sinologist revisionists, in their eagerness to 'correct' history, falling victim to the very kind of preconceptions from which Perdue claims to be seeking to escape. Arrogant Western assumptions that Chinese backwardness in the nineteenth century was based on ingrained cultural factors are not disposed of by assertions of her superiority that smack of a compensatory indulgence towards the country. Such indulgence is itself implicitly *de haut en bas*. That is what condescension means.

If all we are saying is that Chinese technology or social organization was more developed than previously supposed, and that we should revise our estimation of Chinese civilization upwards as a result, then there is no problem. Though even then we should be careful to avoid falling into a familiar trap: the assumption that reactionary or autocratic regimes can be justified by the extent of their material achievements or social control. This is an argument that takes us straight back to Mussolini's Italy, where an authoritarian regime allegedly had the benefit of ensuring that the trains ran on time and the telephones worked.

It seems more than coincidence that a parallel debate is underway about the Mughal Empire in India, as that country too rises to a new prosperity. Again the claim is that a nation destined to fall victim to colonial rapacity was previously a flourishing country. Opponents of this theory say it was the British who brought elements of democracy, modernity and the rule of law; others, like the economist Amartya Sen, insist that a tradition of public discussion and dissent already existed which the British suppressed.

Yet another debate on these lines is bubbling up with regard to imperial Japan. There too American writers have begun suggesting that before Commodore Perry's intrusion into her affairs in 1853 Japanese society was on the road to advancement, and that the America irruption deflected it from progressive change into more dangerous and aggressive directions. In other words (and this has been explicitly suggested) at Pearl Harbour, as on 9/11, the US 'had it coming.'[6]

Many unwholesome factors appear to be at work here, including, one suspects, a compulsion to make American guilt over the invasion of Iraq retrospective, as if the spirit of Donald Rumsfeld had presided over the country's entire history. The invasion, such critics claim or imply, is simply the latest instance of clumsy, brutal, imperialistic efforts to foist an alien system of democracy on non-receptive cultures, who in any event had their own forms of progress and civilization, no less meritorious than (and in China's case superior to) those of the West. On India and Japan I do not know enough to offer a view. I simply note the coincidence with the discussion on China, and wonder at the plausibility of the notion that the lives of virtuous, advanced, peaceable and (in their own way) proto-democratic societies all over Asia were deformed and perverted by the intrusions of the West.

At its most extravagant the suggestion appears to be that before being infected with the debilitating European and American virus Asians formed a higher and wiser species of humanity. So we come back to a notion whose pedigree, as we have seen, runs from Prester John in the twelfth century to the hippies of the '60s, and appears to have life in it yet. Besides the Iraqi connection, and the insecurities inspired by the struggle against terror, its resurgence seems to me to have a good deal to do with a decrease in confidence in American democracy itself, and a tendency, characteristic of the Protestant mentality, to seek out ever new fields for self-chastisement. Claims to a monopoly of sin, practitioners of this vice should remember, are more than a symbol of spiritual pride, they are a perverse form of imperialism too.

A truly fresh look at China's history would break with both the patronizing and idealizing tendencies. Perdue's pronouncements can have the flavour of a retrospective exercise in ethnic apologetics, which the Chinese do not need. Overstated claims of Chinese achievements do not encourage us to revise hardened opinions. Instead they underline the central thesis of this book: that our knowledge of China and the Chinese remains so skewed by subjectivity that radical new claims and theories can be thrown out that promise to do something to open our minds to alternative possibilities, but which are ultimately likely to tell us more about ourselves than China.

In this instance we are assured that the sources of our new knowledge are scientific, but as we have learnt to our cost, science too has its biases and mystifications. Preconceptions can too easily influence conclusions, not least when they are born of remorse. There seems little future in seeking to atone for the past by a kind of posthumous kowtowing.

*

Seen alongside the praise lavished on historical and modern China by members of America's Marxist Left, Perdue's claims are modest. Here the boosting of her past and present shows signs of developing into an ideological industry. For European and American Marxists the 'loss' of a truly communist China was in a sense a greater blow than that of the Soviet Union and Eastern Europe. For all her virtues in their eyes, Russia never had the advantage of being fashionable, even amongst its Western sympathizers; China, on the other hand, exercised a perennial appeal to the imagination, which made her defection to capitalism the more painful. A way had to be found to rescue it from its state of perdition, and the leading voice in this task at present belongs to Giovanni Arrighi, a seasoned, seventy-year-old Marxist professor of sociology of Italian extraction teaching at Johns Hopkins University in the USA.

Arrighi's starting point is not Marx but Adam Smith. Smith was of course a richer and more complex thinker than advocates of the rule of market forces in every sector of our lives claim today, and it is this many-sidedness of his writings that, in Arrighi's interpretation, becomes the basis of his Chinese theory. The gist is that China is on the verge of replacing a doomed Anglo-American civilization by something altogether more economically just, socially enlightened and internationally peaceful. You may object that the same thing used to be said by Marxists about the USSR, but that was then, and in any case it was said in a different way.

Unlike other eighteenth century admirers of China (Arrighi argues) Smith understood its economic dynamics. In particular the Scot was canny enough to foresee that, as distinct from Europe, she was pursuing a 'natural' path to development. By this he meant that the Qing empire had concentrated on agriculture before industry and international trade. The result was that, although the internal market flourished, capitalism with all its evils did not take off, and the state played an important role in the economy. The road chosen by Europe, on the other hand, with its precocious and disruptive industrial revolution and scramble for international trade, was 'unnatural'. In Arrighi's interpretation this original sin set the scene for centuries during which rapacious and militaristic Western capitalism ravaged helpless, harmless (and in China's case superior) cultures.

Following the colonial period and the warlord interlude in the early twentieth century China, the theory goes, was fortunate to revert to her agrarian, statist traditions under Mao Zedong. Indeed it was by building on these traditions that Mao secured his 'extraordinary social achievements' (Arrighi shows no interest in their cost in human lives). As for the Cultural Revolution, far from being a disaster, by reinforcing the importance of the countryside in national economic strategy and in the minds of city-bound cadres it helped lay the basis for the economic successes to come.

The switch from extreme leftism to the state-sponsored, buccaneering capitalism of today turns out to have been part of a grand design directed not just at the empowerment of China, but at helping to free the entire Southern hemisphere from US hegemony. Arrighi's reconciliation of Maoist fundamentalism with the reformism of Deng Xiaoping, the man the Chairman hounded, is a small *chef d'oeuvre* of retrospective rationalization that deserves quotation. His starting point is the paradox that China is a bigger threat to the West today than she ever was in the Maoist era:

> A more accurate version of this assessment is that, as long as China was cut off from global trade by US Cold War policies and felt threatened militarily by the USSR, the CCP was driven to use ideology as the main weapon in the struggle to consolidate its power nationally and internationally. But when, in the latter years of the Cultural Revolution, the ideological weapon began to backfire, at about the same time as the United States sought an alliance with China in the Cold War with the USSR, the stage was set for a pragmatic use of the market as an instrument for the empowerment of the Chinese Communist Party nationally, and of the People's Republic of China internationally.

This surreal interpretation of China's history raises the question of whether Mao was just pretending to be a Maoist all those years, or whether China is just pretending to be capitalist now? But then far from representing any kind of ideological sell-out, Arrighi claims, capitalism in China isn't really capitalism at all. Communal action continues and the state has retained laudable eighteenth century powers to oversee the economy. In China as in India what we are seeing, he insists, is not so much an upsurge of production and prosperity through resort to Western-type market forces as 'a golden age of reformed socialism.'

Once again it is China, the New Atlantis. The cliché is true: Marxism was indeed a religion, and Arrighi's analysis of China's future has millenarian overtones. After the necessary destruction of the Cultural Revolution, China inherits the earth. God will wreak His judgment on the West for centuries of evil-doing, and reward the meek and the suffering of the earth, in this instance the Chinese, who will arise as the benign Middle Kingdom of a just and peaceable world order. We are back to Prester John.

I have given Arrighi's thesis more attention than it deserves for a single reason. China has a perennially seductive power for intellectual *fashionistas,* and it seems to me possible that his views could become modish on the broad, liberal Left. To a twenty-five year old disabused by George W. Bush, appalled by the recession, disappointed by Obama, fearful of more 9/11s to come and looking East for hope and spiritual comfort, his arguments could sound plausible, as well as alluringly paradoxical.

Viewed closer they are crazy stuff, yet the perverse pleasure of seeing America as a nation lost and China as a civilization re-born should not be underrated. This and other versions of the Arrighi line seem to me to have the makings of a neo-Maoist orthodoxy in both guilt-stricken America and in americanophobic Europe. It would be good to be wrong.

*

For the French, the British and the Americans, attitudes to China have never quite lost their whimsical aspect. The Russians, being closer, can afford no such luxury. Except for spiritualist fads, for which they too can have a weakness, there is little record of fanciful or idealizing attitudes towards China before or during the Soviet regime. Even at the height of Sino-Soviet friendship in the '50s there was scant enthusiasm for their Eastern brothers: between the signature of an alliance and mutual defence treaty in the presence of Stalin and Mao in 1950, amidst proclamations of eternal friendship and cooperation, and the mass withdrawal of Soviet technicians from China under Khrushchev a mere nine years were to elapse. While happy to talk grandiloquently of their country having its Far Eastern as well as European destiny, Russians have little desire to be thought oriental; rather the contrary. All they knew in the '50s (or thought they knew) was that industrial aid and expertise to China were costing them a lot of money.

The first time I saw the two peoples together was as a postgraduate at Moscow University in the early '60s. The Chinese students kept to themselves and were not encouraged to fraternize with their supposed brothers. They lived in dormitories, had even less money than Russians, led an ascetic existence (unlike the boozy Soviet students they didn't drink), made no attempt to get alongside Russian girls, and went about in mendicant clothes with a vaguely hostile air.

Whatever fellow-feeling there might have been in earlier times—and I doubt it was ever warm—had evaporated by 1961, as the Sino-Soviet dispute began to fester. Russian students called the Chinese *limonchiki* (little lemons), and jokes about them were incessant, indecent and casually racist. Assuming one got there early enough in the morning to catch them, in the student restaurant the virtuously un-hungover Chinese sat at their breakfast, silently, in groups, eating their *kasha* with sour faces and sipping their over-sweet chicory coffee with the same enthusiasm.

To this day what is most striking about the Sino-Russian relationship is the absence of romance. Despite China being its neighbour and the enlivening of Russia's capital city, Moscow's Chinatown (*Kitaigorod*) remains a small and unattractive enclave compared with those of London, New York or Sydney. In the other direction the '80s and '90s of the last century were to see some small new interest amongst Russians in Chinese culture. One of the results of disillusionment with a Marxist materialism that failed to produce material goods was a new taste for orientalist flummery, especially amongst the middle classes.

The end of censorship after the communist collapse resulted in a plethora of mystic books, alongside translations of Western detective novels. Escapism of this kind—Taoism, Buddhism, Chinese gymnastics, the Book of Changes—has been in fashion in the West since the '60s and before, and like our own gap-year students and drop-outs, Russian youth is now more able to don its back-packs and set out in search of Nirvana. (Meanwhile Chinese bent on their own spiritual renewal have tended to make for Tibet, where before recent troubles the streets of Lhasa were full of instant Chinese artists and religious seekers).

Yet a Chinese Nirvana remains a decidedly minority pursuit. For most Russians China represents not a place to go for a rebirth of the soul, but a hulking and somewhat menacing reality. There is nothing exotic, fashionable or ironic about having a vast, over-populated country of a billion three hundred million people as your neighbours, whose politics lurch alarmingly from one extreme to the other, whose economy is now blossoming mightily along with its military strength, and who have from time to time laid claim to large portions of your territory.

With his tongue in his cheek a Russian historian[8] has identified the trace elements in the Russians' violently changing views of its great neighbour:

- A natural ally in revolutionary Russia's struggle with world imperialism.
- A hostile dictatorship over a people marinated in propaganda willing to lose much of its population in nuclear war and to get its hands on Russian territory.
- A rightwing, revisionist regime, sold out to imperialism and demolishing socialist structures.
- A successful socialist regime that, unlike Gorbachev, has been able to reform itself and improve living standards without restoring capitalism.
- A country of Eastern wisdom, fine poetry and profound philosophy.

After the communist collapse in Russia relations with America and Europe were the country's first priority, and in their enthusiasm to westernize under President Yeltsin the Russians underrated the looming rise of their eastern neighbour. A detail gives the flavour: in 1992 the Minister for Foreign Trade mounted an ill-starred drive to interest the Chinese in Russian-made white goods of such chronic unreliability the Russians themselves refused to buy them. Exporters of Russian arms, badly hit by cuts in the defence budget, had more success. Strategically however a low view of China persisted in the new Russia, with all the old suspicions of her long term intentions in the Far East.

On the face of it there was plenty for them to worry about. The demography of the area is startling. According to a 1993 census the population of the entire Russian Far East was less than eight million, and shrinking. The three North Eastern Chinese provinces opposite numbered over 100 million people and were growing, rapidly. After a visit to the Amur region at the time, one minister opined that it was potentially a rich area, and went on: 'The Chinese and Koreans have understood this quickly enough, which is why they have literally occupied our Far East. Before you know it they'll be pronouncing it their own slit-eyed republic.' In 2000, with his familiar forcefulness, Putin himself told an audience in Blagoveschensk that economic and demographic problems in the Far East were posing a threat to the very future of the region as part of Russia:

> I don't want to be over-dramatic, but if we don't make real efforts quickly, in a few decades even the Russian population will be speaking Japanese, Chinese and Korean.

As President, however, Putin has refrained from playing the anti-China card. On the contrary, he has tried to re-balance Russia's position between East and West in an Easterly direction. 'Russia flies on two wings, the European and the Asiatic' he has written. To complete the metaphor it was stressed that it was not for nothing that the Russian eagle had two heads looking different ways. The Balkans war and NATO's bombing of Belgrade helped strengthen the neuroses of a much-weakened Moscow about America's global hegemony, a concern that was to pull the countries closer.

Meanwhile, after years of negotiations an agreement on the Eastern frontier with China (along the Argun, Amur and Ussuri rivers) had been signed in 1991. Agreement on the shorter, Western side (in China's Xinjiang province) came two years later, followed by yet more frontier agreements with the now independent republics of Kazakhstan, Kyrgyzstan and Tajikistan. But there were new problems.

After the 1969 clashes Moscow had taken swift and energetic measures to develop the frontier areas and beef up their defences, and the locals lived better as a result. Following the fall of Soviet communism, insecurity in the area had taken new forms. Workers lost many of their privileges, such as a premium on their wages and extra supplies of scarce consumer goods. As in Russia as a whole corruption increased, a mafia sprang up, there were electricity and water shortages, and an outflow of the population began. On the positive side frontier controls were weakened, and for a while cross-border trade prospered. Cheap Chinese goods could be bought with a minimum of bureaucracy and Chinese merchants were happy to barter, e.g. for timber.

The honeymoon proved brief. Before long the Russians were in a position to compare Chinese goods with South Korean, Japanese or American produce and found Chinese quality wanting. An influx of Chinese merchants and their families across the unregulated frontier brought anxiety about being swamped. False invitations by Russian institutes, phony marriages, 'tourists' who stayed touring indefinitely— the Chinese, according to inflamed local Russian newspapers, were up to every trick. There were tales of contraband, the Chinese mafia, and the seizure of Russian goods in China. All the Chinese wanted, the increasingly chauvinistic press began to claim, was access to Russian timber, coal, fertilizer, metal and fish. After a dispute between local politicians and Moscow the locals won and the open frontier was closed.

A sober look at the facts suggest that Russian fears about being submerged by Chinese immigrants were seriously overplayed, for predictable racist reasons. Official figures show that the number of Chinese in the Russian Far East as a whole when the visa-free frontier was open was a mere 50-60,000, a figure which sank even lower after the frontier closed in 1994. It is true that some Chinese went further West, though there is no evidence of large-scale clandestine immigration: even in Moscow the numbers are a tiny 20-25,000.

None of this prevented Far Eastern Russians believing that the Chinese government was pushing a programme of a 'shift to the North' and 'quiet expansion.' Anti-Chinese feelings hardened further when it was rumoured that if they were awarded two pieces of land on the Tuman River, as was proposed, the Chinese would gain not only an outlet to the Sea of Japan; they would be in a position to build a sea-going port, lay a railway to Europe across Kazakhstan, and destroy the entire Russian Far Eastern economy.

Paranoia such as this, provincial in every sense, nevertheless reflects a profound Russian unease about China. Russians as a whole are less racially tolerant than Western Europeans, and the further eastwards you go, it seems, the more the race factor comes into play. One statistic sums up the situation neatly: a survey showed that while 6.5 per cent of Muscovites would be happy to have a Chinese spouse, in Khabarovsk the figure fell to 0.9 per cent—though attitudes may be changing.

*

Today a pietistic tone, eerily reminiscent of that prevailing before the great split, has crept into official Sino-Russian relations. Since Putin entered the Kremlin and subsequently became Prime Minister trade has more than tripled, and China has put money into Rosneft, the quasi-nationalized Russian oil company. In 2001 came the formation of the Shanghai Cooperation Organization, a Central Asian grouping of smaller countries led by Russia and China. More significant states in the region like India, Iran, Pakistan and Mongolia are admitted as observers. Initially its aim was to counter the smuggling of drugs and weapons as well as terrorism and separatism. In August 2007 however its remit appears to have been expanded, as Russia and China conducted joint military exercises within the framework of the organization.

Talk of a Sino-Soviet Nato may be wide of the mark, yet there is no doubt that this flamboyant cooperation is meant to signal a joint determination to counter the American presence in the region and its muscle in the world. After a period during which Russia's international power and prestige had shrunk dramatically it suited Putin to put the West on its guard by harking back, albeit with limited plausibility, to the great days of the Sino-Soviet bloc, just as he found it expedient to reinstate the Soviet national anthem.

Reasons for a cooperative approach are not lacking. Economically Russia and China are to an extent interdependent: broadly speaking Russia provides raw materials, machinery and weapons—in 2006 half of Russia's $6 billion of arms sales went to China—and China consumer goods. (This happy complementarity is said to be echoed in marriage arrangements that can prevail along the frontier. Because of China's one-child policy and preference for boys, Chinese men suffer from a dearth of marriageable women. Russian women, on the other hand, endure a dearth of sober, energetic Russian males. For all the statistical reluctance of Far Eastern Russians to countenance mixed unions, the result has apparently been a recent spate of cross-border unions.)

Both countries have terrorist problems, China in Xinjiang (there are some 35 million Muslims in China) and Russia in Chechnya and elsewhere. Both dislike Western hegemony in the world, and each resents being pressured to look to their human rights and develop democracies that pass muster. (The Chinese will have noted Russia's absence from the presentation of the Nobel award to Liu Xiaobo with contentment.) It is in this spirit that they have sometimes linked up on issues such as Iran or the Libyan crisis of 2011 in the United Nations to use whatever means they can contrive to sabotage Western efforts to secure unanimity in the Security Council. Neither country is an adequate counterweight to America by itself, but together their influence could loom increasingly large.

Yet old antipathies seem likely to endure. The fact that Russia is a European country which happens to have its main landmass in Asia makes the Sino-Russian border the frontier between East and West, and it has always been restive. Russians crossed the Urals at the end of the fifteenth century. Beginning at the end of the sixteenth they expanded towards the Pacific Ocean, founding Okhotsk in 1638. At that stage they confined themselves to Northern latitudes, leaving Baikal and the Amur river far to the South. Yet the Amur region appears to have exercised a mysterious attraction over Russian minds, and legends about it spread across Siberia. Around the time of the Manchu occupation of Beijing in 1644 Cossacks made probing raids against the Daurian tribes in the South. Such was their ferocity that when in 1650 Khabarof, a wealthy Siberian, reached the Amur with the intention of subjecting the newly discovered territories, the inhabitants fled.

Racial and civilizational strains in the relationship, there from the beginning, are unlikely to melt away. It is enough to talk to educated, otherwise modern-minded Russians about their Asian neighbour: for all China's prosperity and international efflorescence, and the impression of a new partnership now officially encouraged, the impression that comes across is similar to the one I first encountered some forty years ago. Still today, in the attitude of the average Russian towards China there are intimations of distaste, derision—and apprehension.

China's claim to great swathes of the Russian Far East, albeit in abeyance, is on record. A hint of Russia's continuing disquiet over the problem has come in a detailed study of the frontier that has recently appeared in Russian, worryingly entitled *Four Thousand Kilometres of*

Problems, though its conclusion is that the Chinese are too pragmatic to reassert their historic claims: for the foreseeable future Moscow remains the superior military power, and memories of the near miss of 1969 will not fade quickly.

Moscow's most pressing problem remains the future of the Russian Far East as the population drains away. Post-communist Russians, as well as being more mobile, have gone soft, preferring less rigorous climes. Some 30 per cent of the population has disappeared from the region in a decade. Two-thirds have also gone from the Russian North, and many are leaving Siberia. Russian concern about the long term is revealed by the strikingly defensive language in semi-official documents describing their current idyll with China: 'The Russian and Chinese people, who have never been to war in the past, have no deep historical reason to go to war in the future.'[10]

It is hard not to sympathize with Moscow's underlying nervousness. Its giant neighbour is both prickly and unpredictable. For all her intricate involvement in China, notably in the twenties and thirties of the last century when Stalin was Mao's inconstant ally, Russia was as taken aback as everyone to see the country ricochet from manic leftism to unbridled capitalism within not much more than a decade. To be ideologically lambasted for being renegades to Marxism in the 'goulash communism' debate of the '60s, only to find themselves outdone in the race for more and better goulash, cannot have been a gratifying experience for Moscow. And insofar as China's conversion showed that Russia had been right all along, Beijing's final abandonment of the miserabilist Maoism that had kept her in poverty and isolation was from Moscow's point of view something of a Pyrrhic victory.

The race to modernize began from different starting points—Russia with political reform and China with economic liberation—but they are running the same track. And while for obvious reasons Russia remains ahead in GNP per head, China's economy is three times larger and the days when she could rely on technological superiority to compensate for the disparity of populations are numbered. The prospect of a rich colossus with a population nearly fifteen times larger than her own on her eastern frontier will preoccupy Russia for years to come. Another danger lies in the possible destabilization of China as her national recovery roars unsteadily ahead.

For the moment Russian preoccupations are well concealed. 'From confrontation to partnership' trumpets an official tract celebrating the normalization of relations, and the 65th anniversary of Russia's victory against Nazi Germany in May 2010, attended by President Hu Jintao, served as a public demonstration of amity. 'A model for big-power relations,' China's Foreign Minister Yang Jieqi called the Beijing-Moscow axis.

There is no shortage of cautionary voices on the Russian side. Echoing conservative politicians in America a Russian professor of politics[11] has openly discussed the need for containment. It is strange to see George F. Kennan's recommendation on post-war policy towards the Soviet Union applied by a Russian to China, and of course Russia could not do it alone. The 'containing' countries he sees as including the US and India, which complicates matters.

From both the Russian and Western perspective the term 'containment' seems misplaced in other ways. Kennan's policy was directed against an ideologically-based regime that had just swallowed up Eastern Europe and whose revolutionary aims were global. China today has no ideology to export, unless it is that, in the short term, a mixture of political authoritarianism and economic liberalism can produce the goods.

Containment evokes a measure of isolation that was desirable in the case of Stalin, though not for the new China: most see it as more sensible to draw her out of herself and bind her into a web of international commitments. In any event, economically a policy of containment is not an option. Just as America is addicted to the cheap Chinese imports that help keep down her inflation and interest rates, so in the future whole regions of Russia seem likely to become dependent on Chinese trade, Chinese entrepreneurs and Chinese energies for the development of their economies.

This is true not only of the Russian Far East. In years to come Chinese economic expansionism seems likely to be felt right up to the Urals and the Caucasus. Her influence in Central Asia also seems destined to outweigh that of Russia, Turkey and Iran. In the end everything comes back to numbers. The demography of Russia as a whole is dire. According to UN projections not so long ago the population, currently 146 million, will be between 70-100 million by 2050, and of this as much as a third could be non-Russian. Even Turkey could be larger. One statistic is more imposing than all the rest. On the lowest estimate for Russia and the highest for the United Kingdom, if our own Office of National Statistics are to be believed, due to the effects of mass immigration even the population of Britain could be bigger than hers in a few decades—an extraordinary thought, even if it is notional.

Little wonder President Putin has described his country's demographic decline as its most serious problem, and promised £5000 to any Russian woman who gives birth to a second child. But that is only one side of the question. If the birth rate is bad the death rate is worse: for every 1000 Russians there are 16 deaths and 10.6 births. In America the comparable figure for deaths is almost half, and in Russia many of those dying are men of working age. Putin is ambitious for a resurgent Russia, not least so as to keep pace with China, but how do you develop the potential of such an enormous territory with massively diminishing human resources?

Across the world migration on an unprecedented scale is underway. Mexico is exploding into America, and North Africa overflowing into Europe. A movement appears to be at work which global warming seems likely to intensify. In this connection the British scientist James Lovelock has suggested that the warming underway in Siberia and the Russian Far East could make the Primorskaya (Maritime) region more attractive to Chinese immigrants.[12] (The prospect of mass immigration at some point in the future recalls a Soviet joke from the '70s: 'A rumour is going round that schools will soon teach three foreign languages: English and Hebrew for those who plan to leave, and Chinese for those who plan to stay.')

Could China ever become Russia's Mexico, though infinitely larger and more advanced? The demographic imperative cannot be ignored indefinitely. In one form or another China seems destined to unload some of her population into the wide empty spaces of Far Eastern and, over time, more westerly Russian provinces. For all Putin's bitter words before his election on ethnic Russian inhabitants speaking Chinese, it could be that future Russian governments will be driven to allow a virtual sinification of large tracts of Eastern Russia, rather as Latinos are coming to dominate Florida and the West Coast of the United States. An alternative might be some sort of enterprise zones peopled by guest workers, though in practice that might amount to the same thing.

Seen in the abstract, importing tens of millions of Chinese to populate and energize the country might seem to make sense. The demand for manpower is unlikely to be satisfied by migrants from elsewhere: people from the former Soviet republics to the south, besides being unavailable in the necessary quantities, would in Russian eyes carry the Muslim virus; already an Azerbaijani has a poor time of it in Russia. Russian chauvinism is fanned by high birth rates amongst the Muslim minority: since 1989 Islamic Russians have grown by 40 per cent to 25 millions. Meanwhile the possibility of attracting immigrants from Eastern Europe seems highly improbable; their experiences at Russia's hands in the past have not been of a kind to tempt them, not to speak of climatic and cultural disincentives, and with major countries like Poland now in the European Union there is scant attraction in looking East.

While the economics of mass Chinese immigration would be seductive, the politics of absorbing millions from a country with a history of claims on her territory seem problematic. As the ethnic Russian population contracts even ten million Chinese would form a huge minority, and behind them would stand the power of the resurgent Chinese state. What would be the attitude of a rich, militarily powerful, self-confident China to the perception that Chinese immigrants were being ill-treated or discriminated against somewhere in the region?

Constantly we return to the frontier problem. Theoretically it is settled, but it has a way of coming back. Historic claims can never be entirely withdrawn, and the population imbalance and temperature changes in frontier areas will help keep them psychologically alive. As China's exports develop it will seem increasingly anomalous for her to have no outlet to the Sea of Japan, north of her frontier with North Korea.

There have been Sino-Russian frontier treaties in the past, notably in 1858 and 1860, when Russia took advantage of Western pressures on

China to regain part of the territory the Qing emperors had seized during the seventeenth and eighteenth centuries. But the Chinese never accepted what they had signed, and were later to insinuate that, like the agreements ending the Opium Wars with Britain, these were 'unequal treaties' requiring eventual re-negotiation. It was in 1960, three years after Khrushchev had so generously provided him with nuclear facilities, that Mao began grumbling audibly about a million and a half square kilometres of 'lost territories'.

Russian experts on China[13] have acknowledged that for all the recent border agreements radical attitudes continue to exist among intellectual and political elites on either side. A populist Chinese book of contemporary history that became a best-seller in 1996, and took a stridently nationalist tone, was ominously entitled *China Can Always Say No*. Once again it reverted to lost territories and unequal treaties, and contained a coda almost designed to play on Russian nerves:

> Of course we haven't got the strength to demand them back. But we Chinese reserve to ourselves the right to remember, the right to think back to all this, if not the right to seek them out, then the right of recall.[14]

On the Russian side there are people who persist in believing that the recent frontier agreements were negotiated too hurriedly. Though officially there are still fewer than half a million Chinese nationals in the whole of Russia, mutterings about the 'Yellow Peril' (the Russians have the same expression) that began a century earlier can be heard again. Even a moderate Russian historian has warned of uncertainties in the future:[15]

> Analysis of Russo-Chinese relations allows us to conclude that theories about a Chinese threat always become popular at times when the Russians believe their country to be weak or unable to develop their Far Eastern regions enough to allay the Chinese challenge. If the present Russian government proves unable to arrest the weakening of the country and work out an effective strategy for the development of the Far East, these theories could once again

come to the fore and begin to exercise a definite effect on Russian foreign policy.

A more forthright foreign policy analyst, Andrei Piontkovsky, has put things bluntly. For him the new version of Sino-Soviet brotherhood is 'an alliance between a rabbit and a boa constrictor'.[16]

One way and another the Russians have not made much of a success of their far Eastern enterprise since the seventeenth century. Already in the first years of the twentieth, when the Manchurian War was brewing, observing and comparing the behaviour of the Russians and Chinese at the time a British traveller and writer was not hopeful about the future:

In Manchuria itself every day fresh signs may be seen by the intelligent observer of how the Russian is being bled to death by the Chinaman, and will be ruined in the long run if he is not more careful—war or no war—for the bear is no match for the dragon in times of peace.... One Chinaman is the equivalent of sixty Russians! And observe that the Chinaman I am using as a basis for my calculation is the Chinaman of the North, whose business capacity is insignificant compared to that of the Chekiang and Canton merchant. When these latter make their way up North in increasing numbers, as they are beginning to do, the position of the Russians will be even more parlous than it at present.[17]

DEMOCRACY: CROSSING A RIVER WITHOUT A BRIDGE

4

'China feels like an old tin of beans that, having lain in the dark for forty years, is beginning to burst at the seams.'

Ma Jian, Red Dust

The title of this chapter echoes a Chinese saying, whose full meaning is 'feeling your way across a bridgeless river.' With no precedents to guide them as to how their country should be governed in the post-Mao era, and no foreign model to emulate, assuming they were ready to adopt one, 'feeling its way' is what China appears to be doing. The West has no bridge into China's future either, but we do not feel our way before tendering advice, we plunge straight in.

China is an old and complex culture, yet our view of it is simple. There is no problem deciding what the country needs, we appear to think, or what is likely to happen. An expanding economy run by a corrupt and authoritarian communist party is unsustainable. As the country roars unsteadily ahead a middle class will be thrown up which will demand its rights, and democracy will follow, as day follows night. Some even pinpoint the exact moment of transition. Asked when China would become a democracy, an American expert responded without hesitation: that blessed state would come about in the year 2015, he wrote, because on current performance that would be the year China clocked up a per capita income of between $7000-$8000 annually.

How much of this is true belief, and how much wishful thinking by evangelically-minded Westerners, is immaterial. Of course one is free to take the line that all China has to do to modernize itself is to repeat what has happened in Eastern Europe: abandon the dictatorship of the Party and adopt a full-scale parliamentary constitution. Worthy and self-gratifying as that stance might be, it has the disadvantage of forestalling consideration of what in reality is likely to happen, and therefore gets us nowhere.

It is true that China's authoritarian regime is increasingly out of sync with international trends. 'China is not exotic' it has been said, 'only the Chinese Communist Party is', and as she has opened up to the world financially her political exoticism has become more marked.[1] The number of democracies in the world rose from ten in 1900 to thirty in mid-century, where it stalled. Then came a surge: by 2005 119 of the world's 190 countries were democracies, and events in the Middle East could further improve things. With her one-party state China now finds herself isolated amongst the larger nations of Asia, with democratic India to the West, Japan to the East, and Russia and Indonesia to the North and South.

This would seem to support the theory that it will not be long before China succumbs to domestic and international pressures and falls into line. Perverse as it seems to question a scenario that is devoutly to be wished, it is something I propose to do.

*

The problem with the democratic prognosis is not so much that it projects on China Western values, but Western historical processes. Pressure for representative government, we are assured, will follow automatically on industrial expansion and the creation of wealth. Yet it is unclear why progress towards democracy should mirror Western experience when at every stage the development of China has been different. Liberal democracy in the West matured over several hundred years, and remains imperfect. In this evolution religion was key: the Reformation encouraged the questioning of civil authority and of the power of the landed classes. Seeking parallels between Christianity and Confucius can be diverting, though ultimately pointless, because China is self-evidently *sui generis*. Not only does its history offer few parallels to that of Europe; it is hard to compare to that of other Eastern nations who have developed democracy, such as India or Japan.

A unique history has been followed by a unique present. To give an idea of just how singular the case of China is, it suffices to ask the question: which other country with a billion-plus population and a five thousand year-old civilization, whose proud spirit led it to regard itself till rather recently as the centre of the world, has been catapulted from extreme leftwing totalitarianism to gold-rush capitalism in three decades, while maintaining a communist political structure? The Chinese are not only aware of their difference, they assert their right to it. On the eve of a trip to Britain in 2006 the Prime Minister, Wen Jiabao, said:

> Democracy is a value pursued by all mankind and a fruit of civilization created by mankind. However, in different historical stages and different countries democracy is achieved through different forms and in different ways.

It sounds both high-minded and hard to deny, though we know what the Prime Minister was getting at. Chinese talk of different ways to democracy puts us in mind of the Russian government's neologism, 'managed democracy'. Under the guise of a right to cultural difference each regime is seeking ways to ward off the advent of free, representative government in any meaningful sense. What these Sino-Russian euphemisms come down to is the continuation of a central role for the state, a single party in all but name, highly circumscribed freedom of expression and a readiness to crush dissent.

Russia has its despotic lineage under the Tsars and Stalin, China its Confucian and Maoist models, and although they are distinct cultures at different stages of development, each is groping for ways to combine these autocratic traditions with twenty-first century capitalism. It is a system they have belatedly adopted because only capitalism can produce sufficient wealth to satisfy popular demands, legitimate their power, and make their countries strong. At the same time both the Russians and the Chinese allow it to be understood that a fuller democracy is their eventual goal. Yet the results to date can often smack less of democratic evolution than of a drift towards new authoritarian, corporate models.

What is forgotten by those urging democracy on China is that, theoretically, the structures we would like to see there already exist in Putin's Russia; a discouraging precedent, when you think of it. When Gorbachev opened the country up there was a surge of optimism in the West. China had begun its modernization with the economy. Russia, more sensibly it seemed, laid down democratic foundations on which a market system was to develop.

In their euphoria at having won the Cold War even realists like Mrs Thatcher appeared to believe that, once representative institutions were in place, all that remained was for Russia to sell off her nationalized industries, install free markets, and everything would take care of itself. The legacy of centuries of oppression, briefly interrupted by a liberal period at the turn of the twentieth century, would finally be swept away, and a fully-fledged democracy would emerge. The fact that Russians had been bought and sold as serfs as recently as 1861, or that they had suffered new forms of serfdom under Soviet rule, would cease to have any influence on their mentality: freedom would take root and entrepreneurial zeal would flourish. She knew all this because Gorbachev seemed to her a civilized man with whom she could do business.

What happened to Gorbachev's revolution there is no need to recall.[2] Today we are seeing the renationalization of the country's most powerful industries, a suppression of dissent, a re-imposition of control of the media, a de facto reversion to a one-party state, and a foreign policy increasingly redolent of Soviet days, which is to say a combination of bullying and paranoia. Instead of becoming rich and sophisticated Russia is becoming rich and, in its international style and conduct, increasingly uncouth. The West should not just keep its nose out of Russian elections, Putin advised us in 2007, but its 'snotty nose'. And the average Russian rejoiced in their leader's way with words.

In a country which after 1989 had become freer than it had been in its entire existence, how could all this have happened? Because the West played a poor hand in dealing with the morbid sensitivities of post-Soviet Russia, notably in the Georgia crisis of 2008, but chiefly because a measure of oppression and brutishness conforms to the Russian spirit. There are enlightened souls who deplore what is going on, but satisfaction ratings with Putin remain high, not least over his nationalistic policies, and there is every likelihood that he will regain his country's presidency should he choose. As for his encroachments on the media, according to recent polls 1 per cent of those questioned thought that free speech was a crucial matter, and less than 50 per cent thought that Russia needed a political opposition at all.

In an un-characteristic moment of apology for his increasingly autocratic style, Putin told the West that it would take time for a multi-party system to take root.[3] Meanwhile, like Wen Jiabao, he works to ensure that no alternative party can come to power. Rather than China aspiring to emulate political progress of Russia, such as it has been, it seems more a case of Russia regressing to Chinese norms of single party control.

I reach for the Russian parallel not because of clear-cut historical affinities—in the end China is always on her own—but because it is the only one that occurs to me, and the nearest to hand: a neighbouring country where an overnight switch from Marxism to capitalism has taken place. What is now becoming clearer by the day is that the source of Russia's hostility towards the West was not simply the October Revolution and its aftermath: it is because of who the Russians are. That is why they had the revolution.

Their ambiguities (or antipathy, if you prefer) towards the West spring from a sense of spiritual superiority coupled with the knowledge of an inferior material mode of living, and have deeper and longer roots than Marx, who as in China was after all a Western import. Similarly the gradual eclipse of communism in China could expose more plainly its nationalistic roots, and its reluctance to take the West as a model. True, there are important distinctions between the two countries. China's modernization has not involved divesting herself of an empire, or in a sharp decline in her power *vis à vis* the West, resulting in the poisonous sense of rancour and consequent self-assertion we are seeing in Russia. The Chinese have more confidence in themselves and their future, with good reason, and with millennia of civilization behind them are less wracked by feelings of inferiority.

Yet China is not without her grievances. The legacy of colonialism is there in her sensitivity to Western didacticism about democratic models. Her official comment on the emergency in Kenya following the disputed elections of December 2007 is an example. The problem, China implied, had nothing to do with Africans or tribalism, but resulted from the West's neo-colonialist aspiration to foist its version of democracy on the world. Her reluctance to condemn the despots of the Middle East during the uprisings of early 2011 are the product of the same mindset.

To say that China is doomed to repeat the Russian experience, and that after its recent progress a period of recidivism is unavoidable, would be going too far. But her history makes it plausible to speculate that, with or without democracy, there will be limits to her toleration of political liberties, and that the behaviour of a rich, renascent China is unlikely to be quiescent. Meanwhile the Russian example will not be lost on the CCP. For reformists, the spectacle of an increasingly prosperous country backsliding in an authoritarian direction is a dismal portent of what democracy in China could entail; it also diminishes the pressure for China to embark on democracy at all. The Chinese will see that Russia remains a member of the G8, and that its prickly, recalcitrant and boorish behaviour does little to diminish the West's anxiety to do business with her.

If something that might loosely be called the Sino-Russian model of authoritarian capitalism can be said to exist it seems destined to be extended to other communist countries, such as post-Castro Cuba, and one day perhaps North Korea. Each case has its particularities, yet it appears only a matter of time before the destitute regimes of Pyongyang and Havana come to understand that the choice is not between prosperity and Party control. China is demonstrating that the former can be used to sustain the latter, while the lesson of Russia is that the accoutrements of democracy are by no means incompatible with centralized diktat and single party rule.

*

The question of how far the Chinese temperament is suited to representative government at all is sometimes answered by reference to the democracies existing in Taiwan and Singapore, and to the situation in Hong Kong. Taiwan has directly elected central and local governments and freedom of the press. Though it triumphed in the elections of January 2008, the automatic dominance of the Kuomintang is a thing of the past, even if the prevalence of fraud and corruption and family clans is not. A mayor of Taipei, Ma Yingjeou, inadvertently echoing the Chinese Prime Minister Wen Jiabao, is fond of saying that 'Democracy in China is always a question of degree.' The mainland, with its preference for Western concepts with 'Chinese characteristics', might silently agree.

Singapore, 75 per cent of whose 4.5 million inhabitants are Chinese, is another community where the degree of democracy has been prudently measured. As anyone who has been there quickly comes to feel, its atmosphere of agreeable orderliness is tinged with mild constraint. (This is the kind of place that paternalist British Tories privately admire.) While having universal suffrage it has also contrived to be run by the same party in the forty-four years of its existence, an achievement that owes something to its habit of trimming the freedom of the press and other liberties.

Moreover comparisons between China and Singapore, however close their ethnic affinities, are intrinsically suspect. Whatever its attractions as a model for the mainland, imagining China as an inflated version of the island is a little like saying that Britain's problems could be resolved if only she would become another Sweden. The question is not simply one of culture or political preferences, but of scale, history and dynamics. Just as there are more Londoners than Swedes, there are five times as many Shanghainese as Singaporeans. Even if China's communist leaders were to decide that the Singapore model was for them, what works in a small, tightly controlled island would be difficult to transplant to an entire empire (where are Singapore's Mongols, Tibetans or Uighurs?)

The case of Hong Kong, though another island, is more pertinent. While enjoying free speech and an open system of law it has never been a democracy with universal suffrage for legislative elections. Now that it is under Beijing's indirect control, and the frontier is more porous, some see its peculiar combination of lack of true democracy coupled with a seductively free way of life seeping onto the mainland. This makes the recent history of democracy in the former Colony worth a word.

Democracy under the British was of the paternalist variety, a system of rule that was generous with its individual liberties while sparing its children the chore of voting. Yet it is false to assert that Hong Kong Chinese chafed under the absence of a directly elected Parliament. Before the prospect of returning the territory to the mainland arose, pressure for democratic advance, while present, was limited. Once that return became a certainty it picked up sharply. But for many in Britain these are difficult truths to swallow, so the past has been reinvented. It is now widely believed that before as well as after the Tiananmen killings in 1989 the British willfully stood in the way of the democratic evolution desired by the majority of the population, because of a policy of kowtowing to China.

This is op-ed history. A true democracy in Hong Kong was never possible, irrespective of British wishes. The Colony existed under sufferance and the communists would never have allowed representative government to establish itself, even if the British had been eager to see it happen, which for Realpolitik reasons as well as lack of pressure, they were not.

Real democracy would have entailed a proliferation of parties. Those with anti-Mao (or pro-Taiwan) sympathies would have exercised their right to free speech to agitate against the mainland. Even assuming the communists would have tolerated 'anti-Chinese' political parties on territory they believed (with good reason) to be their own, they would have established their own mass movement to counter them. The likely result would not have been opposing parties peacefully contending for parliamentary power: it would have been blood on the streets. The Colony could easily have been de-stabilized, something neither the British, the mainland Chinese nor the majority of the population wanted.

A move to genuine democracy would also have been seen by a paranoid Beijing as preparation for independence; in Taiwan, as we have seen, any prospect of that brings a blizzard of threats from Beijing. In Hong Kong the risk was that an irritated China might reach out a paw and grab its territory back. During the 1967 disturbances, when to China's fury some communist rioters were shot and many jailed, I recall our constant awareness of the risk of a takeover, which as Deng Xiaoping was to remind Mrs Thatcher in 1982 would be the work of an afternoon. With this in mind officials like myself were issued with emergency evacuation kits during the troubles.

Paradoxically, the risk of invasion was to increase in the more relaxed climate following Mao's death. China had held her hand before because of the economic cost of a takeover; now that a market economy was on the rise on the mainland itself confidence that she could run Hong

Kong without killing the golden goose was growing. In the back of British minds during the negotiations that led to the return of the Colony there was always the thought that if we overplayed our hand, especially on the democracy issue, the Chinese might lose patience and serve notice of occupation overnight.

The case for prudence has now been spectacularly confirmed, and it has nothing to do with kowtowing to China. The danger of a forcible takeover, it turns out, was more imminent than anyone supposed. In 2007 Lu Ping, the senior Chinese official who headed the negotiations, confirmed that invasion was a serious possibility.[4] It appears that Deng Xiaoping, reasonably enough, was afraid that announcing the 1997 handover so far in advance might precipitate unrest in the Colony, a risk which could be pre-empted by implementing his implied threat to Mrs Thatcher.

In these calculations there was always an emotional element. What the British tend to forget is that the Chinese were capable of hard-line behaviour over the Colony because they were Marxists, though also because they felt they had a justified grievance. Our habit of proclaiming Hong Kong a brilliant economic success made China's humiliation worse. There she sat, on the Security Council of the United Nations, the foremost anti-imperialist power obliged to tolerate a British Colony on her territory because it earned her a lot of foreign currency—a fact that the Russians had made much of when the communist giants were at each other's throats.

In the course of the stormy secret negotiations with mainland communist representatives to resolve the 1967 crisis I gained a sense of their personal as well as official resentment at being obliged to negotiate with occupiers of Chinese soil. Years later, in 1981, when as principal private secretary to the Foreign Secretary Lord Carrington I met Deng Xiaoping when the future of Hong Kong was discussed, the force of the Chinese leader's resolution on the issue was tangible.

Handing over a democratic Hong Kong to the mainland was always a non-starter, a fantasy indulged by the Governor and the British media to save British face. 'Face' in this instance meant going out on a moral high, so as to disguise the unavoidable fact that we were handing the Colony back to a regime that had massacred hundreds of its citizens in

Tiananmen Square eight years earlier. In this self-interested charade our stance was as unseemly as its morality was questionable. Holding up a false promise of democracy in the Colony after doing so little about it for the century and a half we were there (even if for good reason) was a disreputable act.

Far from being a display of courage in 'standing up to China', what it showed was a certain gutlessness: real courage would have involved recognizing the realities of the situation and using international concern and diplomatic skills as a lever to get a better deal for Hong Kong citizens than we did. As it was we merely tweaked the tiger's tail, backed off smartly and—smirking in self-satisfaction—called upon the world to admire us.

Because of this self-gratifying factor even today it remains impossible to debate this dingy period in the Colony's history honestly; nothing is less welcome than to be told that you have no right to the moral conceit you feel about something you have done. For a serious consideration we shall have to await historians who are prepared to question both the official and the media line, which is that holding out a phony prospect of representative government to the Hong Kong people on the eve of our departure was in some way heroic.

The relevance of this episode to the debate about reform on the mainland is that it illustrates better than anything I can think of the illicit attractions of a grandstanding approach to Chinese democracy. For reasons of bad conscience over Hong Kong, as well as a natural preachiness in these matters, the British can be more prone than others to self-delusion. To gain a reputation as a person of moral stature in dealing with China it is sufficient, it appears, to pronounce oneself in favour of the immediate installation of full representative government and human rights, and to hell with the practicalities. One might have thought the Iraq adventure would have dented that approach. But then as so often in our dealings with the country, our stance has less to do with Chinese realities than with our own *bella figura*.

*

To discuss the subject in an objective rather than a top-down, self-regarding manner (the paternalistic West visiting its benefits on the backward East) it becomes necessary to envisage precisely how democracy in China would come about, and how it would work. Were it to be miraculously established overnight, in its early years democracy would seem likely to be incomplete, corrupt, and possibly violent. It is not simply a matter of whether or not the Chinese are ready for representative government, but what kind of polity it would be.

Every democracy has its national style. French candidates for the Presidency of their country to this day include latter-day Trotskyites and the crypto-fascists of the *Front National,* who together polled an astonishing 20 per cent of the vote in the first round of the 2007 presidential elections. Increasingly the Americans operate a star system, where money talks and dynasties and celebrity families (the Kennedys, the Bushes, and one day perhaps the Clintons) increasingly seek to parcel out the presidency between themselves. The Russians tend to elect 'strong men' and to applaud nationalistic stances. And the British, proud of their democratic heritage and the least meritocratic society in the West, think it normal for a personable Old Etonian to ease his way into Number Ten with his friends after a brief period in the House of Commons and no ministerial experience whatsoever.

What Wen Jiabao said about there being different historical stages through which democracy was achieved in different countries, and how its characteristics can vary, was in one respect all too true. Any Chinese democracy would have decidedly Chinese characteristics. In a country with almost no experience of elections at national level (those of 1913 ended with the murder of the winner), but a good deal of emperors, warlords and dictators, few of these cultural traits seem likely to be positive. To date the only practice in representative government the CCP has allowed have been elections for village leaders at local level, begun in 1988 and generalized in 1997, in which there are no alternative parties to the CCP. To ensure compliance with Party needs the communists have the additional advantage of vetting the candidates.

Meanwhile expectations of progress are modest. To illustrate how the habit of representative government was catching on, in Beijing recently a young journalist of a liberal disposition told me proudly how the Central Committee of the Party had just reversed a decision concerning traffic regulations in the capital. To him it seemed a giant step forward. For me it was a reminder that an orderly transition to anything resembling genuine democracy in the biggest country in the world would be a huge challenge. Even assuming the will was there, a gradualist programme over a number of years might be prudent if destabilization is to be avoided.

China is a society imbued with a sense of duty but with scant feeling for a system of rights. It took many hundreds of years for these rights to take root in Europe and America. The least one can say is that with the best will in the world (which in China may frequently be lacking) a working democracy is unlikely to be accomplished in a brief historical period. And as Russia has shown things can easily slip into reverse.

If the CCP threw in its hand tomorrow, on the Soviet model, progress could begin—or chaos. In a country with a tradition of struggles for regional autonomy, formerly held in check by Maoist repression, anything would be possible. Powerful local interests would be involved, and if central control were weakened China could revert to regional rule or to a modernized form of warlordism. Now that the army has its own economic interests to defend, it too could become a factor. A loosening of the Chinese Communist Party constraints could also encourage a still more rampant capitalism, which in turn could pave the way for the emergence of a populist, left-wing strongman, or alternatively of a fascistic, military-backed counterpart on the Right.

These are not reasons for not setting out on a democratic journey, but China is a big place and the road could be long and perilous. Some believe it could be smoothed and shortened by the return of a new, modern-minded generation of Chinese educated abroad. The hope is less that they would agitate for the human rights they have enjoyed in Europe or America, and seek to overturn the government, than that they would work from within gradually to reform it.

'Biological evolution' this has been called. It sounds attractive, though the idea that only foreign-trained people can move a culture forward has colonial echoes. In his book *On Liberty*, written in 1859, John Stuart Mill applied it specifically to China: 'They have become stationary; have remained so for thousands of years; and if they are ever to be improved it must be by foreigners.' A form of moral imperialism is what the modern Western attitude to China boils down to.

Foreign-trained young Chinese can clearly be influential, through their up-to-date knowledge and experience and open-minded outlook. (It should be remembered that of a million Chinese who left to study abroad from 1978 to 2006, a mere 273,000 have so far come back, though as the economy expands and opportunities for foreign-trained graduates increase, more could be tempted home). Yet it is a mistake to assume that students educated abroad who take up political positions at home necessarily work for progress. There are too many examples to the contrary. When the local political culture is both powerful and debased, as so frequently in the Middle East and Africa, educated men and women tend to get absorbed by the system in which they pursue their careers.

Examples of corrupt or violent African leaders who are Western-educated are legion; Idi Amin, butcher of Uganda, was Sandhurst-trained. President El-Assad of Syria, an ophthalmologist educated in Britain and friend of Lord Mandelson, has done little to reform a backward and thuggish regime that locks up opponents, blows up politicians who resent its infiltration of the Lebanon, and who arranged for his own re-election as President with 97 per cent of the votes. Next we had the spectacle, in the uprising in Libya of February 2011, of Colonel Gaddafi's son Saif, reputedly a westernized liberal who had written a thesis in favour of democracy during his time at the London School of Economics, and yet another acquaintance of Mandelson, brutally warning unarmed protesters on state television that they would be violently repressed.

So it is no surprise to learn that a number of Western-educated Chinese have returned to forge a career in the CCP. Whether they throw up a Gorbachev or a Yeltsin, or comfortably adapt to the Party's more repressive ways, only time will show.

There is also an assumption, fostered by governments, that Western pressure will help impel China towards her democratic destiny. Certainly such pressure has encouraged the government to release or banish individual dissidents, and Western opinion means far more than it ever did under Mao. Yet it has severe limits.

If ever a single episode brought out the dualism at the centre of

China's world view it was her reaction to the Nobel award to the dissident writer Liu Xiaobo in 2010. Observing Beijing's behaviour can be like looking at one of those trick postcards that offer two pictures, depending on the angle of vision. One is of a reformist China opening itself to the world, whose economic engine helps stoke the global economy in a time of recession. It is a consoling image, yet next thing the CCP seems to have gone back thirty years, denouncing as 'obscene' the Norwegian Nobel Committee's decision honour Liu, a university teacher locked up for eleven years for saying what he thinks, and when the world objects they put his wife under house-arrest for good measure. The venom didn't stop there: a state with a population of over a billion then began issuing threats of retaliation against the five million good people of Norway.

For Beijing Liu's worst crime was his link to the memory of the 1989 uprising in Tiananmen Square, an event it desperately wants the world to forget. A criminal, Beijing calls him, subverting the power of the state. And why? Because along with 303 other inoffensive intellectuals, simple citizens and even communist party members, in 2008 he signed the 08 Charter calling for the end of single-party government and an independent judiciary system.

Upon which the gigantic communist machine took fright. A single spark can start a prairie fire, as Mao Zedong used to say in his revolutionary days, though in modern China that makes no sense. There is no prospect of any mass uprising. Like it or not the Chinese people as a whole do not lay awake at night fretting over the absence of full democracy. Most go to sleep with more contentment and fuller bellies than any generation of Chinese for sixty years.

So why China's grossly disproportionate reaction to the Nobel prize? Anything that interferes in its domestic affairs causes resentment, and in their eyes the decision would appear as a 'provocation' and deliberate humiliation, with colonialist echoes. Liu's stubbornness must also have riled them, together perhaps with the dangerous reasonableness of his approach. They sentenced him to twenty years after Tiananmen, then to three more in 1995, yet still he won't kowtow to the regime. Though what is there to recant? Liu is not preaching violent revolt. On the contrary he insists that the road to democracy must be 'gradual, peaceful, well-ordered and controlled.'

The government's clumsy tactics stirred amazement abroad and some opposition at home: Xia Yeliang, a prominent economics professor at Beijing University, called on people to put photos of Liu in their car windows in silent protest. The bad smell left by the Liu Xiaobo incident will take time to dissipate. Chinese economic policies these last few years have frequently been enlightened and intelligent. The treatment of Liu is neither, and arouses fears for the future. What it tells us is how ready the CCP remains to revert to cave-man tactics the instant it sees its primacy threatened – which on this occasion it never was – and how much nerviness and nationalism is still there under the outwardly reasonable behaviour.

Perhaps we should not have been surprised. Looking back, the attempt by President Clinton in 1993 to speed up the process of China's democratization by direct foreign pressure, giving Beijing a year to improve its human rights record before being faced with the suspension of normal tariff treatment, was a warning. His tactic backfired badly. You do not have to subscribe to the notion that China is uniquely sensitive to matters of 'face' to see that the civil-liberties-for-imports approach would fail, which it did, obliging the Clinton administration to cave in on the eve of the expiry of its ill-advised ultimatum. There have been echoes of this episode in America's pushy approach to encouraging China to revalue its currency upwards.

The fact is that ideological impediments to business on the Western side are few to non-existent, and the Chinese know it. Firms and governments who were eager to trade with Maoist China are unlikely to accept that it is wrong to do business with a country a hundred times richer and (in the Chinese scale of things) several times freer.

The Chinese market is lively, but their purchases of advanced machinery or luxury goods have yet to reach the hoped-for levels, and the billion-plus market remains a gleam in Western governments' eyes. Meanwhile it is not in their interests for anything to be done that might have the effect of disrupting progress, still less destabilizing the country. Businessmen working in China are swift to assure me that precocious political changes, however desirable in theory, would have that effect. In bald terms what this means is that, protestations about human rights notwithstanding, the West has an interest in continuity under the CCP.

A Chinese democrat living in the West, Hu Ping, editor of the New York-based Chinese monthly *Beijing Spring* and a friend of Liu Xiaobo, wrote bitterly on the subject following Liu's Nobel award:

> As they [the CCP] see it, the current strategy works. The formula 'money + violence' works, and we stay on top. We know what the world means by human rights and democracy, but why should we do that? Aren't we getting stronger and richer all the time? Twenty years ago the West wasn't afraid of us, and now they have to be. Why should we change what works?

Earlier he had written in the same magazine:

> One of the major factors in this setback to democracy in Russia was the example of China, because Western investors were showing a preference for autocratic but stable regimes such as China's rather than democratic but turbulent countries, such as Russia. (Indeed, today China has become a model for all the world's antidemocratic powers.)[5]

*

This leads to the question of how great the pressure from below is for full-scale reform in China? To the Western mind, with its media-induced propensity to distil complex situations into a single striking image, it seems an indecent question: a snapshot of the Tiananmen revolt would seem to provide the answer. When we think of politics in communist China the picture that presents itself to this day is of a defiant young man single-handedly confronting a tank in the cause of democratic revolution.

The image is powerful, poignant, and as we tend to interpret it, in important respects false. The objective of the large majority of those involved was never to overthrow the Communist Party, but to reform it. And it must be doubted how far the young man's heroic gesture symbolized the country's mood. Tiananmen was never Budapest in

1956, Czechoslovakia in 1968, or Poland in the '80s, not least since the Chinese tyranny was home-grown.

None of these truths detract from the boldness of the protest, or from the feelings of revulsion its suppression aroused. I was in Hong Kong in the immediate aftermath and nothing could have been more moving than the silent display of mourning, such as black bows on taxi aerials, or the collective dignity of the people. But it is what happens in China that matters, and if we are to face sober truths we must recognize that on the mainland sympathy for the demonstrators was limited, as was any appetite for revolution, which in any case the students were not demanding. Certainly they were joined at some points by workers—the late '80s had seen a slump in growth and consumer price inflation of 20 per cent—though not enough to turn the tide.

What I remember best are the ugly TV images of the manhandling of those arrested in the security sweep that followed the crushing of the demonstration. Westerners can be puzzled by the way the Chinese authorities openly show the mistreatment of the regime's victims by soldiers or police on state media. In this case the reason for the ostentatiously brutal behaviour was twofold: *pour encourager les autres* - a warning to other people of the consequences of challenging the Party; and because the Party knew that the reaction to these images of a majority of the population, notably in the countryside, would be to deride the protesters, and take pleasure in seeing them bullied.

Mass mentality exists the world over; in China it is strong and can be cruel. The reaction of the average Chinese to what they saw was probably that the victims were spoiled middle-class students, urbanized and Westernized, who deserved what they got. It is true that city populations have grown stupendously since that time, to around 50 per cent of the whole, so one might expect a more sympathetic attitude today. But then the average townee is now a lot better off than in 1989, and has more to lose in any disorder.

The Tiananmen revolt was never broad-based. There were lesser disturbances in major towns though none in the countryside. Nor did the leaks that followed years later, in the form of official records published in the West in *The Tiananmen Papers*, suggest a leadership determined on ruthless suppression from the start.[6] Instead we saw the

Chinese Communist Party as a group of hesitant, confused and fearful gerontocrats. The chief villain was not however Deng Xiaoping, 85 years old but a reforming spirit; it was the younger and singularly unattractive Li Peng, then Prime Minister. In the internal debates Li played adroitly on his elders' fears of the kind of disorder that had accompanied the Cultural Revolution, in which Deng himself had almost died and his son had been crippled.

Deng comes across as initially wavering, though ultimately determined. Terrified of allowing the country to fall into anarchy, he is nevertheless loathe to initiate bloodshed and concerned for China's world image. Yet in the end he gives the order to 'clear the Square before sunset.' Official records tell us what the prime movers say, not what they think, and there seems an element of disingenuousness in the wily Deng's insistence that no one should be killed when martial law was finally declared.

The PLA, never a namby-pamby organization and not in the habit of the peaceful management of demonstrations, was in any event not well-placed to clear the Square by riot police and water canon alone. A hardened communist seeing authority collapsing around him, Deng would have known the value of decisive action to a country conditioned to respect power. He could hardly have failed to calculate that there would be resistance and deaths, but had decided these were inevitable to preserve the dictatorship of the Party in a country he himself had set on the capitalist road.

That underlying contradiction—the idea that you can have economic without political freedom—explains everything that happened in Tiananmen Square. China has become a wealthier and in some respects freer country since, there will be compromises of every description, but in the long term that central conflict will not go away. No doubt it was this knowledge that motivated the passing of *The Tiananmen Papers*, allegedly by a senior Chinese official, to an American sinologist. In the course of the discussions Deng gives a classic statement of the contradictions of China's communist/capitalist system and the limits of what the Old Men of Beijing would allow in the way of liberalization:

Of course we want to build socialist democracy, but we can't possibly do it in a hurry, and still less do we want that Western-style stuff. If our one billion people jumped into multiparty elections, we'd get chaos like the all-out civil war we saw during the Cultural Revolution.

For all his modernizing image in the West, and his clowning in a Stetson, Deng was revealed in *The Tiananmen Papers* as an old-fashioned CCP patriot: what the West were really after when they prated about human rights, he believed, was the destruction of China's sovereignty. The triumph of Maoism in 1949, we are reminded yet again, unlike that of communism in Russia, was as much a nationalist as a Marxist revolution.

Of course the protesters were heroes who showed great courage. The painful paradox of this historic event is however that it illustrated, not the widespread desire of the Chinese for democracy and human rights, but its opposite: the weakness of the reformist camp. Its magnification by global television should not blind us to the fact. Today the students of the time, like other Chinese, enjoy more personal liberties than they did in 1989. They are freer to travel and get rich, which many a former radical-minded student is doing, freer to voice their opinions, with due caution, freer too in sexual and artistic matters. Some of those involved in Tiananmen are now engaged in the business of business rather than of subversion. This is not to devalue their motives or the utility of their actions; on the contrary, it suggests their demonstration was not wholly in vain.

*

Much of the optimism about China's progression to democracy rests on the premise that a growing middle class will demand it. The glibness of this assumption should put us on our guard. The least one can say is that the transfer of this sociological term of art from one culture to another is in danger of being simplistic. If the exact definition of the 'middle classes' in Britain and other Western countries is a matter of controversy, in China their status is doubly uncertain. They may have surface similarities with the intermediate sections of society who have emerged over centuries in the West, but they cannot be the same. Under Mao China was as near as any society in history has ever come to being classless. Today's middle classes have sprouted since Deng Xiaoping's invitation to the nation to get rich, but that was a mere couple of decades ago.

I do not wish to underplay the magnitude of what has happened. In that time several hundred million people, primarily in the towns, have enjoyed a sharply rising standard of living. To the author the rapidity of the change from the poor, ugly, hostile, aggrieved and willfully grim nation he saw in the late '60s, to the infinitely more relaxed, informed, consumerist society of today is a miracle reminiscent—insofar as any parallel fits—of that in post-war Germany.

It is enough to go to a popular evening restaurant, with its sumptuously diverse menu, its noisy, cheery crowd, chatting away loudly to make themselves heard over the live music. Compared to the cowed, browbeaten, poverty-stricken country eking out a living on subsistence rations, who except when instructed to shriek idolatry at the great dictator in compulsory street marches kept their voices low, this is a country reborn.

Nor is progress entirely material. Along with rampant consumer appetites there has been a loosening of tongues and a diminution of fear. To that extent the middle classes, already enjoy a measure of freedom, relative admittedly, though in terms of recent Chinese history a major advance. It is equally true that China has gone from a country of drab monotony to one of glaring contrasts, not just between town and country but rich and poor in the towns themselves. Another incongruity is that between the sophistication of urban life—the cheap, smart clothes, the electronic gear, the Hong Kong-style shops and malls—and the po-faced functionaries who continue to run the country.

Progress towards greater liberty can never be fast enough, it is easy to feel, and to those most conscious of the weight of the state, or who become victims of its arbitrary powers, it is hard to say 'be patient.' Yet unless our purpose is to flag up correct stances, so as to feel good about ourselves, patience is likely to be needed.

Those who lament the slow pace of reform invite the question: in a matter of a few decades since the demise of the world's largest and (outside North Korea) most vicious despotism, how much did you expect? Nor should we forget that in neither Russia nor China do political elites and their clients relinquish control without reinventing themselves in forms designed to perpetuate their power. In Russia we are seeing it in the transformation of the KGB into a ruling clique, and in China in the appropriation by the CCP and the army of financial interests.

Now that a certain progress has nonetheless been made in establishing a civil society, how anxious are the Chinese middle classes, however defined, to push forward? The first thing to be said is that Party cadres and government officials who have done well out of what in many respects has been a counter-revolution themselves form a good chunk of these classes (there is one of them for every 26 people in the country), and while some can be enlightened folk, the majority will be in no hurry for change. The folk memory of China in the twentieth century is likely to be an inducement to caution. It is a history of endless strife and upheaval, from the end of the Imperial dynasty in 1911 and the rule of warlords to the anti-Japanese War, then the civil war between Mao and the Kuomintang, and finally the communist victory, and what followed. Even the social order totalitarianism imposed failed to bring respite, as Mao indulged his taste for permanent revolution.

By no means all Chinese are benefiting from the best times the country has enjoyed for over a century. The livelihoods of the rural population are lagging badly (half of China's people subsists on around $10 a day or less) and hundreds of millions are driven to roam the land in search of work. Yet it is safe to say that more Chinese are better fed and housed and live more peaceable lives than at any time within living memory. For all the corruption and imbalance between coastal and inner regions that the vertiginous growth rate has brought, it will take a serious national setback to undermine the regime and inspire a mass movement for some more worthy though probably less orderly democratic alternative.

In this very recent society the middle classes, recent themselves, will be aware of the fragility of these changes for the better, and will not take them for granted. However self-serving the message in the CCP's propaganda—that the country's prime concern for the next twenty years must be economic development rather than political reform—it will find an echo amongst many of the newly well-to-do. Hence the suggestion that the middle classes have done an unspoken deal with the government, whereby liberty is sacrificed to economics, but even that is not quite right.

At a certain level of political consciousness it may well be true, though in another sense it is misleading, since it assumes that personal liberties, such as freedom of expression, are close to the top of the average civil servant, teacher or shopkeeper's agenda. Interpreting Chinese political culture with Western mindsets gets us nowhere. It may make us feel good to ascribe democratic impulses to people who, for the moment at least, may not give them the priority we would wish, or whose interest in freedom is highly selective (e.g. freedom to own land rather than freedom of expression), but feeling good is not the purpose of the exercise.

To us it seems unthinkable, against nature, that educated, modern-seeming and often modern-minded Chinese citizens, many of them free to travel, should not enjoy democratic freedoms commensurate with our own. But it will seem less strange to them. The older ones will have lived through harrowing times; many may have experienced real hunger. Their priority at present will be the ability to enjoy the relative plenty under the current regime. The younger generation in the towns have never had it so good, or so free, and insofar as they are the beneficiaries of a conscious policy of bread and circuses, it is an approach that appears to be working.

The rights of man are a western invention which has shallow roots in China. It is this that makes it easier for the CCP to suggest that there are two kinds of human rights: the right to food and clothes and, for richer countries, to absolute freedom of expression. In China's case, the official line goes, it is clear which is the more urgent. The argument is crude, if only in the sense that prosperity and the equitable distribution of wealth, to say nothing of justice, will in the long term depend on representative government. But in a country imbued by tradition with an excess of deference to authority, and where life for many is getting better, for the moment the official position appears to be persuasive. That is why Chinese spokesmen so frequently resort to it. 'In China human rights means having gas for your car' was one Minister's recent version.

*

What should the West do? In which countries is it right to demand instant democracy, and where should we desist, or go easy? A differential view of the degree to which democracy is exportable is one of the curiosities of contemporary Western politics. In 1975 George F. Kennan reflected that truly representative government seemed a monopoly of Europe and America, and that 'the evidence has yet to be produced that it is the natural form of rule for people outside those narrow perimeters'.

His opinion has been out of favour for several decades, and would today be described by many as intrinsically racist. Now there seems to be a pick and mix approach. As I write everyone, Barack Obama included, seems enthused in the cause of Western-style democracy in Egypt, Tunisia and Libya. On the other hand the view that the invasion of Iraq was a mistake, not least because conditions were not ripe for the establishment of democracy in that country, is one that commanded support across the political spectrum, including the liberal left, despite their preoccupation with human rights. At the same time the proposition that full democracy in China is overdue and must be urgently promoted and secured will be equally warmly endorsed, often by the same people.

Like Iraq – and Egypt for that matter - China is short on experience of elected government. In common with Iraq, till recently she was a brutal dictatorship. The only thing China has over Iraq and Egypt is that its politics are not plagued by religious schisms, though that advantage is mitigated by its regional tensions and daunting size: Iraq has a population roughly equivalent to the Shanghai conurbation.

The truth is that for self-evident cultural reasons, as Iraq and Afghanistan remind us, transplanting democracy is a fraught business, while propagating it from scratch in such countries is likely to take whole historical eras. A demand for the full panoply of human rights and political freedoms in China presupposes a level of civic consciousness that appears to be widely lacking. It is enough to glance at the evolution of the country's social mores in the short time during which totalitarian shackles have been loosened. The speed with which gangsterism, pornography, graft, prostitution, official corruption, drugs and sundry other vices have revived do not point to a nation emerging purified from its forty years immersion in ascetic Maoism.

The moral vacuum the Cultural Revolution induced has been filled with a ferocious egotism, ruthless materialism, and a deeply unsentimental society. The spirit of sacrifice is wanting, if only because the past was about nothing else. China's period of what was sometimes seen as heroic poverty was never heroic for the untold millions who hungered or starved to death, and in any case it is over. The brutalities of the capitalistic Great Leap Forward we are seeing today are evidence enough of that.

It could be that the strains this lurch into the future is producing will erupt in popular disorder and topple the CCP. Change appears more likely however to come from the top. Compared to the Long March veterans and Party loyalists of the past, Party cadres are getting not just younger but smarter, less like the ideological visionaries and placemen of the old days and more in the mould of technocratic managers.

As the CCP becomes de-proletarianized there are fewer ill-educated folk from poor backgrounds whom the Party trained, all too successfully, in blind obedience. As one commentator has put it, 'the elite is thickening', and their knowledge of the world is thickening too. We cannot assume that younger and better-educated necessarily means reformist-minded, for reasons I have sought to explain, yet nor can we discount the possibility of a modernizing spirit developing amongst rising party and government bureaucrats and ministers, a gradual understanding that the days of state coercion as the answer to every problem are over. The more enlightened may even draw forward-looking lessons about the advantages of a top-down approach, rather than waiting for the crowds to force change, from what has been happening in the Middle East – though much depends on the outcome of what is happening there.

The experience of other nations, while not necessarily applicable, is worthy of note. In more advanced countries most of the transitions to democracy since the '70s (Spain, Russia, Eastern Europe, Taiwan) have not come about primarily through popular agitation or upheaval, but by the actions of the governing powers. China can never be seen as part of

the mainstream – her society is neither Third World, Western or Middle
Eastern - yet when it comes to change from the top, she has form. The
impulse behind the economic revolution of the late '70s and '80s did not
come from a disempowered and inert populace: it was a palace
revolution in which Deng Xiaoping carried the majority of his comrades
with him, and the world was pleasantly surprised at the abruptness and
profundity of the changes.

Could the same thing happen, politically? Might a Chinese leader
decide in five or ten years time that the only way to make permanent its
economic gains was to secure them with political underpinning? It
sounds unlikely, though there are events that encourage out-of-the box
thinking. Early in 2007 a remarkable text was published in Hong Kong,
recording the private opinions of Zhao Ziyang, Chinese premier from
1980-87 and the seventy-year old General Secretary of the Party when
Tiananmen erupted in 1989, on China's future.[7]

It was Zhao who advocated an accommodation with the students.
When he personally went to meet them in the square the world was privy
to something it had seen in no communist country before, least of all
China: a top leader shedding tears. Declining to confess his mistakes
after the demonstration was crushed, Zhao was put under house arrest
which lasted till his death in 2005 at the age of 86. Zong Feng-ming, a
friend and a retired Party Secretary of the Beijing University department
of aeronautics, managed to continue to see him under the pretext of
administering Chinese medicine, and secretly recorded his thoughts over
several years.

The results are remarkable. Zhao Ziyang, who for all his tears had for
decades worked at high levels of one of the harshest regimes in the
world, had not been persuaded by China's enrichment under the
communist party to see the error of his ways. Nor did he want piecemeal
political reform, but a full-scale revolution from above. 'So-called
political reform means eliminating the Party's monopoly on power…
The only way to solve China's social ills is to establish democracy and the
rule of law.'

Airy as his comments may appear, Zhao has thought through
modalities. Aware that an abrupt move towards full democracy might
bring about the condition all Chinese administrations most fear—*luan*,

or disorder—he recommends beginning by removing censorship and allowing independent media to operate. Multi-party elections would come later.

Most unusual from a Communist Party veteran is his open-minded attitude to the West. More extraordinary still, Zhao turns out to be an Americanophile, an endangered species even in Europe, in his case for cogent reasons:

> What is referred to as modernization is actually Westernization, which requires a convergence with modern Western civilization... If China is to develop it needs to cultivate good relations with the US... Cultivating good relations with the US means cultivating the American people, because the policies of the American government are influenced and restricted by the American people. In any case, the American government and the American people are equally sensitive to the issues of democracy, freedom, human rights, and autocracy. They believe that autocracy is characterized by a lack of human rights guarantees, and for that reason they regard China's autocracy as a threat. Only democratic government can preserve world peace and development... For that reason neither the American government nor the American people will tolerate the ascendancy of an autocratic country.

The tone of stratospheric simplicity in these and other statements, as Zhao argues his case from first principles, help them ring true. (In a more opaque vein, Mao himself could talk like this: 'Some say the situation is very bad. I say it is very good.') Zhao's radicalism is also a reminder of the element of volatility that can characterize CCP thinking at the highest levels: Mao's opening to America, Lin Biao's defection, and Deng Xiaoping's unashamed pragmatism are examples. Arbitrariness and totalitarianism, it is easy to forget, like the monarch's whim go together.

Zhao could be dismissed as some wise, endearing crank, except that cranks do not usually make it to the position of General Secretary of the Party. Two other senior communists contributed prefaces to the book (banned, of course, in China). One is Li Rui, once a secretary to Mao and a former minister. Stigmatized as a 'right-wing opportunist' he was rehabilitated after Mao's death. The other was Bao Tong, director of the CCP Central Committee Office of Political Reform, and Zhao's political secretary. By virtue of their age and experience such folk cannot be regarded as jejune reformists.

Might Zhao's book exercise a posthumous influence amongst the Party elite? Optimists will be reminded of how Deng Xiaoping, Zhao's jailor, also suffered imprisonment, though his ideas were destined to make a dramatic comeback. It is an enticing prospect, though Zhao himself had few illusions. In a shrewd if gloomy analysis he recalls how he used to believe that the end of the Party strongmen like Mao or Deng Xiaoping would see the rise of different political tendencies in the regime that would co-exist. By the time of his death in 2005, however, he feared that a corporate elite now ran China, a tight-knit group that would defend its own interests to the last. Nor was he sanguine about a younger generation of managers: even leaders who have studied abroad and been influenced by the West had been 'co-opted into this mutual interest group and made part of the power elite.'

The most acute of his perceptions concerns nationalism and the 'neo-leftists.', namely Party members with reservations about the pace and direction of economic reform and the opening of the country who hark back to Maoist times. His views here are a warning to the West, which has tended to assume that China can only go forward:

The neo-leftists use the pretext of 'protecting state industry and defending the sovereignty of the state for the sake of a stronger nation and a more prosperous people' as a reason to resist globalization and progress towards a modern world culture. This ideological trend appeals to those whose nationalist sentiments still feel the sting of China's past century of foreign encroachment and bullying, and can easily ignite parochial ethnic hatred. It can also easily lend cohesive power to the authorities' efforts against 'westernization' and 'splitism', and contribute towards the internal unity required to preserve stability and consolidate rule, causing repeated attacks on China's progress towards a modern civilization... Nationalism will be the greatest threat.

In advocating a step-by-step approach, rather than the grand slam that took place in Russia and tore its empire apart, Zhao no doubt had in mind the potential for disruption that a move to democracy can bring, not least on the nationalities front. China is not of course the Balkans, nor can its peripheral peoples be easily compared with the swathe of states and provinces that used to form part of the Soviet Union. But a fearsomely repressive policy has kept the lid on ethnic discontent so successfully for so long that it is easily forgotten that China too remains an empire.

As we have recently been reminded, Tibet is an example of the relentlessness of its repression, though China's domineering spirit is today disguised by economic progress for an impoverished region. (The Tibet Autonomous Region has been growing faster than China as a whole. It has just acquired a high altitude railway, whose effect will of course be to enhance Beijing's control and the sinification of the province.)

The East-West clash of cultures over attitudes to Tibet was apparent in the disturbances in the run-up to the Olympic Games. At one extreme was the quasi-mystical fascination of the denizens of Hollywood with Tibet and the Dalai Lama; at the other the contempt of the average Chinese for what they see as a backward, superstitious people whose homeland rightly belongs to them, and who should be eternally grateful for Chinese colonization and the enlightenment, investment and modernization that come with it.

As for the regime itself, it is noteworthy how swiftly it reverts to the crudest Maoist invective where Tibet is concerned: 'The Dalai Llama is a jackal in Buddhist monk's robes and an evil spirit with a human face and the heart of a beast', in the words of the CCP leadership in the Tibet Autonomous region. Whilst these are unlovely sentiments, the central government's impatience with the moralizing of the British press in particular can be understandable in the light of history: it was after all British forces under Colonel Younghusband who first intruded into Lhasa in 1903-4, killing many in the process. As a nation we do not seem especially contrite about it. It was all part of the Great Game, whose victims just happened to include Chinese and Tibetans.

The restive, strategic North Western province of Xinjiang, where 8 of the 19 million population are Turkic-speaking Muslim Uighurs, is another instance of China's determination to impose stability on her frontier regions. On a visit there in 2010 I had an acrid whiff of the problem. In July 2009 murderous clashes between Han Chinese and Muslim Uighurs had erupted over nothing more than a dubious rumour that a girl in a faraway southern province had been raped by migrant labourers. The viciousness of the violence – hundreds were killed and many more wounded as the two ethnicities turned on one another - and the uncertainty about its cause are a reflection of the depth of mutual hatreds. The roots go back centuries, and as millions of Han settlers pour in Muslim resentment festers.

As in Tibet the Chinese have invested huge sums to improve the infrastructure of a province that, with its oil and gas and gold and mineral deposits could one day become a kind of Chinese Texas. Its capital, Urumqi, is already a city of over two million. Despite its veneer of modernity - glass towers, fashionable shops, smart hotels, excellent restaurants - and the fact that almost a year had passed since the lethal riots, the Chinese were taking no chances. The internet was still switched off, and after sundown troops and armed police lurked on the streets.

Venerable voices urging democratic reform in the country from above have not been completely silenced following Zhao's death, even on the mainland. In November 2007 Li Rui, now 92, wrote an essay in a small intellectual magazine named *Spring and Autumn* contributing what he called ideas for the CCP's self-criticism during its Congress. His analysis and prescription were simple enough:

> From 1949 to the end of the Cultural Revolution, hundreds of millions of innocent people were purged by mistake and tens of millions died of hunger. This makes us bitter with hatred. It was all because our Party failed to counterbalance power with democracy.

Less ancient that Li Rui, though equally forthright, was Hu Deping, the 65-year-old son of a reformist leader active in the '80s, who is Vice-Chairman of the CCP's United Front Work Department. In a meeting on the margins of the Congress he pronounced himself completely in favour of a democratic system.

Seen in the round however Zhao Ziyang's thinking turns out to be less encouraging than it appeared. Instead of inspiring hope that even hardened communist leaders can open their eyes to the world and recognize the stabilizing and peace-inducing qualities of democracy, the message he left is that China was likely to take a different path.

*

The problem with reform from above runs deeper. The fact that the will is likely to be lacking amongst power-hungry and frequently corrupt Party leaders is just one problem: the truth is that, in the short or medium term, the CCP would find it next to impossible to democratize in any serious way even if it wanted to. The reason is economic. Were it to hold free and fair elections, the peasantry, with their huge weight in the population, would be able to make their voices heard for the first time in history, and a national change of course favouring rural areas would in all likelihood result.

One of the most memorable conversations I have had in post-Maoist China was with an economic minister in 1987. Two things impressed me about the strategy he outlined for abandoning the quest for uniform development and concentrating on the urban coastal areas. The first was his strength of conviction. For him this was an earnest of his country's resolution to throw off China's peasant image once and for all and join the modern world.

The second thing that struck me was his disregard for the consequences of this policy in terms of entrenching unequal standards of living for hundreds of millions of rural folk; he acknowledged that this would be the result of the policy but (literally) waved it aside. The fact is that, for all its harshness, from the regime's viewpoint to date the strategy of coastal preference and of feeding the towns with cheap labour from a semi-indigent countryside has been a success, not least for China's international standing. The disequilibrium was colossal but then so were the productive gains.

The rewards were swift to appear. By the beginning of the '90s production in the three eastern provinces of Jiangsu, Zhejiang and

Shandong was ten times more than the total for the nine provinces and autonomous regions to the West, and they account for an overwhelming percentage of foreign investment.[8] The benefits feed through to the urban population, who are less likely to question the political backwardness of their country as a result. The central paradox of China, it could be said, is that stability depends on the CCP's readiness to keep the towns happy by exploiting the rural majority of its people, who if things deteriorate too far could themselves undermine the regime.

A wiser, more humane strategy might be to cool the economy, develop the towns more gradually while investing in public services in the countryside, notably health and education, and take other expensive measures to relieve its distress. Gestures in this direction aimed at re-balancing the CCP's policies have been made, such as the abolition of agricultural taxes, and a new health care system. But there is a limit to how far the government can go. Were it to divert large funds to needy peasants, to the point where growth rates and urban standards of living stagnated or were significantly reversed, the Party could see its mandate from heaven come under question where it matters.

The appointment of two younger men to the CCP Politburo Standing Committee in 2007, though welcome enough, does not suggest any great break with the recent past. On paper the new entrants have encouraging profiles. Xi Jinping, the likely new president, a mere 54 at the time of his promotion to the Standing Committee, was a Party boss of Shanghai and the son of a reformist ally of Deng Xiaoping who condemned the killings in Tiananmen Square. (It is amazing how often in supposedly egalitarian, meritocratic China top people turn out to be someone's son or daughter. 90 per cent of the richest Chinese are said to be the offspring of Party cadres and government servants).

A fan of American films, Xi also has a daughter enrolled at Harvard. More startlingly his wife, Peng Liyuan, is a glossy popular singer, better known than her husband. Before concluding that she will act as a bridge to the nation's youth by furthering the democratic cause it is worth remembering that, as we have seen in Italy and Serbia, leaders with show-biz connections are by no means necessarily democracy-mongers. Mao Zedong's actress wife Jiang Qing is the strongest argument against excessive expectations. I do not know if Xi, by all accounts a more amiable and easy-going personality than Hun Jintao, will turn out to be as populist as his wife (she is especially appreciated by the military), but the prospect of him in the country's top job brings to mind a Russian description of a new style of authoritarian leader, in this case the Russian President, Dmitry Medvedev:

> Medvedev is a representative of a new generation of Russian bureaucrats. They listen to Western rock music, speak foreign languages, wear Brioni suits. But deep inside they are strong Russian national conservatives... They buy the advantages of Western civilization but they do not buy its values. They are generally afraid of the West as a competing system.[9]

Xi's swift ascent was confirmed in late 2010 when a Communist Party Central Committee Plenum appointed him vice-chair of the military affairs committee which oversees China's forces. This makes him even more likely to be the heir to Hu Jintao when he reaches the end of his 10-year term in 2012.

The second youngster on the rise is Li Keqiang, now 56 and a probable successor to Prime Minister Wen Jiabao. The fact that he is a lawyer who is said to have mixed with liberal thinkers, was involved with democracy experiments in his student days, and helped translate *The Due Process of Law* by Lord Denning into Chinese also raises hopes. Clearly it is progress that both men have matured in an era where their minds will have been directed more towards the West than to the Soviet Union.

Yet we should beware of attributing reformist sentiments to men whose background suggests that they are essentially career apparatchiks. The very fact that these two form a balance, with Xi being intimate with business affairs and Li's experience lying more with the rural poor, suggests that, politically speaking, the current leaders are seeking to line up successors who will continue their policy of steady as she goes. It is hard to disagree with the well-known artist and dissident Ai Weiwei on prospects for democratic advance: 'We are not expecting much from the next generation of leaders. Maybe the generation after. After another decade they will be more open in their ideas.'

*

All this may seem dispiriting news for Westerners who prefer to believe that change will be forced on the country before long. The economist Will Hutton is one of those convinced that for the Chinese Communist Party the game is almost up. His argument (see his book *The Writing on the Wall*) is that the current Chinese model is unsustainable.[10] Only if it embraces the economic and political pluralism of the West and adopts our Enlightenment values and institutions, he believes, can the country stake its claim to be at the centre of our century.

The appeal of his message, I fear, is that what Hutton says about China's future is what we would like to believe. To affirm that the country can only resolve its problems by adopting a Western system of parliamentary government and entrenched human rights is a little like saying that going straight is in the best interests of a persistent crook. Everyone will nod sagely and no one will contradict you.

Hutton is right to argue that economic success and nationalism are the CCP's twin legitimating factors. He is correct too in labelling the system that has brought China where it is today as one of 'Leninist corporatism', rather than capitalism as the West knows it, though its idiosyncratic nature has invited other descriptions, such as authoritarian bureaucratic capitalism. And it is true that the system creates a chronic disequilibrium in the country. Building a more normal knowledge economy with sensible levels of investment and consumption would involve constitutional changes that would be inconsistent with one-party rule. How to perpetuate the claim to one-party rule itself when the class war is over is another problem.

Nor can Hutton easily be criticized for his desire to project Enlightenment values to China. Presumably he feels that the same values should apply across the globe, though I do not recall many people on the Left saying that Enlightenment values should be gospel in for example Muslim countries, a proposal that would undermine the teachings of most brands of Islam. In any event a little more humility in this area would be advisable. It was after all Enlightenment values such as rationalism and scientism that, carried to extremes, were part of a way of thinking that led to communism, a Western ideology implanted in

China, with the results we have seen. In that sense it could be argued, mischievously, that in China 'Enlightenment values' have been tested to destruction.

Ultimately however Hutton gets things wrong because his premises are almost exclusively economic. Politics subsumes economics, which is in turn subsumed by culture, and Hutton gives insufficient weight to elements of continuity in the present scene with China's cultural and political inheritance. Modern China never really had what we would regard as a free enterprise system even before communism, though there are plenty of precedents for the bureaucratic capitalism, corporate management, *dirigisme* (centralism) and corruption of which Hutton complains.

In the Qing period the state exercised a large measure of control over the economy (one reason why, as we have seen, Western left-wingers tend to give a glowing account of what in truth was still a fiercely autocratic period.) Even in the early twentieth century, of a total of twenty-six cotton mills set up between 1890 and 1913, almost all had official connections with the state, a fact that makes the hybrid system of ownership and management of today a little more comprehensible. However outlandish 'Leninist corporatism' may appear to the West, it represents a form of continuity.

If you are setting up an enterprise in modern China your first thought is likely to be not the banks and the market, but official connections; good *guanxi* (contacts) can help fix both. A Chinese form of inter-dependence, in which the individual entrepreneur, like the individual personality in the communist system, is never wholly free of authority, and where his entrepreneurial activities are seen as depending on and benefiting the state as well as himself, makes a kind of Chinese sense. So do the giant enterprises who offer their workers schools, libraries and sports facilities. Corporate, communal capitalism of this kind may be something we deprecate, sometimes with good reason, but in China, for the moment, it can produce the goods.

On democracy Hutton is in danger of confusing the desirable with the attainable. Free markets and free elections may be excellent companions, but one does not always imply the other. Historically there is no lack of cases of an uneasy but rather durable coexistence between authoritarian government and the market, or open government and centralized, semi-closed markets. (In socialist Britain, to look no further, the Cabinet ran car and steel companies, and foreign exchange regulations obliged holidaymakers to limit the amount of currency they could take abroad). Where he is least convincing is on the timescale of the advent of democracy in China, supposing it happens. And in this instance to get the timing wrong is to lose the argument.

When Prime Minister Wen Jiabao said that China would find her own way to democracy he might have added 'and in her own good time.' Chinese timescales are notoriously elastic—in a civilization that has continued unbroken for five thousand years that is natural—and by the time a respectable democracy is in place many of us could be dead. To me it seems conceivable that 'Leninist corporatism', an absence of pluralism and a tough line on human rights will continue in one form or another, even if not under the communist party, for decades.

Like generals who promise a return to democracy after a coup, Chinese leaders suggest that political reform will come, eventually. In the interim, the theory goes, China will become stronger and therefore fitter to take the strains of a transfer to a more representative regime. But how long are the timescales in question? If the CCP holds out for another twenty years and the economy continues to leap ahead, however fitfully, the country will have experienced huge and continuous growth under Party management for half a century with none of the radical reforms Chinese dissidents and the West would like to see. If that were to show signs of happening—and it is surely on the cards—how could we continue to speak of the system as inherently unstable? At what point can a regime that could last as long as Queen Victoria's reign cease to be stable?

This is not a case of Hutton's optimism versus my pessimism, but of his voluntarism versus what I prefer to see as my realism. We do not differ simply because he is not a China specialist: that can be an advantage, by encouraging a cold-eyed view of the economic risks and discarding any form of sentimentalism in a culture whose peculiarities can be seductive. Yet it is a drawback in the sense that his analysis tends to omit not only the human factor, but the Chinese factor. The contradictions he points up in the present system are flagrant enough, but the Chinese have a gift for tolerating contradictions, over long periods. (So have we: the House of Lords, a grossly undemocratic mixture of appointment by patronage, by bloodline and by merit, endures to this day).

Living with contradictions is central to being Daoist in private and Confucian in public, which in the case of the Communist Party has come to mean letting money-making rip while preaching political and social control. The Chinese for contradiction, incidentally, is *mao dun*, meaning sword/shield, said to refer to a shopkeeper who claimed that his shields were as impenetrable as the blades of his swords were irresistible. The sword of capitalism and the shield of communist control may coexist longer than we suspect. There is a fine but crucial line between arguing that the Chinese are not interested in freedom— something I do not believe—and that their thirst for liberties identical to our own is urgent and insatiable.

In advocating changes we would all like to see Hutton is presumably meant to influence policy, though it is not clear how this influence is to be achieved. In the world governments have to deal with, rather than comment on, whether you regard the Chinese miracle as sustainable or not makes little difference. The only practical choice is to wait and see, and to work and trade with the regime as fully as possible meanwhile. Hutton's diagnosis seems to me unsuited to a situation that is without precedent and not susceptible to mechanical analysis or remedy. Though here an important qualification to my own analysis must be made. This is that, for the same reason of intrinsic unpredictability, he could turn out, against the odds, to be right.

Where he is undoubtedly wrong is in discounting so heavily the possibility of a continuation of the status quo. It seems altogether conceivable that China under the CCP might lurch and stumble forwards, wracked perhaps by crises of various descriptions but holding onto power and growing ever richer and more powerful as she goes. France takes pride in being *l'exception française*, American exceptionalism is a cliché, the British constitution fits no pattern, and I suspect we are going to see a lot of exceptional things occur in China too. One could be a regime that clever men and women write off as theoretically kaput soldiering on for decades.

Before Deng Xiaoping launched his economic counter-revolution the notion that there could be such a thing as a halfway house between communism and capitalism that did not involve a radical loosening up politically would have appeared absurd. Yet the ideological camel cobbled together by the CCP Central Committee, ungainly as it is with its triple humps – capitalism, corporatism, Leninism - has carried the country forward for several decades, surmounting two major financial crisis (that of 1997, and the 2008 recession) in the process.

The advantage of half-way houses, however unstable or irrational they appear, is that they avoid extremes. In China's case these are Maoist despotism and autarky on one hand, and what the CCP sees as a dangerous and premature lurch into a full-blown parliamentary multi-party system on the other. A pragmatic aspect to the situation that is often ignored needs to be mentioned. The one certainty about the situation in China, it seems to me, is that the system will endure, not as briefly as textbook capitalism says that it should, but as long as the CCP can get away with it. And to that the answer is I suspect: longer than it should and longer than we think.

The impressive Australian sinologist Ross Terrill echoes Hutton when he says that 'Economic growth and crude nationalism are insufficient supports for the long-term continuance of a regime.'[11] The sentiments are impeccable, though I would replace 'are' by 'ought to be'. And as in Hutton the crucial question—how long is long-term?—is begged in his work.

Throughout history China has been the butt of our moralizing impulses, and on that score little has changed. Now that she is more powerful than ever before it would be a mistake to expect China to hasten to bow to our will. If a clash occurs between her domestic and international interests the maintenance of the regime will predominate, in the knowledge that the West will condemn and protest and fulminate, as it did over Tiananmen, and in the last resort stand aside.

*

None of this means that we should despair of progress. Michael Mandelbaum, one of America's leading foreign policy thinkers, has an encouraging theory about markets and dictatorships which it is tempting to apply to China.[12] Markets, he writes, have two appeals to dictators: they not only make their countries richer, they increase the spoils for themselves and their cronies and enhance the means of repression. And insofar as they are obliged to demonstrate economic progress to their people, they can help provide the cash to improve schools, social services and infrastructure. In the short or medium-long term free markets can therefore help to secure both the welfare of dictators and the stability of their regimes.

But that is not the whole theory. However well or badly the dictator's economy performs, it goes on, the regime will eventually find itself under pressure to cede ground to democracy. If it does poorly popular support declines and pressure against the regime builds up. And if market institutions thrive people 'acquire the habits and attitudes that foster democracy.' By this Mandelbaum means that as commerce and free choice develop the sovereignty of the citizen takes root as owner and as consumer. Habits of trust and compromise, without which a free market cannot operate, are also promoted.

So it is that democracies can emerge from free markets like a butterfly from a chrysalis. The optimism of this analysis is attractive, and it would be pleasant to think that in the long term, for once China might not be an exception. Though looking at what is currently happening in Russia, we can't be sure. Maybe it just takes time.

*

What do Chinese democrats themselves think about democracy's chances? The voices of leading reformists are mixed. The father of modern Chinese dissidents is Wei Jingshen, formerly an electrician. His notoriety began in 1978, at the age of twenty-nine. When Deng Xiaoping was fighting against the left wing of the Party for his 'four modernizations', in agriculture, industry, education and science, it was Wei who had the courage to put up a poster in Beijing demanding a fifth: political reform. Normally such posters are not signed, for self-evident reasons, but Wei had the audacity to put his name to his: a deliberate gesture, he later explained, to help restore the dignity of the individual in China.

'Democracy Wall' was born—and within a few weeks, obliterated. Wei was condemned to fifteen years in prison and in labour camps, a terrifying experience during which he was tortured and lost all his teeth through ill health. On his release he was arrested again, accused of trying to establish a trade union, and disappeared for two more years. An international outcry obliged the Chinese government to expel him to America in 1997. From there he has broadcast frequently to China on Voice of America.

Wei insists the Chinese people do want democracy, rather than some softened form of Party dictatorship. It is not an ideological choice, he believes, but a preference for what works over what doesn't. The CCP is fond of quoting Confucius, yet Confucius guaranteed social peace while respecting the autonomy of the family and the clan, and the emperor did not interfere in private lives. Mao destroyed the Confucian system and replaced it with police surveillance every instant of the day, so that individuals were mere robots at the service of the Party.

Wei's thinking has now ricocheted in the reverse direction. Today he does not believe China needs a centralized authority at all. He sees the country as more diverse than America, though less than Europe. Hong Kong, Taiwan, Tibet, Xinjiang and Inner Mongolia he believes should be autonomous. For self-evident reasons his programme for dismantling the Chinese state does not recommend itself to American broadcasters or institutions concerned with China. After meeting President Clinton in the early days of his stay in America, and receiving help from various foundations, officially, Wei was dropped.

Another prominent exile is the self-described commandant of the Tiananmen uprising, Wuer Kaixi. Originally a Uighur from a Muslim family, he now lives in Taiwan. For him Tiananmen is the turning point of modern Chinese history. Since 1989, he contends, the Chinese are no longer slaves, either in their own eyes or in those of the world. But there are different analyses of the meaning of the event, and the democrats are divided. The dissidents retain a certain influence amongst their peers, but the revolt was over a quarter of a century ago, its leaders have been scattered, and Wuer Kaixi is honest about the softening effects of exile:

In China we were ignorant of what individualism, love and consumerism were. Everything was communal and political. In the West we discovered all that. We were twenty years old and we had a taste for it.

In allowing dissidents to leave the country the CCP calculated that they would not be unified enough to establish a movement in exile, and they were right. The younger generation, operating in a more permissive political climate, can be more moral than political. Yu Jie, thirty years old, declines to go abroad. So far the worst he has suffered have been police intimidation and ten-hour long interrogations. An admirer of de Tocqueville and a convert to Christianity, his books invite the Chinese to read nineteenth century novels in order to rediscover their humanity and inner identity.

He believes that the era of Wei Jingshen, a veteran of the Cultural Revolution when everything was black and white, has passed. The CCP is still cruel but more subtle. The democratic revolution that the Wei generation hoped for will not happen, but change would come. It was hopeless to expect the Party to evolve, it would do everything to cling to power, even if it meant having recourse to the army. The answer was prayer, and moral redemption

Yu Jie pulls no punches on Mao. When the CCP was celebrating the anniversary of its victory over the Japanese in 1945 he published an article in Hong Kong pointing out that Mao Zedong had killed more Chinese people than their enemies. He also announced that 'A civilized Olympic Games cannot be held in Beijing so long as the corpse of this murderer remains here.'[13]

Meanwhile, beyond the internationally publicized cases of repression, signs of significant change, large and small, are mounting. Class struggle has officially been declared 'an incorrect concept', as the Party has concluded, correctly, that it is people themselves who matter. Instead of being shot or clapped in labour camps (*lao gai*) Chinese citizens seeking to import forbidden books may merely have them confiscated. Old timers from the Party openly call for democracy. A young professor, Gua Quan, has announced the formation of a political party allegedly supported by millions called The New Democracy Party.

Instantly he ceased to be a professor. But he was not arrested.

At the end of 2007 a movement sprang up in the North East of the country for the seizure and redistribution of state-owned farming land, which was excluded from a new law on property ownership. There were signs of hesitancy in the authorities' response. And though it is rarely reported in the West, there are intimations of progress in China's long road to becoming a country ruled by law. Between 1987 and 2003 the number of legal judgments almost tripled, in roughly the same period the number of judges went from 70,000 to 180,000, and the trend continues. Many of the new cases they try are no doubt commercial, but there is no lack of civil and even privacy cases too: not long ago a young Shanghai couple successfully complained when they were photographed embracing on the Underground after the photo found its way onto the Internet.[14]

Meanwhile executions, it has been announced, are henceforth to be by lethal injection rather than shooting, because the Party considers this method of disposing of criminals more humane. Their number has also begun to decline now that each death sentence must be confirmed by the Supreme Court. Direct universal elections for the Chief Executive in Hong Kong have been promised by 2017, which would make elections to the legislative Council possible as early as 2020. (On that score, we shall see.)

In an unprecedented gesture that must have taken aback those on the receiving end, when vast numbers of people were stranded by breakdowns in service during the severe weather at the beginning of 2008, the nine highest Chinese leaders went to railway stations to express their compassion: given official fears of large congregations of people getting out of hand it was a demonstration of concern, in two senses. One of the extraordinary changes I have noted in the last thirty years has been how quickly the Chinese have changed from being a cowed to a pushy people. In Beijing and the coastal cities 'small spaces for dissent' (in Pankaj Mishra's phrase) have opened up. And finally, in a quite different field, contemporary art of a kind that must be genuinely 'challenging' for Party apparatchiks has been officially embraced by the state.

Beneath the harsh rhetoric and exemplary punishments, is China going soft? If so, and piecemeal liberalization proves terminal for the CCP, what will emerge in its place? In the view of one activist, Wang Li Xiong, the Party is operating a dog in the manger policy. It was no longer in a position to control the country, yet by refusing to allow any other political institutions to grow it risked the whole structure crumbling when the CCP itself collapsed.[15]

When it was seeking to secure the Games for China, the country's Olympic committee, aware of misgivings amongst foreigners about Beijing's record of suppressing dissent, thought it would be smart to suggest that awarding China the Games would help the development of human rights. The argument proved an own goal: it was instantly taken up by intellectuals and others as an excuse to advertise their dissatisfactions.

The experience should be borne in mind as the country moves forward. Again, there is a Soviet precedent. On a far larger scale something not dissimilar happened in Soviet Russia at the beginning of the '70s. At the time Moscow was keen to sign an agreement on security and cooperation in Europe, partly to fix in aspic the borders of the German Democratic Republic. In the prolonged negotiations in Helsinki that followed (the CSCE – Conference on Security and Cooperation in Europe) the West was determined to force Moscow to pay a price in terms of agreements on the free exchange of people, ideas and information (I was the British delegate at the CSCE preparatory meeting in Helsinki dealing with these subjects).

Reluctantly the Russians signed up to what came to be known as the Helsinki Documents, giving the West what many of us believed at the time was a purely paper victory. We were wrong: the victory was real. The Russians could not keep secret what they had signed, dissidents fell on the documents to legitimate their actions and a 'Helsinki movement' developed that was to play a role in the collapse of the Soviet regime some fourteen years later. It would be wrong to overplay it, but in a smaller way, and despite the efforts of the security authorities, simply by promoting international contacts and putting China in the spotlight of world opinion, events like the Olympic Games and Expo 2010 will have had something of a liberating effect. If the regime is rash enough to talk the talk about human rights, as occasionally it is obliged to do, as in

Russia people could one day begin to take them at their word.

Will China conform to the law of autocracies, whereby the most perilous thing the power-holders can do is to relax their grip? Again the obvious parallel is with Russia, where what began as perestroika led swiftly to the entire country falling apart. In the longer term it is possible, but China is China and nothing can be assumed. Conventions are everything in this culture, and it is equally conceivable that something like a *modus vivendi* between government and opposition may emerge. The dissidents would take care not to overstep the mark in their proclamations and activities, while for their part the authorities would finesse their punishments (a Chinese speciality) and refrain from implementing the full gamut of repressive measures.

Assuming there is no drastic economic reversal, the temptations of the good life described by Wuer Kaixi will meanwhile have the effect of wearing down the will of some dissidents to resist. The latest indicator pointing in this direction is the failure of young Chinese to respond in any significant numbers to the so-called Arab Spring in early 2011, despite (or perhaps because of) the echoes in Egypt or Tunisia of Tiananmen Square.

*

When I was learning Chinese in Hong Kong and grumbled to a Western business friend about the sweat of mastering my quota of 3000 characters, by way of encouragement he told me that memorizing ideograms was the perfect training for computer literacy. For that reason the Chinese, he said, would one day dominate the industry. Because they had been memorizing characters from the age of four, with their complex network of radicals and phonemes, meaning and sound, pattern recognition—a key feature of computer literacy—was bred in the bone.

That was in the '60s. Today it is clearer what he meant. There is something about the sight of Chinese children at work on computers— their concentration, their dexterity, their alert posture—that gives the impression that they have fused with their machines, and in a sense they have. Whether or not they are more culturally predisposed than us to the workings of the keyboard the Chinese have certainly taken to personal computers in a big way, and to the Internet in particular. At the beginning of 2008 the country was reckoned to have 221 million surfers, a number superior to America's. The most extraordinary thing about that figure is that it had increased from 137 million (i.e. by 61 per cent) in the preceding year. By 2011 it had grown to encompass a third of the population.

The devotees of game shows and chat rooms are often the young, and 10 per cent of under twenty-fives are addicts, as against 1 per cent in Britain. Officially, in China the condition is defined as spending five or more hours a day on the Internet for purposes other than work, to the neglect of the addict's health. So concerned are the authorities that they launched a televised programme of education on the damage caused by the Internet. 'The electronic opium of the people' the official media has called it - a phrase that neatly combines Marx's views on religion with memories of the imports of opium which helped rot the Qing empire. In Beijing there is even a clinic where the young can go— or be sent—for treatment and where electric shock therapy and calming agents feature amongst the cures. The most inventive form of therapy is one that could exist nowhere but in China: adolescent addicts of war games are dispatched to do military service once a week and exercised to the point of exhaustion.

Officially the causes of computer addiction are said to be one-child families where, with no siblings to talk to, children can spend many hours on their own, and at lower social levels computers are a form of escape for young people without a future. But at the forefront of government minds are of course political worries.[16]

Satellite TV and the foreign press are already restricted to international compounds, and towards the end of 2006 China took the radical step of banning all foreign news agency reports distributed in China which had not been cleared by the state. New powers of censorship were conferred on the New China News Agency (NCNA), first established in 1931 and the CCP's official organ ever since. Its remit was at once simple and all-pervasive: anything that undermined the country's social or economic order, or its stability, would be banned.

Yet even in a country with tens of thousands of internet censors and snoopers, implementation is not easy. Looking for banned material on the screen is like seeking out risky wall-posters put up overnight: whether or not you catch a glimpse of them in the morning depends on how long it took the authorities to get wise and tear them down.

In the new corporate China commercial and political motives are intertwined, with a high admixture of cronyism. The head of NCNA, Tian Congming, has spoken frankly of his aim to put Reuters and Bloomberg out of business in China and replace the booming market of financial services. The potential for Mr Tian personally is promising. As it happens he is an old associate of the Chinese President Hu Jintao, with whom he has worked in Tibet; Hu was Party boss there and Tian his deputy. In terms of business access it is as if Rupert Murdoch were a near-relative of George W. Bush.

For NCNA the economic potential is as unlimited as the number of Chinese shareholders. One of the most striking things I have seen in the new China was a share shop in Shanghai. Hundreds of bicycles were parked outside, a sight one is unlikely to see in the City of London. Inside their humble-looking owners were seated in front of screens of prices, ravenously monitoring the flickering figures.

As the country is torn between censorship and modernization, a knowledge economy and the rationing of information, the stakes are high in money terms. Clearly a relaxing of controls overall would bring an even bigger burst of activity, but for the CCP politics comes first. In 2002 China established a system by which foreign Internet servers who wanted to do business in China were obliged to sign a charter promising to cooperate with state security. This was China's first Internet purge.

To monitor, control and root out offenders in a country this size requires a vast manpower; it is thought that some 30,000 people, leaving aside law enforcement, are engaged in this gigantic censorship machine. Presumably they are highly trained English-speakers as well as computer literate, a fact that brought to mind what a Russian once said to me while we surveyed an endless queue outside a shop in a Moscow high street in the communist era: 'Think what all those people could be accomplishing if they weren't doing that.'

The opportunity costs of China's great cybernetic wall are huge, but their work of stamping out anything resembling organized dissent is crucial for the Party. They are engaged in offensive as well as defensive operations: their officers orchestrate public acclamation for the Government on chat sites, advertise the Party's alleged successes, and generally manipulate opinion. The regime may be less harsh than it was, but thanks to technology it can be more efficient; the very mention in blogs of the names of the country's leaders, President Hu Jintao and Prime Minister Wen Jaibao can be impeded, and non-persons are erased from existence more quickly and thoroughly than in the old days. When the Shanghai Party boss Chen Liangyu was fired for corruption, computer agents sprang into action, obliterating tens of thousands of official references to the former top flight official within minutes.

A market system that excludes the free flow of information makes little sense in Western eyes. It makes even less when the West colludes in the suppression. Some Western Internet companies have been playing by China's rules, to the indignation of some of their shareholders and of politicians. As a consequence there was a minor shareholder revolt at Google. Cisco systems, which supplied equipment to the Great Chinese Firewall, also had trouble. Yahoo! is alleged to have gone further by allowing its search engine to supply information which helped the Chinese authorities to convict and imprison a pro-democracy Chinese journalist, leading the House of Representatives Foreign Affairs Committee to call its chief executive a 'moral pygmy.'[17]

The executive's excuse was that its local employees in Beijing had no choice but to comply with legal Chinese demands. The only defence for these companies is that they are in there for the long haul, which means some difficult choices while getting established. 'China is a nation with a 5000 year history' Google's chief executive remarked in 2006. 'That could indicate the duration of our patience.' It wasn't: just a few years later it accused China of attacks on its systems to identify and pursue dissidents. In January 2010 Google abruptly decided it could no longer live with the moral ambiguity of its position and resolved to close down its operations. Subsequently it moved to Hong Kong, but there is talk of a new arrangement with China.

There will be no lack of Chinese officials who must have said good riddance to Google, and all who surfed on her. And not a few Americans will have smiled. When Google agreed in 2006 to censor its services in accordance with Chinese security desiderata in return for agreement to set up in China, it had previously fought off attempts by the US Department of Justice for information on what domestic users were searching for.

As Google saw it, its agreement with China could be justified on the grounds that the short-term moral ambiguity would be justified by a long-term engagement with a progressively more open and enlightened regime, which its internet service would itself foster. It was then that its chief executive spoke rashly about patience.

In 2006 Google had a case, if only because its argument was opposed to the absolutist view: that the choice lay between censoring some information and offering no information at all. Businesses – especially big ones - are in this respect like countries. In the Cold War the British and the American governments never stopped sponsoring Western plays or exhibitions in the Soviet Union because the Russians declined to open the gates to everything we produced. When Google opened up in Beijing things looked promising enough, not just financially but in the context of a hesitantly modernizing China, for it to place its bet, holding its nose as it signed.

If you are going to operate in a sovereign country at all, it also argued, you have to respect local laws. What some must have thought but could never have said was 'look at the compromises Western governments and businesses make in Muslim countries every day of the week, on freedom of Christian worship or the repression of women in Saudi Arabia, before you condemn the cyber folk in China out of hand.' The most recent awkwardness in this field was the unilateral closure of the Internet by the Egyptian government during the protest movement in January 2011: an embarrassment, this time, to Vodaphone.

Maybe the whole experience will cure Google of its tendency to go on talking quite so loudly about its 'mission' - a habit uncomfortably reminiscent of bankers talking about doing God's work in the world.

*

The possibility of instant communication across a vast and disparate country raises nightmare scenarios in Party minds. It is easy to see why, and events in the Middle East, where people have spoken of an internet revolution, will have intensified their fears. The 74,000 incidents of disorder the Chinese have admitted to in recent years have two things in common: the clashes with law and order agencies were mostly provoked by corrupt or high-handed behaviour by local Party officials; and they were mostly isolated cases, with few ties between local protesters.

Fear of the establishment of links between the violently discontented haunts the Chinese mind. Ultimately the reason goes back to the Tai-ping rebellion. The greatest recorded revolt in Chinese history began in 1851 and was not suppressed until 1865. In the process eleven provinces were ravaged and some twenty million lives were lost. The leader, Hong Xiuquan, was a Christian convert who had visions in which he saw himself as divinely ordained to rule China. The government only won after demoralized and ineffective imperial troops were reformed into a serious fighting force, by General Gordon amongst others.

Millions flocked to Hong, partly through ignorance and superstition, though mainly, as so frequently in China, from grievances against officials that went un-remedied by distant government. His importance lay less in his religious teachings than in his ability to act as a catalyst against authority. Seen through anxious official eyes the Tai-ping revolt has several things in common with the present situation, notably the religious factor.

It is not difficult to understand their apprehension at the spread of the Falun Gong, a quirky and inoffensive cult in Western eyes, but for the paranoid Chinese Communist Party a more serious matter. Its membership includes professors, generals and students, and its teachings are imbued with Taoism and Buddhism. Nor has the fact that Christianity in China is spreading gone unnoticed. Estimates range from 40 to 70 million; if it is closer to the latter there would be as many Christians as Communist Party members. All that is lacking, the CCP might fear, are ways to bring aggrieved and marauding locals together. Hence their vigilance about the internet.

A single confrontation that took place in 2005 contained every element of the malaise in rural China that makes the Communist Party nervous. An electricity station was to be built in an area of Hebei province. A hundred peasants refused to vacate the land without compensation. The local authorities recruited a militia to drive them out. The peasants resisted and twelve were killed. There was nothing in the press—a journalist got wind of the story but when he turned up on site he was arrested—yet the killings featured on the web in the form of a petition to the government. It turned out that a government allocation had been made to compensate the peasants, but almost all of it had been siphoned off by officials.

Most cases of this type are never published at all. A website pulling them together would be a powerful indictment against the regime, and an incitement to others to act.

*

Progress towards democracy in China will be closely linked with the official view of the past. A fascinating, previously secret account of recent Party discussions on the question was published in Hong Kong in 2007 by Song Ke (pseudonym Xin Xiling), a Professor at the Defence University, an establishment which has a rich store of Party materials. The official view that Mao's actions were 70 per cent correct and 30 per cent erroneous was arrived at during an evaluation of the historical record in 1981. At an enlarged meeting of the Politburo's Standing Committee in 1993 Deng Xiaoping said that determining the exact position on the balance between errors and achievements had been limited by the situation. Some of the history was not true, he admitted, and some comrades had accepted it against their wishes.

Victims of the Cultural Revolution, such as the former Mayor of Beijing Peng Zhen, were told that although their reservations were correct, things had to rest where they were for now because of the overall situation. To go further might risk negating the CCP's historical achievements and damaging its leading position. Deng proposed that a true evaluation of Mao should await a new generation of leaders at the beginning of the next century. Not only would the political climate be more advantageous, but comrades would be less stubborn in their views. Communists were materialists and the correction of past errors was a sign of confidence. The decision was read into the record of the standing committee meeting.

A year after Hu Jintao became president in 2003 another leading moderate and victim of the Cultural Revolution, Wan Li, former President of the National People's Congress, asked Hu when he planned to do something about Mao's record. Hu told him he totally understood the importance of the resolution passed under Deng Xiaoping and assured him that the problem would be solved sooner or later. It was a major political issue and must be sorted out at a time when they were not hemmed in by too many problems which needed to be resolved first. The Mao question was best approached in a calm political atmosphere, he insisted, when there would be more common ground. Hu Jintao appears to have promised Wan Li that something would be done during his period in the Presidency. He is now coming to the end of his tenure, with no sign of action.

It is almost possible to sympathize with Hu's position. There is never a good time for governments to broach such subjects, and no lack of pretexts to postpone the day of historical reckoning. Yet there seems reason to hope that at some stage in the future a sharp retrospective adjustment of Mao's record will be made, either officially or—more likely perhaps—in publications sanctioned by the Party. When it happens there will be protests from a minority of conservatives and Party old-timers, but that is to be expected. More entertaining will be the reaction amongst non-Chinese admirers of Mao. It would be ironic to reach a situation where Western aficionados of the Chairman opposed further concessions to the truth by the Chinese communists themselves, not a few of whom suffered from his depredations.

Meanwhile, the regime can depend for support for the 70/30 formula on many a Western sinologist, a good slice of intellectual opinion, and a gaggle of hopelessly impressionable show-biz figures. Even when his memory is finally dethroned in his own country, millions in the West will remain sentimentally loyal to the memory of the Chairman Mao of their youth. Again, one can almost sympathize. Such folk were never too concerned with the reality of China in the first place, so why change their view today?

'Strong winds make noises no-one has heard before.'
Chinese proverb

If it is true that the arts foreshadow the future, then there are worse ways to speculate about what we can expect from China than to glance at what is happening in opera, in films, in literature, in architecture, or in the Chinese art market. Trends here can be powerful indicators not only of where the country has reached, but where it may be going. China itself is increasingly conscious of the power of its cultural reputation: hence the decision to open 500 'Confucius Institutes' across the globe by 2010, a form of image-making that would have horrified the imperial government, with its implication that China cared what barbarians thought of it, or was keen for them to pry out the secrets of its language.

Opera is one of the most characteristic forms of Chinese art, not least because, unlike its equivalent in the West, it enjoys popular appeal. To us the most striking fact about Chinese opera is that, however elaborate the staging, essentially it is caricatural. The painted faces are masks, coloured according to character. Sixteen designs exist for the main types of personality. Red means uncomplicated and loyal. White indicates a cunning, resourceful fellow. Black is sound, honest and upright. Yellow denotes intelligence, brown stubbornness, green means ghostly, blue suggests vigorousness and courage, and so on.

Such type-casting is not unknown in other cultures: the English, after all, can be tediously devoted to their stereotypical 'character actors'. But in China stylization is absolute—the military are stiff, erect and proud, the statesman will invariably have stooped, rounded shoulders—and is reflected in the rigours of the apprenticeship system for performers. Till recently the student had to train for six years holding a stick upright in front of him, so that the body leans neither too far forward or back. Allegedly connected with the Yin and Yang symbols of Taoist philosophy, to the Western eye the movements are staccato and not especially subtle: hands and body tremble all over to show fear, and an infinitely rehearsed flicking of the sleeve—a highly prized gesture often evoking applause in itself—displays anger or indignation.

It is not too fanciful to see in the rigorous conformities of Chinese opera reflections of national states of mind. Like the blue-faced character on the stage the Chinese government can be quick to anger and imperious in the shaking of its sleeve. Relations with Westerners, though a little more relaxed nowadays, are still characterized by stiffness and formality. And a tendency to extremes, you sometimes reflect, watching the controlled explosions of emotion on stage, and the singers' harsh expressions, may be embedded in the culture. Chinese art itself can be refined and exquisite or, like some late Qing pottery, graceless and garish.

In the economy and social relations too something in the Chinese temperament appears to draw it to extremes. It is there in the rigidities of Marxist diction and interpretation, where the Chinese showed themselves even more dogmatic than the Russians. China went much further than its European comrades, or indeed any society in history, in its manic egalitarianism, insisting that a peasant might know more about medicine than a doctor and abolishing military insignia denoting rank (you learned to tell a soldier's seniority by the number of his pockets). As a convert to capitalism its excesses have been caricatural too, a throwback to what we would see as Victorian times.

Extremes are present in the whole pattern of Chinese commerce, whether in the wild lurches of stock markets or the dramatic shift from autarky to exports in a matter of years, and a ruthless determination to corner entire global markets. The town of Xiaoshan makes 80 per cent of all duvets in the world. Fenshui does 80 per cent of ballpoint pens. Qiatou makes 29 billion buttons, 90 per cent of the global supply. Donguan does 75 per cent of the world's toys.

Chinese society itself is another example of massive sways between opposite states of being. For anyone who has known the country over several decades the change in atmospherics is extraordinary. It is sometimes hard to believe that this is the same nation. 'My assessment of these people', said Henry Kissinger before he went there, 'is that they

are deeply ideological, close to fanatic in the intensity of their beliefs.'
Surveying their behaviour in the '60s that was certainly my experience.
Yet in the space of a few years these same ideological fanatics have
produced a generation who sit around in swanky clothes tranquilly
sipping their Starbucks coffee. How can a national temperament change
so fast?

The swing from an egalitarian to a widely divided society has been
similarly stark. The British insist that the legendary public notice in a
park in colonial Shanghai saying 'no dogs or Chinese allowed' is
apocryphal, the Chinese believe it. What is certain is that the dogs of
rich Shanghainese today have a lot more spent on them than the average
peasant. Rarely in history can there have been such dramatic—one
might say operatic—changes between one generation and the next. In
Maoist days there was an average of one restaurant per three million
people; now it is one per four hundred. Extremes meet again in the
townscapes, as the drear homogeneity of the Mao era is replaced across
China by the tinsel uniformity of replica Hong Kongs.

China is not a relaxed country. As in its opera tensions can be sensed
in every scene. Gradualism and evolution, you are left thinking, are not
in China's blood. Periods of paralysis followed by moments of epilepsy
are more evident in its history. It is scarcely necessary to say which
period we are in today.

*

Epilepsy is evident again in the Chinese art market. The art trade has
boomed in recent years, from a standing start, with both Chinese and
foreign auction houses setting up in the capital. None of this should
surprise us: the Chinese are more than mere art lovers, they are the
world's most compulsive and discerning connoisseurs. Today what is
happening however goes beyond traditional criticism and
connoisseurship. In many ways it is a manic reaction to what went
before.

During the Cultural Revolution almost all art and antique shops
closed, anything old being *ipso facto* out of favour. In the single scroll
shop that stayed open in Beijing and which I visited regularly I saw no

Chinese customers at all in nearly three years; indeed there were only two or three buyers (all foreign) besides myself. This was hard on the old experts who manned the shop; the fewer customers there were the more time they were forced to spend in the inner courtyard reading out confessions of their bourgeois thoughts and reciting the Chairman's scriptures before a distinctly unaesthetic-looking group of Red Guards.

At the time there was of course no 'contemporary' art, in fact little that would qualify as art at all. No one would have dared to paint any subject except Mao, the PLA and the virtuous masses, and even then it could be a risky business: one unorthodox element and the artist could be accused of counter-revolutionary tendencies and find him or herself dragged off to a struggle meeting for a beating-up. The only other outlet for artistic expression at the time was calligraphy on big character posters—the *dazebao*—and the manufacture of coloured posters and cut-outs, usually in praise of Mao.

The denunciatory calligraphy scrawled by Red Guards had a certain angry vigour, being splashy and dramatic ('crush his dog's head', 'who is blowing up a black wind?', 'struggle this imperialist agent'). The posters were mostly kitsch in Soviet realist style, though the intricate paper cut-outs, a Chinese specialty, would have pleased Matisse. Despite their limited range of propaganda themes they could be technically brilliant and startlingly well designed. All in all however it was woeful stuff: a wretched residue of a five-millennia old culture.

There has been no lack of cultural putsches in history, from the burning of books by the second century Emperor Qin Shi Huangdi to Savonarola and the Nazis, but this was something else. As so often the regime distinguished itself by its thoroughness. I once bought some ornate writing paper manufactured before the Cultural Revolution in which charming, half-inch square coloured prints of paintings by the grand old man of twentieth century Chinese art, Qi Baishi, who specialized in birds, insects and other harmless subjects, had been ritually crossed out by censors, page by page. On the front was stamped: 'Sold off as criticized material.' It was certainly cheap. For good measure Red Guards, we heard, had gone to the trouble of vandalizing the artist's grave. Then, no sooner was Mao dead and the Cultural Revolution over than a colossal swing took place in Chinese art.

When communism collapsed in Russia a Moscow artist friend foresaw what would happen. For years, he said, many artists had been working metaphorically and literally underground. The only studios they could afford were places like disused basement car parks, with no natural light but the advantage of privacy from the police. This underground mentality encouraged the belief that genius abounded, and would eventually emerge into the daylight and be publicly recognized and rewarded. My friend's prediction was that, now they were free to surface and mount shows of their work, it would become painfully apparent that repression does not necessarily guarantee artistic genius, and that talent would be sparse.

Worse, the realization would dawn that the 'subversive' styles in which many artists had painted were more often than not pallid imitations of innovative work done in the West. The pain would be all the greater when it was realized that the inspiration behind the foreign artists they were sub-consciously copying had often been the Russian avant-garde of the early years of the twentieth century: Malevich, Kandinsky, Tatlin. And so, very often, it came to pass, as one 'liberated' exhibition after another turned out to have doubly derivative echoes: of the great age of Russian modernism and of its development in the West.

In China, when art began again in the late '70s, it was starting from a clean slate, in a way without parallel in other cultures. Yet there has been something of the Russian experience in this resuscitation of China's talents. Here too there has been a lot of catching up to be done—more than in Russia—and foreign influences are stark. The difference is that, derivative or not, some of it has been striking work, and commercially speaking a huge success. The tens of thousands of items of export porcelain recently recovered from wrecks that foundered en route from China to Europe remind us of the extent of the taste for *chinoiserie* in the eighteenth century. The wave of Chinese contemporary art that has hit Western salerooms has a little of that feeling. China, once again, is in vogue.

In the climate of the late '70s and '80s artists had no inclination to return to the frozen conventions that had pertained since 1949: bird-and-flower paintings, innocuous landscapes, model proletarians, pictures of anti-Japanese soldier-heroes. Cut off from the world for a third of a century, many artists lunged into cosmopolitan modernity.

The spectacle of an imprisoned imagination exuberantly breaking free has been remarkable, and the excess of zeal in the search for novel effects understandable. Chinese artists could be said to be lucky in their timing, to the extent that their emergence onto the international stage has coincided with a boom. In another sense they have been unfortunate, as the international craze for novelty and the lack of critical discipline has encouraged a wave of modish mediocrity or charlatanism. The question is how much of what contemporary Chinese artists are producing has to do with art, and how much with meeting the insatiable demands for exoticism in an over-heated market?

It was bad luck on China that the rediscovery in the West of ideas pioneered by Dada and Marcel Duchamp almost a hundred years ago should have led to so much outright plagiarizing or clumsy kitsch. It seems particularly sad that young Chinese should find themselves looking for inspiration to a British movement that, for all the self-interested hype by dealers and public galleries in search of Treasury cash and a new public, was itself so backward-looking and derivative. Never mind: hedge-funders and other speculators in the genre were not too well up on Duchamp or Dada, and it sold.

Some of the principles behind abstract and conceptual art were not new to China. 'Xe yi' (paint the idea) has long been a recognized Chinese style: it is enough to think of paintings composed of a few, exquisite abstract strokes, with their Zen or Taoist echoes. As for aleatory art, such as Damian Hirst's spin paintings, as early as the eighteenth century the Chinese were dipping women's long hair in paint and sloshing it about to see what chance effects might be procured. They were also early adepts at finger or tongue painting, for what it was worth, which was usually little.

Installations, a long-established genre in mainland Europe though seen in Britain as excitingly modern, were also nothing new to the Chinese mind. Xu Bing, the new vice-president of the Central Academy of Fine Arts in Beijing and a distinguished artist himself, has explained:

Duchamp's attitude towards art and life is in step with Chinese Chan (Zen) Buddhist methods... Warhol really understood the idea that

Buddha is everywhere, right next to you. There is a Chan saying: 'Only in the complete absence of reference to (or conception of) him will Buddha appear.' That is how Warhol approached art.[1]

This style of thinking will inevitably be a big influence on emerging Chinese artists, who after years of enforced silence feel that they have a lot to say, or 'signify'. The force of their imagination in this genre, combined with the dramatic social changes in their country, and the fact that their work was sprung on the world from a previously closed culture, gave it extra allure. Yet for all the philosophical parallels highlighted by Xu Bing the cold truth is that the often dated nature of the Western styles they were copying, in which old clothes were so frequently sold as new, meant that a good deal of the inspiration behind their work was not just second-hand, but third. As Gore Vidal has remarked, 'everything changes except the avant-garde.'

An example is the well-known artist Ai Weiwei, one of the driving forces behind the revival of the late '70s. The work in question is a performance piece called *Dropping a Han Dynasty Urn,* which is what he does, to camera. It is no secret what he is getting at: destroying an ancient artifact is designed to offend our delicate sensibilities and shock us into thinking about Chinese art anew. For a Westerner however the shock is that it is possible for an artist blatantly to repeat something we have seen so often before; it is almost a century since Duchamp painted a moustache on the Mona Lisa. As Sir Ernst Gombrich pointed out many years ago, when he welcomed modern work but wondered where it could go, it is the kind of gesture that it can become tedious to repeat.

Maybe every country has to ceremonially trash a bit of its venerated art to make the point about 'challenging rigidified cultures', and in China, pre- and post-Mao, there has been no lack of rigidity. Yet this particular performance carries unfortunate echoes. The Red Guards too smashed many an ancient piece of porcelain, burned many a scroll and took hammers to many a temple carving to make a similar point from an ultra-leftist angle, but the porcelain was still in bits at the end of it. If totalitarians and libertarians like Ai Weiwei are to indulge in a potlatch of China's heritage, that would be a shame.

A problem with prominent artists who are well-known dissidents is that being on the right side of the political argument and persecuted by the authorities (Ai's Weiwei's new studio was closed in 2011) can make them immune to aesthetic evaluation. This (in my opinion) is what happened at Ai Weiwei's show at Tate Modern in London in 2010, consisting of a myriad sunflower seeds, each separately painted. It ought to be possible to object that, while the message about the Chinese being individuals as much as anyone else is not something anyone would contest, his massive installation is a cumbrous and unimaginative way of making the point, except perhaps in the eyes of Tate Modern which has an empty turbine hall to fill and a public in search of novelty to amuse, together with their children.

One pities the hundreds of Chinese whose un-individual and somewhat humiliating task it was to paint millions of virtually identical seeds. But there we are: when contemporary art, political rectitude and celebrity coincide criticism of any kind becomes unacceptable, and reviewers righteously applauded, as they had when Ai Weiwei produced an exhibition in Shanghai in 2000 with the title 'Fuck Off!'

There is no doubt about the artist's talent—it was Ai Weiwei who helped design the enchanting, latticed 'bird's nest' Olympic Stadium in Beijing for the Swiss architects Herzog and de Meuron. He vowed he would have nothing further to do with the Olympics because of the Chinese government's use of the event for propaganda. This seems reasonable, but then political stances are one thing and their enduring translation into artistic expression another. W.H. Auden was amongst those who saw the dangers of mistaking political gestures for art:

> To do this is to reduce art to an endless series of momentary and arbitrary 'happenings' and to produce in artists and public alike a conformation to the tyranny of the passing moment, which is far more enslaving, far more destructive of integrity and originality, than any thoughtless copying of the past.

Which covers the antique pot and the sunflower seeds neatly.

The flourishing trade in contemporary Chinese art is suggestive of the country's state of mind in other fields. Its spectacular entry into the art market mirrors its economic globalization as a whole, in more than the financial sense. As in the textile or white goods business there has been a tendency amongst Chinese artists to over-production, and the temptation to turn out replicas on demand. One area in which Chinese art remains distinctive however lies in the technical quality of the work. Whether in photography, installations, or the scrupulously exact, hyper-realistic painting at which the Chinese excel, age old traditions of application shine through. A combination of respect for craftsmanship, a new vision of China and the world, and freedom to create could prove promising for the future, unless of course everything succumbs to rampant commercialism.

It is the styles and themes that can be the problem, rather than the execution. In the early days antinomian work, rarely without its post-Maoist jokiness, thrilled impressionable Western collectors eager for new pastures. The difficulty is that 'political pop' or 'cynical realist' styles tend by their nature to be ephemeral, especially when they are churned out on demand, and rely too much on adolescent irony or stunt-value. This does not mean there is nothing of value in the genre. Positive and negative elements come together in the work of Yue Minjun, whose major work to date is *Execution*, in which a quartet of eerily laughing young men in underpants face a mimed execution.

Here there is technical ability, a striking construction—and a large debt to Goya, Delacroix and Manet, who have all painted firing squads. The original aspect of the painting—presumably an evocation of the Tiananmen massacre—is the vapid hilarity of the 'pretend' executioners and their victims. The phony side of protest in a consumerist society where nothing is real is one of several possible interpretations. One problem with Yue is that this highly successful artist (this painting was sold for £2.9 million, the most ever paid for a contemporary Chinese work at the time) has tended to repeat himself in paintings with sundry other grinning figures. Cynical realism *seriatim* can quickly descend to sarcasm, and wear thin.

For all the booster talk that has frequently replaced serious art criticism in the West, the revival of Chinese art does not automatically equate with 'an explosion of creativity.' The images can often be striking (like the Russians the Chinese can excel at poster art) but as one discerning critic has said, too often the pictures or artifacts degenerate into market products:

> Visiting Shanghai in late 2005 I was overwhelmed by China's sharp
> and pervasive social contrasts. But a canvas by Wang Guangyi that
> interposes workers wearing the gleaming strained smile that the
> Cultural Revolution required for propaganda painting imagery with
> the names of luxury Western brands does not satirize these cultural
> contradictions—it transforms art into another cheaply made and too
> easily consumed, high-priced commodity.[2]

A similar critique could of course equally be made of much
contemporary Western art. The impudence of Chinese 'political pop'
echoes a strand of heavy-footed, message-laden work, like Mark
Wallinger's anti-Iraq war gesturing in Britain. To a Western audience at
least, the Chinese work looks new. Produced in what is technically still a
communist country it also has an aura of daring, and some artists run
the risk of persecution. No one is going to come looking for Mark
Wallinger in the night. Yet given the regime's increasing forbearance
where art is concerned, even that element of authenticity is wearing thin.
The credit crunch has also encouraged more critical views, and as of
2010 the contemporary market is no longer floating on a sea of
undiscriminating cash.

In the thirty or so years that contemporary Chinese art has been
evolving its progress has gone, like much else in the new China, by fits
and starts. In the early '80s exhibitions were banned, and in the '90s
'apartment art' - private shows in a flat - became a way of displaying
more difficult material. Now official tolerance is greater, not least
because of the market aspect. National pride in seeing China occupy a
prominent place on the artistic map, and her auction houses begin to
compete seriously with the biggest in the West, has also played its part
in making the genre respectable.

Chinese leaders want to be able to do more than grin sourly when
congratulated by their foreign hosts on their country's artistic
rejuvenation. The former President Jiang Zemin was embarrassed
during his official visit to France in 2002 when he was unable to respond
to the President Chirac on the subject. Back in China he is said to have

arranged tutorials for himself—a surreal notion in itself. How entertaining it would have been to be present at these sessions. What the aging communist functionary made of the sub-Duchampian or neo-Warholian products of contemporary Chinese artists passes understanding.

Signs that the Party, gratified if mystified by their country's international prominence in the field, is ready to take contemporary artists into its embrace are yet another echo of Western, and especially British practice. In Britain work that is trumpeted as subversive of everything the Government stands for—public decency, the market system, the use of military force to parry the terrorist threat—is lavishly praised and funded by that same Government and its cultural agencies. Meanwhile the works themselves sell to profoundly non-subversive multi-millionaires, and the artists flaunt their riches. Not for nothing is British contemporary art called 'state art' by its critics. In Russia the famous joke about the Soviet Government's attitude to its people was 'You pretend to work and we pretend to pay you.' In the case of Young British Artists the message to the political, social and financial establishment is 'We pretend to attack you and you pretend to bleed.'

The Chinese authorities could come to find such a simulacrum of protest very much to their satisfaction. Socially critical art that is patronized by government agencies blunts its edge. It remains to be seen how enthusiastically contemporary artists respond to the state's embrace. The local government in Sichuan, the province celebrated as much for its scenery and painters as for its spicy food, offered eight contemporary artists under the age of 60 their own premises. All accepted and their individual museums opened in 2008. We await their products. British arts ministers have perfected a bland expressionlessness when touring galleries crammed with sexual or politically-loaded material, but it would be interesting to see the faces of local worthies at the opening ceremony at the nude performance art of Wu Shanzhuan, one of the lucky eight, or of paintings, installations or multi-media items satirizing authoritarian government. Perhaps there will be an unspoken agreement that in return for their free premises, and the public money invested in them, the artists will refrain from provocation.

There are long traditions of connivance between Chinese artists and authority, and authority has lucrative commissions for public art to dangle. At the same time, in a field where assaults on dissidents are bad for China's image, artists are well placed to call the government's bluff.

The big question about Chinese contemporary art today is similar to that hanging over the country's economy as a whole: will it endure, or is it, like Shanghai's housing market, hugely overblown and destined for collapse? As for the West, the art market's fling with Chinese contemporary work fits the tradition of sporadic engagement with China all too snugly. Market-making is a form of myth-making, and in China's case of orientalism. One only has to think of the matter of Mao, so frequently the satirical subject of Chinese painters today. When he was alive many in the West made a profitable fetish out of the cult of the Chairman. Now they make a cut from his demise.

In China itself, where contemporary work has limited appeal, the wider art market shows signs of prospering mightily. New-rich countries like Russia have a tendency to buy back their artifacts from abroad, and like Moscow's billionaires China has the money. Financial prudence comes into it too. When banks and stock markets are unstable art can be a more reliable—and more discreet—form of currency. An additional incentive to buy is that, with an increasing number of multi millionaires but severe foreign exchange restrictions, art can be a legitimate means of exporting capital. If the Qing dynasty scroll or Ming vase or antique rosewood furniture at auction in Beijing has been abroad for many years and is re-imported for the sale, the buyer will have the right to re-export it, and so stash some of his wealth abroad.

The art trade invites corruption, and China's traditions of high quality fakery (or 'painted in the style of...' if you will) are imposing. In addition, the rich find it convenient to reward officials who have allowed them to underpay workers, evade customs duties or export controls, erect unsafe structures or ignore health legislation in kind, rather than in traceable notes or bank transfers. As well as being a symbol of a culture's spiritual values, art launders cash. And currently cash is China's pre-eminent spiritual value.

A reason the fate of art in the new China will continue to be tantalizing even if the present boom subsides is that, as in the economy, politics and international affairs nobody has a clear idea of what is going to happen. Suggesting that China presented the world's most suitable environment for the development of contemporary art, the artist and critic Xu Bing has said:

> It is an entirely unprecedented, completely new situation. Westerners don't know, we Chinese people don't know exactly where it [art] is headed, what it will become. Nobody knows what it will produce. Anything of value is so because of its unknownness.[3]

The last sentence of course makes no sense. The problem with unprecedented situations, as Xu Bing, now an official spokesman, is no longer at liberty to acknowledge, is that in art as in politics they can take negative as well as positive directions. To say that the situation is excellent for artistic production of any kind is a little too close to ministerial assurances that the outlook for the economy has rarely been so good. True or not, the ministers have to say it, but contrary to the impression that the contemporary market sometimes gives, art is not economics.

*

In architecture too the country has gone from paralysis to epilepsy, as the inertia of Maoist China has been replaced by the biggest building site in the history of the world. Nowhere was Oswald Spengler's early vision of dwellers in the modern megalopolis to prove more apt than in contemporary Chinese cities:

> A new sort of nomad, cohering unstably in fluid masses, the parasitical city-dweller, tradition-less, utterly matter-of-fact, clever, unfruitful, deeply contemptuous of the countryman...[4]

Instantly one imagines the towers arising in countless Chinese cities and the hundreds of millions of *mingong*—the new nomads—flocking from the country to construct and settle them. Nowhere are the masses more fluid than in their swift streets and tumultuous department stores. No people are so quickly lost to tradition as the Chinese in their Western cars and clothes, or so clever in their resourcefulness. And no-one is as contemptuous of the countryside as those who have recently escaped it.

Architecturally, the losses from this frenzy of space-clearing and construction have been terrible. For centuries generations of travellers have marvelled at the beauty and idiosyncrasy of the Chinese city. Today there is little that is Chinese about most Chinese towns, beyond the Hong Kong-style advertisements that save them from clean-lined anonymity. Mao hated old China, and was happy to see city walls or ancient monuments pulled down. His successors are indifferent, but the results are the same. For half a century now China has been engaged in an orgy of casual or deliberate self-destruction.

Again the mood is manic, an all or nothing approach. For two decades no one thought to suggest that modernization does not have to be at the expense of the best of the country's past. Too late its current leaders have begun waking up to what they are losing. Qiu Baoxing, a Vice Construction Minister, has deplored the destruction of his country's architectural heritage, but it was a Deputy Director of the State Administration of Cultural Heritage, Tong Mingkang, who put it best: 'What we are doing is like tearing up an invaluable painting and replacing it with a cheap print,' Why has it taken the country's elite so long to see what is happening beneath their noses? Because the New China is in a hurry, and aesthetic qualms could fractionally delay the day when the middle kingdom comes into her global inheritance.

With her change of ideology has come a dramatic change of style. Nothing is more symbolic of today's China, its social and economic relations and its ambitions than a new skyscraper. If it is in the centre of a town like Beijing or Shanghai the land it has been built on will probably be reclaimed *hutongs*. Some included attractive courtyards, though more often they were shabby, tumbledown single-storey houses. In the few that are left men crouch outside in the stifling summer months playing mah-jong or cards.

Many were little more than huts, others had a distinctive, traditional style which made them worth preserving. Sanitation-wise they were nothing to be proud of, but without excessive romanticism they could be described as having charm, and as being the heart of their communities. A terrible sadness afflicts such places when in the throes of demolition. After looking round one I made the mistake of trying to say a few words of consolation to an old woman still holding out in the semi-ruins. Too proud to accept comfort, she told me to be on my way.

No one appears to have given a thought to how to conserve the most characteristic type of popular dwelling in modernized form. It is not only formerly charming lanes that are gone in the race for city space; in the country of ancestor worship cemeteries are being built over. Arrangements whereby the developers acquire potentially valuable downtown land, and the planning permission to transform a centuries old corner of a Chinese city into a bland block of flats or offices 50 stories high, are obscure, for the usual reasons.

Those who lived there would be promised compensation, either in the form of cash or of a flat in the new development, and some of them might receive it. Others might find themselves with less than they hoped, or disposed of in a new high-rise way out on the edge of the city. Depending on the type and age of tenancy, the scrupulosity of the developers and the local officials, some could find themselves on the streets, with nothing.

The number and height of the skyscrapers proclaim that China has joined the world. They may be a standard product, or like those in Pudong in Shanghai or in the best parts of Beijing, by figures like Rem Koolhaas, Paul Andreu (designer of 'The Egg', the new national theatre) or Norman Foster, have architectural distinction. In either case the speed of erection has been phenomenal, especially in pre-Olympic and pre-EXPO 2010 days. Builders are often migrant workers who scarcely leave the site. Working conditions are reminiscent of indentured labour and the truck system. They live on site in hut-like dormitories, sleep on pallets, and are fed basic food.

Again extremes are to the fore. The result of the mass demolition of *hutongs* has been a drastic change in the nature of neighbourhoods, often from low-class, low-paid, elderly or unemployed people to yuppie types. It is not as if we were unacquainted with the pattern. But seeing it happening on such a phenomenal scale leaves you aghast, and somehow apprehensive.

*

Prospects for the Chinese film industry are good. In addition to the talents of their actors and cineastes they have two pluses that no other country enjoys: a national landscape and townscape scarcely known to the outside world, and a largely untold story. Here is an area of the arts where decades of censorship and national isolation have stored up visual treats for the future. In an art form where overproduction can feed banality and boredom, unfamiliarity is a powerful plus. It is sufficient to place a camera in front of Chinese rural scenes, with their idiosyncratic geology, vertical mountains and dramatic gorges, their architecturally distinctive villages (many now disfigured by rural industrialization, it is true) and exquisitely fashioned traditional household and agricultural implements, to dazzle a Western audience.

There are not one but two main untold stories to tell, neither of which has anything to do with orientalist, box-office nonsense: the first is the truth (as distinct from the hints the authorities have so far allowed) about China's communist past, the second about the Wild West atmosphere in the new China. There can be no country on earth where human dramas are so plentiful, because nowhere else has society been transformed so radically and mercilessly in so short a period. And nowhere else, not even in Russia, have the chasms between social and economic classes reopened so abruptly and become so wide and deep. Nor can anywhere compare with China's sheer dynamism, mobility and vivacity.

Politically the potential of film in China, a country which has never in modern times seen the truth about its history on screen, is awesome. That is why the authorities are on the watch, though things are done somewhat less brutally than in the past. A favourite pretext for censorship are nowadays trumped-up problems of quality. A young filmmaker, Lou Ye, who risked telling a story against the background of Tiananmen Square, was told that it could not be shown for 'technical' reasons arising from inadequate quality. To improve things would involve recourse to larger funds, which a controversial filmmaker is unlikely to have at his disposal.

Yet at least films can be made, and Jia Zhangke, a thirty-seven-year-old director, is a good example of where things stand. He was awarded a Lion d'Or at Venice for *Still Life*, filmed on the site of the Three Gorges Dam, whose construction brought about the exile of over a million people. The film will have had as many viewers in France (200,000) as in China. Shunned by the big distributors, he has had to set up his own production company and personally take his work to private audiences, and to 50 universities.

In his view the problem lies in the tension between a willingness to allow the system to evolve and a determination to secure the ideology on which it rests. The situation however, as in the visual arts, is slowly improving, and his last films have been authorized for release. Quantitatively, the fact that a mere 20 foreign films a year are allowed a public showing will doubtless help domestic production. But there is little doubt of the country's genius in the field, and before long we could be seeing serial masterpieces from China.[5]

*

It is rare that the prospects for an entire country are summed up in a novel, but Jiang Rong's *Wolf Totem* does this neatly, if at length. In 2005 it won the biggest foreign rights deal ever negotiated for an Asian novel. Two years later it was awarded the Man Asia Literary Prize, and appeared in English translation in early 2008. Inspired by the author's experiences as a young Beijing intellectual vulnerable in the Cultural Revolution, it tells the story of how he thought it wise to volunteer to go to Inner Mongolia to herd sheep, learn from the masses, and purge his bourgeois soul.

His stay leads him to ponder the meaning of existence, which he finds in the nomadic life of the untamed Mongolian grasslands. Above all he discovers it in the wolf, whose freedom and ferocious energy he contrasts with the sheep-like Chinese. It is the wolf who becomes the true hero of the book. When he returns to the scene of his exile twenty years later the wolves have been exterminated, the grasslands have turned to dust which blows down on Beijing, and the nomads are riding motorbikes.

As so often where China is concerned, Western readers have

frequently missed the point. A critic in the *Times Literary Supplement* offers a typically cosy misreading:

> Harsh and beautiful, *Wolf Totem* reminds us that nature is not always kind and bears witness to the tragic rejection of that lesson in the name of progress in the 1960s, and offers a warning about the consequences of China's rapid industrial development today.[6]

In fact Jiang Rong is a sociologist, and this is a highly political book about national destiny and the Chinese character. Above all it is a patriotic call for a more confident and assertive nation. That is why the People's Liberation Army and China's big employers are recommending the novel to their staff, and why it was allowed to be published in the first place. The notion that China's military, political and financial elites would actively encourage the public to read a novel whose message was confined to the sanctity of wildlife, the desecration of the Inner Mongolian grasslands and the ravages of industrialization is quaint.

A few passages help to explain the enthusiasm of the authorities. The author's voice is heard clearly throughout the book, and his sentiments can be startling:

> 'In world history', Chen continued the thought, 'nomads have been the only Easterners capable of taking the fight to the Europeans, and the three people who really shook the West to its foundations were the Huns, the Turks and the Mongols. The Westerners who fought their way back to the East were all descendants of nomads. The builders of ancient Rome were a pair of brothers raised by a wolf... The later Teutons, Germans and Anglo-Saxons grew increasingly powerful, and the blood of wolves ran in their veins. The Chinese, with their weak dispositions, are in desperate need of a transfusion of that vigorous, unrestrained blood.'

One does not think of Maoist, or indeed post-Maoist China as lacking the military spirit. Nor are current Chinese military spending plans modest. But then the effort is necessary, Chen appears to believe, to keep up with the wolfish West:

Learning their progressive skills isn't hard. China launched her own satellites didn't it? What's hard to learn are the militancy and aggressiveness, the courage and willingness to take risks that flow in nomadic veins.

Yet Jiang Rong is clearly conscious of objections. To this end he gives Chen some soothing lines:

There'd be hope for China if our national character could be rebuilt by cutting away the decaying parts of Confucianism and grafting a wolf totem sapling onto it. It could be combined with such Confucian traditions as pacifism, an emphasis on education, and devotion to study.

Is this passage meant to ally fears of militarism? If so it appears contradictory with what has gone before: a call for pacifism does not sit well alongside praise for a more vulpine view of the world and for Genghis Khan. The fact that Jiang is a democrat, who has said in an interview that China without democracy would be in danger of becoming like Germany in the Thirties, confounds the confusion of Western readers, and makes his message ambivalent to say the least. (As it happens Germany was a democracy of sorts when Hitler triumphed in the Thirties, but never mind.)

A good deal of the book reads like a eulogy of nationalism and raw power. Maybe Jiang Rong was once again trying to dilute that impression when he has Chen say 'Neither food nor killing was the purpose of the wolf's existence: rather it was their sacred, inviolable freedom, their independence and their dignity.' One is not instantly reassured.

The book's contradictions can be squared and Western susceptibilities soothed by arguing that what Jiang Rong is saying is that Confucius and communism broke the spine of the Chinese individual, as well as marginalizing the country's power and influence in the world, and that a new, democratic China would be free, vital and assertive. The trouble is that the message comes across rather more wolfishly than that, and that Chinese readers appear to like it.

Official critics have oscillated nervously between praise and blame, uncomfortable with the guilt ascribed to Han Chinese for destroying Mongolian nature, and with the idea that the Chinese are sheep who need to become more wolf-like; perhaps we need a touch of both, one critic concluded demurely. Probably the novel scraped through censorship because it can be read as a patriotic as well as a democratic call to arms, and the regime is not averse to a bit of ecological correctness. The author has a foot in all camps. His book can be interpreted as a summons to the Chinese to throw off their subservience to authority, while military and business circles presumably read it as a call to steel themselves for the market or military challenges that lie ahead. Both reformist and official readings look forward to a more assertive China. And that is the point.

PROPHECIES

6

'I see arise, far in the East, the cold bright sun.'
The Tang poet Han Yu

As an adviser on Russia and China to an American bank at the time
when the Soviet Union was collapsing and China opening up, I was
pressed to say exactly what I thought would happen in each country. The
bank—a large one—was thinking of investing large amounts, so where
should they put it? Being forced to stop seeing too many sides of a
question and come up with a straightforward recommendation is a
useful discipline. Driven to the wall, my prophesy was that China would
roar ahead, whereas Russia would be a case of two steps forward and
one step back. So I would go more for China. Looking back I suppose
that makes me half-right and half-wrong, in the sense that Russia too is
now moving ahead on the basis of its energy wealth. What the bank
eventually did I do not know. So far it hasn't collapsed.

The question today is different. The enigma is less how China will
fare economically—on that we have form—than the stability of the
regime, on which there is none. In this uncertainty basic questions arise.
Who are the real Chinese? The unisex, boiler-suited men and women of
the '60s, or their slick-tied or high-heeled successors? Even if her leftist
interlude is over, could virulent nationalism return? And as her
economic and military might and international self-assurance mount
might China—bullied by the West in the not so distant past—herself
become a bully, if only on the economic front?

Might we even come to regret the old hostile and resentful though
mercifully self-sealing China of the Maoist years, when in global terms
the country was scarcely on the map? Napoleon warned that 'When she
wakes up the world will be sorry', but you do not need to be a general
to realize that the awakening of more than a fifth of humanity, armed
with the energy, intelligence and sense of cultural identity peculiar to her,
not to speak of a historic grudge against the West and the third largest

nuclear arsenal in the world, could have adverse implications.

On China prophets face a double hazard. First, the novelty of the situation: in the history of humanity, it must be said again, there has been no conjuncture like the one we face, or at least none that I have seen suggested and none that I can think of. This alone makes it tempting to nuance our judgements. If the English and the French are prone to getting each other wrong, despite being neighbouring powers, how likely is it that Europeans can decipher the future of a country whose past and recent history are without parallel? But then in unprecedented circumstances everyone's hunch can be as valid as everyone else's—a reason for not hedging one's bets too much and saying what one thinks.

*

Sinologists and other informed observers have come to a rough consensus, not on what is going to happen, but on a span of possibilities.

1 A gradual transition to democracy, in which political parties emerge, as the CCP breaks down into opposing factions of conservatives and reformists. The result would be a more benign, internationally-minded China.
2 Bankruptcy and chaos, as an unreformed, over-heated Chinese economy hits the wall, partly for environmental reasons, taking the CCP with it. Result: a tumultuously formed democracy, or a strongman of the left or right takes over, or both.
3 Popular revolution. Local rebellions coalesce into a national challenge to the regime. Result: as in 2.
4 The status quo, as the CCP conclude that any serious move towards democracy would be disastrous for its authority, let alone the interests of Party members. Result: a country sailing on a sea of intermittent storms, financial and political, but one that could continue to forge ahead longer than we might like.

Ross Terrill does not believe that a repressive China, however well-equipped with machines, missiles and dollars, can play a dominant international role. Eventually he sees her emerging as a leading force in the world and a fruitful partner in Asia. The trouble with this scenario is that it is difficult to dissent, if only because in the end we all want the best for the country, and for ourselves. A free-minded and cooperative China would be a boon to the world—but when? The usual figure of speech for the time it takes to turn round unpromising situations are oil tankers, but no mere tanker is big enough to serve as a metaphor for a country this size. So while hoping—and to an extent believing—in the eventual emergence of a reformed and smiling China, who has finally discarded old hang-ups, I fear we face a long haul.

Surely her quickening engagement with the world will bring swifter results? Progress here has certainly come fast. In 1978 she had relations with 113 countries; by the year 2000 it was 161. In the '70s she belonged to 21 international organizations and 71 non-governmental organizations; now both figures have roughly doubled. Again the situation has been one of long-term paralysis followed by epileptic change. The speed of normalization of China's place in the world is reminiscent of the establishment of the first Chinese Foreign ministry, the Tsungli-Yamen, in 1861. Then it was the shock of foreign invasions and the Taiping revolt that forced some opening up. Today it was the collapse of Maoism that has brought about a more internationally-minded foreign service.

What was in Chinese minds when they first crept from their shell in 1861? The spirit of some reformists was high-minded. In the words of the new Chinese Foreign Ministry at the time commenting on the reasons for stationing officials abroad, the aim was:

... not simply the transaction of business in which Chinese and foreigners may be jointly concerned... Men's minds, in fact, must have free access to each other before angry collisions between them can be prevented. If there are to be no collisions between them they must thoroughly acquaint themselves each with the other.[1]

Enlightened words, which seem to give grounds for hope this time round. How can the experience of being out there in the world today fail to head off 'angry collisions' and hasten the happy hour of China's integration? In some ways it already has. Her involvement in Africa is an example. At first all she saw was a compliant source of raw materials—33 per cent of her tropical woods, 24 per cent of her oil and 22 per cent of her industrial diamonds. Blundering about the continent, in cahoots with some of the nastiest regimes on the planet, and to the devil with any humanitarian considerations, her behaviour there presented a primitive image of neo-colonialist selfishness.

Now her diplomats seem to have got a small say. As the biggest investor in oil in Sudan, a major supplier of arms, and a protector of the country against international pressures to stop the killing her indirect complicity with the genocide in Darfur, her conduct has been shameful. Under pressure, China softened her support. Though she remains one of a group of countries (Libya, Russia, Vietnam, South Africa) who continue to do dirty work for the regime, she has also finally begun backing away from her friendship with President Mugabe of Zimbabwe, which goes back to 1970. Her position on sanctions on Iran's nuclear ambitions (she has oil interests there too) has become less uniformly obstructive, and she has become more conscious of the cost of her cosy relationship with the military regime in Burma, source of timber and mineral supplies. She has even attempted to take some of the edge off her hostility towards Japan (though it has a habit of coming back.) A greater readiness to show willing on intellectual property rights and on the international aspects of pollution are further examples of a new suavity in her dealings with the world.

But there is another view. Some suspect that there is a tactical feel to much of this, notably on Darfur, and that to a greater extent than other countries caught up in a modernizing maelstrom, China is likely to remain China. An astute specialist has remarked that:

> The Chinese are receptive to globalization as a means to become modern—it is not a goal, it is a means. Policy and behaviour have changed more than Beijing's worldview.[2]

There is nothing anti-Chinese about this observation. For all their surface transformation national political cultures do not change as quickly as we might wish, and there is a history of the Chinese jobbing back. The heyday of an open door China was at the beginning of the twentieth century, and look what happened to that: by the 1960s there were fewer foreigners there and fewer Chinese citizens abroad than fifty years earlier. And what was the long-term purpose of this opening up? At around the same time those pious words about foreign contacts being 'not simply the transaction of business' were written, Foreign Minister Li Hongzhang submitted a memorial to the Emperor trying to rescue a steamship-building programme that was under threat, in terms that might have had some appeal for Chairman Mao:

> The method of self-strengthening lies in learning what they [the barbarians] can do and in taking over what they rely on… If we can really and thoroughly understand their methods—and the more we learn the more we can improve—and promote them further and further can we not expect that after a century or so we can reject the barbarians and stand on our own feet?

This of course was written in colonial times, when the Chinese had a legitimate aspiration to rid themselves of the Western incubus. Yet the psychology has not wholly changed. The tradition of 'Chinese learning for substance, Western learning for function' has never quite gone away. When the phrase was first coined by Zhang Zhidong, another late nineteenth century official, it was meant to encapsulate the case for moderate reform, but the separation of function and substance has persisted. The Chairman was keen on Western and Soviet learning when it came to the nuclear arming of his country, but the Chinese 'substance' was Mao Zedong's thought, a key aspect of which was that correct political thinking trumped science and technology.

For all the changes in the last thirty years, a kernel of this idea of the West as a mere repository of functional knowledge remains. Today the substance/function split is that between politics and economics. In insisting on 'socialism with Chinese characteristics' the CCP is in effect defending the old authoritarian order handed down from the Qing or Maoist dynasties. As previously its essence is discipline, nationalism, corporatism, and centralized control. These reflexes are more than circumstantial, arising from outside pressures; they pre-date the Western intrusion into the Middle Kingdom and are in that sense genetic. Yet more reasons why a benign revolution, should one come, is going to take time.

*

I make no apology for glancing, once more, backwards. We shall get nowhere in predicting the future behaviour of China unless we bear in mind her resentments, ancient and modern, and recognize the extent to which they are justified. China herself will not forget. It is this heritage of humiliation this makes her touchy about being pushed around, whether about her treatment of dissidents or the environment. An example. Now for the first time she is the world's biggest emitter of greenhouse gases, but when she complains that she has been growing for a mere thirty years, whereas the West has been polluting for two centuries, China has a point. No one is going to feel good when the music is stopped just when they join the dance, especially if they have only just taken up dancing.

As a further caution against expecting to see China clamber onto the international stage like some amiable giant panda, it is worth posing a simple question: what modern example is there of a newly powerful nation, or in China's case an old one re-born, failing to assert itself in a forceful way, especially if it had colonial and cultural scores to settle, as China does?

When it comes to having regard to the susceptibilities of other nations, why should a newly confident China behave in a more restrained manner than the Romans, the Turks, or the British and Americans in their heydays? I am not speaking of wars of conquest, but of more modern ways of imposing one's will in the world. The world into which China is emerging moreover is in an unprecedented state of flux: globalization, the recession, the environment and terrorism are just four factors. Its re-entry has been at speed and turbulence is inevitable.

On the plus side I admit to surprise at the extent of the *de facto* loosening-up happening internally at present—a reflection I believe not so much of the tolerance of the state as the tendency of people to take some matters into their own hands and get away with it. In the Maoist years of absolutism things were easier to police; now that there is a modicum of freedom even China's repressive apparatus appears to be stretched, as well as more corrupt and inefficient than in the past.

I do not exclude the possibility that as the atmosphere softens it becomes conceivable that a reformist revolution may sweep the country in the shorter rather than the longer term, and prove reasonably successful. Yet my lack of optimism in this area remains undimmed, and for me one of the least attractive futures for the country seems the most plausible.

I can picture a China run by the CCP, or something very like it, that with some first aid and one or two surgical interventions by the government along the way, could endure and prosper for decades. The fundamentals of the regime would be the same two ingredients that are keeping President Putin aloft in the polls in Russia: money and the motherland. Economically it could be more of a roller coaster than Russia, though the eventual rewards could be greater. Politically it would remain an authoritarian regime, though adept at avoiding confrontation by giving some leeway here and there.

There seems likely to be a good deal of lurching about, as the CCP attempts to push the country forward while holding its people back— willing the horse onwards while keeping a tight grip on the reins. Yet the horse may prove unruly. An impression has formed in the West of the Chinese as a supremely disciplined people, but as one writer has remarked, this is a radical misunderstanding: under Mao 'China was not in essence disciplined, but temporarily terrorized.'[3] A particular eye should be kept on the huge output of students, only 50 per cent of whom were finding satisfactory jobs on graduation a few years ago. If it hits trouble the CCP will only have itself to blame: it is after all the Communist Party who, in its first 27 years in power, accustomed the country to the rule of violence in politics.

Another source of tension will be between the government's wish to encourage entrepreneurial capitalism while inclining social policy to the left. As successive Party Congresses have shown, a kind of politics is already operating within the CCP in this regard. Most notable has been a new law of contracts to give workers more stability of employment.

At the same time firing procedures have been made less easy and compensation increased. The new law came into force in January 2007, amidst rumours of a cataclysm in the Chinese economy. To date it hasn't happened, but that has not prevented a wave of strikes in mid-2010 by workers determined to improve their often miserable lot in a country where differentials are increasingly glaring.

China seems headed in the right direction, though we should not underestimate the intrinsic volatility of the situation as the country hurls itself at the future. Domestically and internationally its politics are like some huge jelly that has yet to set. It is enough to look at China at the beginning of 2010. Till then the assumption was growing that the country would assume her rightful place in the world smoothly, peaceably, and without expansionist aspirations. Then something seemed to be change, suddenly, between East and West. All at once Obama's America appeared weaker, a melting glacier to China's erupting volcano. You didn't have to listen very hard to detect the tectonic shifts as American power subsided and that of China rose. Obama's cancellation of NASA's Constellation programme that was eventually to return astronauts to the moon at a cost of $100 billion, may have seemed commonsense to us. But for China, with her eye on space, the decision must have looked hugely symbolic.

Her indignation at Obama's decision to welcome the Dalai Llama to the White House was to be expected, but her rage was vehement, with threats of economic repercussions. These seemed more than ritualistic displays of anger. For all their new sophistication many Chinese nurture irrational suspicions of the West, which surface at the slightest setback in relations. This is because they are rooted in a conviction that foreigners are intent on derailing the country's rise by undermining the unity of the Chinese nation, notably in Tibet and Taiwan.

Actually all America wants in Tibet are more rights and more autonomy for an oppressed people. It stops short of proclaiming the province's right to independence, China's greatest fear. As for Taiwan, advances in its economic and political ties with the mainland have gone a long way to defuse tensions. Yet around the same time China chose to mount a hue and cry around America's sale of up-to-date weapons to its Taiwanese ally, to whom it is bound by treaty, mainly as a balance to

China's own colossal military expansion.

Then there was her obstructionism on ways to stop Iran's development of nuclear weapons, a vital Western interest if ever there was one. Even the Russians were coming round to the inevitability of tougher sanctions, but the Chinese were holding back. What explained this attitude? A cynical readiness to do business with anyone anywhere, in pursuit of oil and in defence of Beijing's dogma of non-interference in other countries' internal affairs.

Next we saw her execution of Akmal Shaikh, a British citizen, for drug-running, in the face of top-level pleas for mercy from the British Government, on account of his mental condition. The Chinese had a case, but it was as if Beijing was determined to show the British first and foremost who was who in the post-colonial world.

Then a senior Chinese rear-admiral proposed that his country should establish a permanent military base in the Gulf of Aden, to help its anti-piracy operations. Nothing wrong with that: anything that promises to curtail the hostage-grabbing off the Somalian coast would be good for all. (During the Libyan crisis in early 2011 she was also to dispatch her first frigate to the Mediterranean). How can we complain? What China was doing was what we ourselves had done in our imperial heyday: plead the need to secure our vital trade routes as a means to expand our international power and influence, and in the Libyan case, protect our nationals.

Taken together, what all these incidents seemed to show was that China is a country growing in confidence at a dizzying rate, a nation that had begun feeling its oats. With its growth rates and position as America's number one creditor, it would be strange if her success in overriding the recession had not made her more conscious of her international muscle, and more ready to wield it.

After this strained period the atmosphere seemed to change, relations between China and the West becoming suddenly smoother. First came Beijing's backing for another round of UN sanctions against Iran over the nuclear issue. Then they cheered the US Government and Western stock markets by allowing the yuan to slide upwards against the dollar, within limits. Finally came the overdue but nonetheless welcome acknowledgement of North Korean culpability in the launching of the

Korean War, an admission that made nonsense of years of Chinese diplomatic history and decades of propaganda vituperation against the United States – not to speak of the position of pro-Chinese, anti-American opponents of the war in Europe. And to round off these months of see-sawing attitudes towards China, stock markets retreated sharply at the end of June on news that the growth of her economy might be winding down: a reminder of global interdependence that put other events in the shade.

To say we must expect more ups and downs in relations would be an understatement: in October 2010 came the award of the Nobel Prize to the dissident Liu Xiaobo, and China's fluorescent geyser of indignation. With memories of the disdain of the world fresh in its subconscious ('No fightee, my coward John Chinaman'), the Chinese will push the boundaries of their influence ever outwards and not be deterred by Western complaints. The size of their standing army –over two million men—and the rate of increase in the military budget—18 per cent in 2007, and planned to increase by 12.7 per cent in 2011—are awesome. The launch of a stealth fighter at the beginning of 2011 also dramatized the improvement in technical quality in her armed forces.

Despite what China says it is not simply the Taiwan standoff that drives her policy. She will not be above some soothing gestures (the Chinese Minister of Defence has visited a worried Japan). Yet until someone comes up with a compelling reason why China should not aim in the long term to approach the level of military power enjoyed by Russia or the United States, and finds the means to stop her, rearmament will roll on.

Relations with Russia seem likely to follow a similar course to the last century, but in a lower key. A joint counter-terrorism exercise in Moscow was code-named, nostalgically, 'Friendship 2007.' Yet for all the two countries' protestations of amity there can be no going back to the grand old days of the Sino-Soviet alliance, when for a brief moment the Chinese seriously considered abandoning their millennia-old script and adopting a Cyrillic alphabet. Tactically they share an interest in frustrating the United States. Strategically there is no longer an ideology to glue them together. In the short term, we can expect more displays of solidarity from our authoritarian giants. Geo-politically and racially however it is hard to see how new tensions can be avoided. In the past Russia the communist superpower bestrode large parts of the world, with China as a junior partner. Today the concept of big and little brother is patently outdated. Nobody is going to call the Chinese 'little lemons' now.

It will take time to reach the point where no major international question can be resolved without China, but that will be the aim. While avoiding confrontations, even over Taiwan, she will be a prickly and willful power. As her strength and influence grow she will promote them with increasing finesse but also determination, by means short of war.

Will Hutton's policy recipe—that China requires 'our understanding and engagement, not our enmity and suspicion'—adds nothing to the argument, since it is a view shared by most. Individual politicians exist who are keen to pursue a Cold War agenda and manufacture imminent military threats, but officially no Western government regards China with enmity and suspicion. They can't afford to. Any perception that the world is ganging up on China, whether in Darfur or Tibet, is likely to be met by the Chinese not by dissatisfaction with their own Government, but a wave of nationalism the Government would no doubt encourage. There is no need for the West to pull its punches on Chinese actions on Tibet or anything else, always remembering that our interests and those of the Chinese themselves are best served by a China that is outward rather than inward-looking.

The truth is that on policy towards Beijing we face the illusion of options. There is no option of a fundamentally hostile stance, just as there is no option of significantly speeding up reforms everyone would like to see. Push too hard for change and the Chinese will recoil; push not hard enough and even token gestures (such as the release of dissidents) will cease. On the need for 'engagement' about which we hear so much, an absurdist logic is beginning to prevail. The more westernized China becomes the better the case for engagement, and should she show signs of slipping into atavistic habits (as in Russia) the more urgent it will become for engagement to be reinforced. What this means in reality is that there are no circumstances short of war in which the case for engagement ceases to apply.

While professing concern about her politics Western governments will have their eyes trained on her economy. In a country where GDP grew 30 per cent from 2004 to 2006, and that has continued to lope ahead despite the recession, no one can say that the CCP has not shown results, or staying power. For all the forest of construction and the evidence of vastly improved living standards in the towns however, the rate of progress must eventually slow. As noted, one thing that could stop the Chinese miracle in its tracks is pollution, and the Chinese know it. Previously they had given the impression of being resolved to plough ahead with their dirty development regardless of the ecological cost, but that is no longer true. Not that they are romantic about these matters: they have simply understood that unless they act their entire national advance could be aborted, or even reversed. Their colossal investment in wind power is one example of a new realism.

The 'Chinese house of cards' argument cannot be totally ignored, if only because we have never seen a house this size built at this speed. Of course the ricketiness of the country's in some areas of the economic structure is alarming: its technically insolvent banks, its manically inflated housing market, its lack of national brands. A glance back at what she went through under Mao however confirms the truth of Edmund Burke's observation about there being 'a deal of ruin in a nation.'

In today's China, come the worst, there is scope for greater ruin still, without the country toppling over. (The CIA's 'descending spiral', mentioned earlier, is relevant here.) National unity, ruthlessly enforced by Mao, can no longer be taken for granted: 'China is united', it has been pointed out, 'mainly by its political order, its motorways, and its hatred of Japan.'[4] Yet even if the worst should happen and the country is pulled apart by economic strains and regional conflict, in terms of population each of those regions—centred on Beijing, Shanghai or Canton—would be bigger than Japan.

*

Meanwhile it would be a mistake to overlook the human factor. By shutting themselves off from the world for almost half a century the Chinese have spared us their competition in numerous fields, and their abrupt resurgence will provide the world with a vast increment of talent. This has implications for the American and European psyche that are rarely discussed; it is one of those things we prefer not to think about, since thinking makes us uneasy in any number of ways.

In the past we have recognized China's historical achievements, though in a somewhat condescending, archaizing manner, as if all this belonged to the past. Parity of esteem in the contemporary world will be a new experience for us. We are a long way from the days when Lord Napier could call a senior Chinese official a 'presumptuous savage', and remind him that the King of England ruled over an empire greater than the whole of China. A top-down approach will no longer work.

Whatever form it takes—military, financial or diplomatic—the spectacle of individual Chinese wielding power or influence over us will in some measure feel belittling to the West. For centuries our supremacy as leading spirits in the modern seemed assured, a god-given ascendancy. It wasn't racism in the virulent, aggressive sense; it was just that even the most mediocre specimen of Western civilization was deemed a cut above the average 'Chinaman.' The former doyen of American China studies John K. Fairbank put it well:

> Even the most undistinguished American citizens—dead beats escaping their failures, remittance men sent abroad for their families' sakes, stowaways and adventurers—once they disembarked at Shanghai had upper class status thrust upon them. Like the Chinese gentry, they were set above the masses, not subject to local police coercion. Embarrassed at first to be pulled by a human horse in a rickshaw, the average American soon accepted his superiority and found Oriental life and its inexpensive personal services enjoyable.

Now we are going to have to get used to a different kind of relationship, in which Westerners could find themselves more often, metaphorically speaking, between the rickshaw's shafts. It was Spengler again who foresaw this, almost a hundred years ago:

> And so presently the 'natives' saw into our secrets and understood them, and used them to the full. The innumerable hands of the

coloured races—at least as clever, and far less exigent—will shatter the economic organization of the whites to its foundations.[5]

Suddenly there are rich mainland Chinese travelling the globe as tourists or businessmen, some of them sophisticated folk and some with a lot more cash than culture (one of the wealthiest Chinese of recent times, Lai Changxin, could hardly write his name.) In the first months of 2007 alone sixteen million Chinese (equivalent to a quarter of the French or UK population) went abroad, and many more have followed since.[6] Within a few years many more Chinese will be visible in the West, not just as moneyed travellers but at the highest social, intellectual and artistic levels, in our schools, our universities, our concert halls, as well as our banks and international institutions. Already Chinese academic distinction in American and British universities is legendary. As their numbers mount there will no longer be anything 'exotic' about the Chinese presence in the West.

Currently about 50 million people of Chinese descent live abroad. And whereas previous generations often felt alienated from their country for obvious political reasons, now they will feel themselves to be cultural (if not passport-holding) citizens of one of the world's proudest and most prosperous powers. The counter-demonstration mounted by Chinese inhabitants of San Francisco— home to the biggest overseas Chinese community in America—during the protest about Tibet when the Olympic torch was carried through the city in April 2008 was significant in this regard. When it reached Canberra, Australia, pro-China demonstrators outnumbered the protesters.

As more passports are issued, students opt to stay on abroad and people smugglers prosper, Chinatowns the world over seem destined to grow. It would be absurd to see the flourishing overseas Chinese community as a fifth column, though with the internationalization of Beijing's interests and influence questions of dual allegiance will inevitably arise, as they can with other nationalities. There have already been instances of the involvement of overseas Chinese in industrial and defence equipment espionage. Jung Chang's experiences over publicizing her biography of Mao in Asia tell us something else. A schedule of interviews with a number of Chinese-language papers in

South East Asia had to be scrapped when, one after another, the newspapers withdrew. A recommendation appears to have come from Beijing to ignore the book. The local newspapers in question were not communist dupes; whatever their politics they were dependent on the mainland for advertising, news or supplies.

As the numbers and wealth of overseas Chinese grow, much will depend on the degree of integration they seek, or avoid. Currently this appears to vary: in North America and Canada especially, where the Chinese are the biggest minority, ahead of the Indians, there is a good deal of mixing. In Europe and Australia, less so, though the Chinese presence is growing: in Sydney they are more than seven percent of the population, and in Melbourne 5 per cent.

Perhaps it is the relative proximity to China, and the fact that an increasing number of immigrants and students come from the mainland rather than Hong Kong and South East Asia, but as we saw over the Olympics feelings of patriotism there appear to be on the increase. This is hardly surprising: today there is more for an overseas Chinese to take pride in. In the longer term, however, as an increasingly powerful China stretches its limbs in the world, there could be problems.

*

Assuming we shall see one, a stable, secure, satisfied China from which the scars of resentment and itch for historical vengeance have faded is decades away. In the meantime I foresee some difficult times. A Soviet-era Russian joke is apposite:

> *Question:* The East-West situation is getting tense. Will there be a war?
> *Answer:* No, no war, but such a struggle for peace that there won't be a stone left standing.

A large part of that 'struggle for peace' could be economic. To date however it is extraordinary how swiftly and un-contentiously China has begun to join in the global market and place large investments in major Western firms. *Prima facie* there is no reason why she should not: it will reinforce her position in the financial world as an international player and partner. The entire Western strategy towards China has been one of involvement, and today she is involving herself in in the most tangible way possible: by buying large slices of our businesses, a trend that the recession has speeded up.

The first big step was the acquisition by the China Investment Corporation of a stake of some 10 per cent in Blackstone, the private equity group, a sudden and somewhat quixotic decision which turned out to be at the beginning of a bad year, 2007. Having taken a hit from that when things turned sour after intimations of a credit crunch began, you might have thought the CIC would retire for a period to treat its burned fingers. It is a measure of China's aggressive global strategy that the corporation should have come back for more a mere six months later, this time buying a $5 billion stake in Morgan Stanley on advantageous terms, after the firm felt the need of capital to shore up its holdings after sub-prime market losses.

It tells you something about the relative smoothness of China's 'coming out' into world financial markets that nobody joked, or even smiled at the irony of a communist party riding to the aid of global capitalism in its hour of need. Lenin had said that capitalists would sell you the rope to hang them, and here was Mao Zedong's party pouring in money to ease plutocratic anxieties that a noose might be tightening around their necks.

Next it was the China Development Bank putting money into Barclays Securities, together with a Singapore institution. Given that the CIC alone have hundreds of billions of dollars in foreign exchange funds produced by the country's trade surplus with the West to play with, more will follow. And naturally enough, like any old-fashioned imperialistic power, the Chinese are seeking secure supplies of raw materials at the lowest prices they can engineer. It is estimated that China will consume more than half of the world's key resources, such as copper, nickel, coal and iron ore, within a decade. (In 1990 China accounted for a mere 5 per cent of copper and 3 per cent of iron ore). No wonder she is engaged in high-level financial and diplomatic manoeuvres to ensure supplies.

If deals of this magnitude are done in a single year, how big could China's stake in Western companies become—assuming continued growth and high export performance—in the next decade? Would Western nonchalance hold as Chinese communist sovereign wealth investment in major Western firms powered ahead? As I write there is speculation about Beijing buying a piece of the stricken oil company BP. Should it happen it would be hugely symbolic from the British and American point of view, since vast numbers of people have BP shares in their pension funds. How would they feel about the future worth of these pensions being decided to some extent by a notionally communist regime in Beijing?

To date there has been no objection to such deals of the kind of that scuppered the acquisition by a Dubai-owned firm of P&O ports in America, on an appeal to Congress, citing security reasons. Nor has Taiwan featured prominently, not least because its businessmen are happy to work with China themselves. Yet if Chinese investments and takeovers grow on the scale promised, the atmosphere could change. At present, when many a Western financial institution is on its uppers, relief at new money coming in from China or the Gulf States is the instinctive response. Once the credit crisis abates, anxieties about what has happened could follow. It seems hard to believe that her investments in key Western companies will not at some stage be described as 'predatory', or that Beijing's motives will not be questioned.

Another worry could be the stability and reliability of Chinese investment institutions themselves. The CIC has a pedigree as long as its first investments, namely five or six years. Chinese banks are looked at askance in the West, not least because of their government-enforced duty to prop up loss-making nationalized industries for fear of massive unemployment, and Chinese investment vehicles could also come under suspicion of not operating on market considerations alone.

Again one thinks of Russia. In Moscow there is little doubt that the Kremlin and its business agents are increasingly in charge of financial strategy, and that foreign policy is closely intertwined. The starkest case was the Ukraine, where Russia applied the simplest of blackmail measures: as part of her effort to bring it to heel she played the energy card, threatening to jack up prices even more than she eventually did and briefly interrupting supplies. As our reliance on her goods becomes greater than our power to influence her decisions, a similar indifference to international opinion could spread to China.

So the doubts pile up. On top of the problem of the state direction of sovereign wealth funds and the potential misuse of financial powers for political purposes comes the question of corruption. Although China appears to lack a mafia as murderously imposing as that of Russia, there have been huge financial scandals. The greater China's involvement in the outside financial world, where the rewards come in pounds, yen and dollars rather then non-exportable *renminbi*, the larger the risk, somewhere in the world, of Chinese Enrons.

What can be done to forestall this risk? The Chinese will not take kindly to any suggestion of discrimination against their investments, and retaliation could follow. Despite the quiescent reception so far there has already been some tough talk by the head of CIC, Lou Jiwei, pre-emptively warning Western governments not to stand in the way of deals for protectionist or security reasons. As a former deputy minister of finance, Lou spoke with authority. His warning did not prevent the American Senate establishing an enquiry into sovereign wealth funds controlled by foreign governments. I doubt whether the Chinese liked that.

*

Anyone who wants to make our skin creep about the Chinese challenge has merely to quote Sir Robert Hart. The day would come, wrote the most famous Westerner in nineteenth century China, when China would:

> ... take back from foreigners everything foreigners have taken from China, will pay off old grudges with interest, and will carry the Chinese flag and Chinese arms to many places... thus preparing for the future disasters and upheavals never dreamt of.

We must hope that, insofar as Hart's prophesy was true, we have seen the worst under the old-style CCP. When it comes to assessing the future Chinese threat, if any, the heart of the matter is not so much economic or military as political, cultural and psychological. Russia sees herself as a powerful regional state with a national destiny as overlord of Europe. Perhaps the only reason we do not think of China as another Russia is that any threat by her of a *droit de regard* in the affairs of other countries would be aimed not so much at us, as at her Asian neighbours. Zones of influence could include the erstwhile tribute-paying countries of South-East Asia, and one day perhaps Japan.

There is a school of thought that it is fundamentally mistaken to attempt to see Chinese actions in Asia through Western eyes.[7] According to this view China may now revert to the stable and peaceful dominance of Eastern Asia she exercised from 1300 to 1800, before Western intrusion demolished this benign system. The benefits of a hierarchical structure were that, since each country knew its place and happily paid tribute, China did not need to indulge in foreign wars of expansion, to which she was in any case uniquely disinclined. Meanwhile there was no need to construct balances of power favoured amongst Europeans, since nobody challenged their hegemonic Chinese master.

Those who uphold this theory argue that the (to date) peaceful rise of China and the speed with which countries such as Malaysia or South Korea have moved to accommodate themselves suggest that East Asian states are reverting to a successful pre-modern form of collective security under China's smiling aegis. Huge new opportunities for trade, it is emphasized, and for mutual Asian enrichment will cement the new commonwealth of nations.

It is right to look at the foreign policy future of China in Asian rather than simply European or American terms, yet this optimistic prognosis for much of Asia, in which China once again emerges in idealized terms and the West as crude-minded 'Realists' and balance-of-power villains, concerned merely with military power to the exclusion of cultural factors, leaves a number of questions unanswered. One is whether independent nations, especially Japan, will be as content to kowtow to China as they were centuries ago. Another concerns the readiness of Far Eastern states to establish friendly relations.

The main reason South East Asian countries are currently establishing cooperative ties with Beijing is that China has ceased denouncing them as US lackeys and threatening them with the export of revolution, while demonstrating her belligerence by provoking conflicts with India, Vietnam and Russia. When the regional dragon stops breathing fire and smoke and takes to commerce instead, as China appears to have done, people feel good. Yet that leaves the question of how long it might last, and how great a burden China's dominance might become, when her GDP overtakes that of the US.

There is a more basic reason for widening our eyes at this best-of-all-possible-worlds theory. For obvious reasons it is one that tends to be promoted by some of the most radical American critics of American foreign policy. But look at it another way. If it were to be seriously suggested that peace and stability could best be secured in the world by less powerful states simply accepting American domination and acting as tributaries to Washington, as befits their intrinsically inferior status in the hierarchy of peoples, many of these self-same critics would have something to say on the theme of neo-imperialism and the rights and dignity of nations.

For the present China's care to project a 'peaceful rise' image is winning her friends. It is not hard however to conjure scenarios in which she might be tempted to make her muscle felt. They could range from regional security to environmental issues or fishery rights, or the treatment of overseas Chinese minorities. Precedents for friction are not lacking In 1965 Mao had to watch passively while thousands of Indonesian communists (the PKI), the majority of them Chinese, as well as innocent overseas Chinese were slaughtered by General Suharto after a failed uprising abetted by China. Vietnam, whose reluctance to behave as a tributary to China and taste for evolving tributaries of her own in South East Asia has caused conflict in the recent past, is another example. In 1979, following Hanoi's invasion of Cambodia and the alleged mistreatment of overseas Chinese, causing them to pour northwards across the Vietnam/China frontier, China launched a punitive strike against North Vietnam which, militarily speaking, turned out to be less than imposing. Today, the problem of the Paracel and Spratly Islands, south of Hainan, claimed by both countries but occupied by the Chinese, remains outstanding.

Malaysia, a country in which the Chinese once led a communist insurgency, where Islamicization is in progress and where resentment against Chinese economic dominance simmers, could be another flashpoint in the region. India, China's chief rival in the Asian explosion of wealth, is a case to herself. Though both sides are striving to keep up appearances there is a legacy of mistrust and hostility expressed in frontier claims and clashes, and by China's closeness to Pakistan. Meanwhile the tensions we have been seeing over Tibet appear set to last. It seems inconceivable that two giant Asian nations can expand in harmony without a feeling that each is somehow cramping the other. The least that can be said is that these two cultures are not made to get along.

Finally there is Japan, where despite mutual assurances of a more friendly era, new frictions can easily occur. In late 2010 Chinese and Japanese boats confronted each other near the islands called Diaoyu by the Chinese and Senkaku by the Japanese in the East China Sea. This was more than a fishing rights squabble: deposits of oil and natural gas lie in an area claimed by both sides. Currently Japan administers the islands, and normally chases Chinese fishing vessels away. But not this time, as the Chinese, aided by a naval vessel, declined to comply. Another symbol of growing power and confidence.

*

The way to gain a clearer perspective on the future is to put our preferences aside, forego moralizing, and ask quite simply what seems most likely to happen? Is the West in for trouble? If we put the question the other way around—will China's integration into global affairs run smoothly?—the answer appears obvious. Given the historical and racial background, and the way others have behaved before them, how can we expect the Chinese to refrain from the misuse of their economic power in their national interest? If they were to refrain it would be a first for the world.

Without going so far as to promote the 'accept Chinese hegemony in Asia' thesis, one of America's foremost sinologists, David M. Lampton, argues that successive US administrations have tended to see Chinese power too much in coercive terms.[8] By this he means their concentration on the growth of the Chinese military, Beijing's intrusion into African or South American markets and politics, and the aggressive strength of its exports. (In Europe China now exports more than America and imports less than Switzerland). Lampton's view nevertheless is that America underestimates China's importance as a buyer, importer and investor, as well as her diplomatic and cultural powers:

> If US policymakers continue to view China's power in substantially coercive terms when it is actually growing most rapidly in the economic and intellectual domains they will be playing the wrong game, on the wrong field, with the wrong team.

Maybe. But the attractions of 'soft power' in a country hardened by generations of conflict may prove finite. A reason for the bestiality displayed by the insurgents in the Iraq war is that its people were for years brutalized by a savage dictatorship and have no modern civic traditions to speak of. Something similar (though less extreme) is true of the post-communist Russians, who lumber about the world like a man with a pit-bull for a pet, because for centuries their lives have been brutal too, and subject to invasion. And for all its layers of civilization something similar could be true of China, whose relative stability and wellbeing are a mere thirty years old. There is a limit to how much delicacy and restraint can be expected from a country where war, starvation, cannibalism, dictatorship, merciless repression and the practice of barbaric cruelty on a vast scale are matters of living memory. Hardness of heart and a steely, self-seeking ambition would be a more natural reaction to the past. That is what we are seeing inside a wolfishly capitalist China, and it would be odd if her behaviour abroad were totally different.

Other American critics, such as Robert D. Kaplan, have made the same point as Lampton, while drawing different conclusions.[9] Whenever great new powers have arrived on the world scene, such as Germany or Japan, the argument goes, they have tended to be particularly assertive, throwing international affairs into violent turmoil. Such people anticipate either a new Cold War with China, expressed in a series of sporadic clashes, or one big hot one, and advocate a policy of containment. How this is to be achieved they do not say.

Somewhere between Lampton's 'soft power' thesis and this harder position lies Henry Kissinger. The former Secretary of State doubts the relevance in our day of both European experience of expansionism and, in a nuclear age, of the conflicts of the past. China, he believes, operates on a different level altogether. She does not go in for a strategy of winner-takes-all, preferring to pursue the psychological weakening of the adversary over time—a prediction that is at once soothing and alarming.[10]

The most famous description of late imperial China was by Lord Macartney: 'The Empire of China is an old, crazy, first-rate man-of-war', who may drift on for a while before being dashed to pieces, and 'could never be rebuilt on the old bottom.' Today China behaves like a country who knows where she is going and is moving at reckless speed. The analogy now would be with the first-rate Maglev train that takes you from downtown Shanghai to the airport at 430 kilometres per hour. It is a slightly frenzied trip, where the passengers, strangely alert, gaze at the scenery zooming past part in wonderment, part in apprehension. In many ways we are all aboard. While marveling at the ride it is natural for us too to be alert and somewhat apprehensive.

POSTSCRIPT

A TALE OF TWO BOOKS

'The Chinese is never an isolated individual, he is always
the representative of a collectivity.'
Paul Claudel, 19th century French diplomat and writer

Of the books on China I have read in the past four decades two in particular have stuck in my mind. One was *The Chinese Chameleon: an Analysis of European Conceptions of Chinese Civilization* by an Oxford sinologist, Raymond Dawson.[1] The other was *Mao, The Unknown Story*, by Jung Chang and Jon Halliday. They were published at an interval of nearly forty years, their views of the Mao era could not be more different, yet the books and their reception tell us a great deal about China, as well as ourselves.

I heard about Dawson's book on my return from Beijing in 1969. As I began reading it I wished I had known about it before going. It had come out in the middle of the Cultural Revolution, in 1967, but we were too busy monitoring the reality of China on the ground to read theories about it. As I progressed through the book my enthusiasm for it grew. It seemed a wonderfully informed, highly readable and frequently amusing account about how the West had so often got China wrong.

'They have no beards, and agree partly with the Mongols in the disposition of their countenance' noted Marco Polo, who as a Venetian was the first to spot that this was also a merchants' paradise. 'The custom of swathing women's feet is very good for keeping females at home,' a Dominical missionary opined in the seventeenth century. 'An example and a model even for Christians' said some Jesuits at the same period, who appear to have been more understanding and imaginative than their narrow-minded Protestant rivals for the souls of the 'heathen Chinee.'

'A contemptible herd of ignorant sordid slaves, subjected to a government qualified only to rule such people' said Daniel Defoe, through the mouth of Robinson Crusoe. 'So gay, friendly, beautiful, sane, Hellenic, choice, human' wrote the critic Goldsworthy Lowes Dickinson in the Thirties. 'If such a people could be lifted onto a higher economic level without losing these qualities, we should have the best society this planet admits of.'

By drawing together widely different and wildly subjective views on the country, Dawson's aim seemed to his admiring reader less to teach us about China (though of course he does) than about ourselves: our Eurocentrism, our casual cynicism or racism, our gullibility, our invariable condescension where China was concerned. A wise, necessary, enlightening work I recall thinking as I was half-way through, and a warning to all who deal in China as a commodity on which to put our stamp, rather than a distinctive and complex culture.

Then something extraordinary happened. In the final chapter on twentieth century China, Dawson's book falls apart. The professor who has spent the last two hundred pages reminding us of our perilous illusions about the country reveals himself as a hopelessly deluded apologist for the Mao regime.

At the time his book was published Dawson was 44. He had been a student in Oxford during the war, and broken off his studies to join the RAF and train as a navigator. In the last months of the war he found himself on a Japanese course. He graduated from Oxford in Greats, but the East had left its mark and he came back to read Chinese. After a spell setting up Chinese studies at Durham he returned to teach at Wadham College, Oxford.

Dawson was no fevered-eyed revolutionary. In many senses his was a conventional background, his career and opinions typical of his generation. A genial soul by all accounts, like many privileged Oxbridge academics who had seen something of the war he was a socialist, and for half a century till his death in 2002 he set crosswords for *The New Statesman*. Many of his readers, friends and colleagues would have known his views on China, and in the climate of the '60s few would have found reason for complaint. Such people moved in cosy circles, and to them there would have appeared no inconsistency between his warning against misreading China in the past and his own gullibility where Mao was concerned.

Fresh from seeing the country in the throes of an ideological frenzy which had brought it close to war, my reading of this part of the book was different. I was (perhaps naively) shocked to discover that a professor in Britain's most prestigious seat of learning could smile at the fables and fabrications of the past while himself being in thrall to some of the basest falsehoods of his times. The Professor could not plead ignorance. China was a closed country, but he was a specialist and anyone who wanted to get an idea of what was going on could do so. At the age of twenty-three, before I had set foot on the mainland, or learned Chinese, I knew pretty much what was happening. Admittedly this was because I was working on Russia and China in the Foreign Office Research Department, but the raw material that gave us most of our information was not secret, but available to anyone who genuinely wanted to know.

Oirs was our bureaucratic name for the papers we produced—overt intelligence reports—and they were collected by the simple means of systematically interviewing a sample of the tens of thousands of Chinese refugees making their way to Hong Kong. The fact that they came in such numbers – these were the early Sixties - told its own story. Some had exceptional permission to leave, or to come on official business, but the majority contrived to make their way illegally across the land frontier. Alternatively they spent months getting themselves in condition in a Canton pool, before laying their hands on a couple of inner tubes or a tyre, choosing an overcast night to avoid British and Chinese patrol boats, and swimming across Deep Bay into the Colony.

Mostly the refugees were from Guangdong, the province adjacent to Hong Kong, though the most desperate and determined came from as far away as Xinjiang in the North West. The information they provided was not by and large of military significance; it was more important. In a society as closed as China's the West's most urgent need was quite simply to know how people lived: how many calories a day they consumed, the availability of meat, the intensity of the family planning campaigns, attitudes to the Party. Through these facts we sought to judge the growth of the population, how the agricultural communes introduced during the Great Leap Forward were working and the behaviour of the communist regime. In other words it was the kind of 'intelligence' that would have been common knowledge in a normal country.

Frequently it included harrowing accounts of why the individual had left: often it was because of hunger, persecution by communist cadres, a sense of desperation and a determination to join relatives abroad, or in the case of a scattering of intellectuals, writers and journalists, the impossibility of living their daily lies. It was my job to condense these reports into regular surveys of mainland life. As I brought it all together I used to try to imagine daily life in a Chinese commune. For all the mass of first-hand information that crossed my desk during the two years I wrote these reports, somehow I failed.

Our Cantonese-speaking soldiers in Hong Kong were not the only ones interrogating refugees: the Hong Kong and international media were doing it too, some for sensationalist headlines, others to write honest, detailed reportage. But the raw facts were available to all. So there was no excuse whatsoever for Western intellectuals choosing to believe primitive mainland myths rather than balanced accounts that appeared.

Having been to China himself, Dawson had even less. After spending six months in the country during 1958, the year the Great Leap Forward was launched, one might have thought he would find space for a word about the most momentous of Mao's political campaigns till that date, and one that was to prove the most costly in human victims. Designed to secure in years economically what it had taken other countries decades or a century to achieve, the campaign was pursued with an absolute disregard for life. In the famines of 1959-1961 that followed the campaign the fortunate in stricken areas stayed alive by eating leaves and bark. As in the famine of 1942, some resorted to cannibalism, in which children were killed and boiled for food.

When Dawson published his book six years later the facts were already known, yet his response was silence, even though it was commonplace at the time to observe that in 1966 Mao was in danger of repeating the extremist follies of 1958. Yet in a sense Dawson had no choice but to ignore the truth, not only on The Great Leap but about the Cultural Revolution as well. To be faithful to the theme of his book—how the West repeatedly and culpably misunderstood China—

he would have had to cite praise from himself and his scholarly milieu for Mao's disastrous policies as an example of the West's habit of giving precedence to its fantasies about the country over the facts.

So numerous were the victims of starvation in these years that Marshal Peng Dehuai, defence minister at the time, had dared raise a voice in dissent. It was not as if he had little experience of seeing death in the mass: he had led Chinese troops into the Korean War. Mao did not forget. When the time came to square accounts in the Cultural Revolution he was denounced as a Rightist, brutally interrogated and beaten up before dying in jail.

By speaking out honestly in his book the Oxford professor would have risked nothing more than his reputation in the eyes of Chinese officialdom as a reliable Western defender of the regime. As so often in his generation, however, where communism was concerned intellectual courage was notable by its absence, most obviously in France but also in high places in Britain.

So much for Dawson's dishonourable silences. When he speaks, it is worse:

> Finally I think that hostility to [Chinese] communism can be partly explained by the fact that for the Western European nations and the United States, which not long ago thought that the future of the world lay with their mode of living, it has been a traumatic experience to find an entirely alien way of life having an immense success in Soviet Russia.

Again my experience and Dawson's had been different. I don't know how much he had seen of Russia, or whether he ever went there, but having lived for a year as a postgraduate student at Moscow University not so long before this was written I had been conscious of no 'immense success.' True, Khrushchev was in charge and things were less awful than under Stalin. Dissidents were no longer shot, just put away. Yet thinking of the time I had spent queuing to buy basic food from half-empty shops, seeing Russian friends harassed by the KGB for consorting with foreigners, or waiting for an hour in the snow for a place in a restaurant where I would wait another hour to be served, or seeing the gloom and penury amongst which the average Russian lived, not to speak of the mendacious propaganda, I failed to recognize the country the Professor spoke of. I also found it strange that a distinguished academic should speak about politics in such didactic, uninformed simplicities. But then I was young.

Worst was to come. There is a moment in the defence of repressive regimes by highly educated men and women at which the argument turns from loyalty to the cause through silence and evasion to intellectual mendacity pure and simple. With Dawson it happens when he touches, gingerly, on the question of 'struggle meetings'. Here only the professor's words will do:

> Underlying this distrust of Communism is the more fundamental antipathy of an individualistic society towards one that emphasizes group activities... Communal activity in contemporary China, whether by neighbourhood or street groups or Party or workers' organisations, seem to many Westerners to involve an intolerable intrusion on individual liberty, especially when members of such groups take part in self-criticism or criticism of their fellows.

He admits that these self-criticism sessions can have a propaganda purpose 'which can be abused', but remains very much in favour. 'The benefit in human terms of group activity as opposed to isolation is not always understood by the outsider. The therapeutic value of group activity is, however, well recognized by psychologists.' Things turn from the lamentable to the tragi-comic when he quotes a Professor Sprott as having made an 'on-the-spot' study of these matters, which concluded that such meetings engendered 'a tremendous force of collective conscientiousness.'

By choosing to publish his defence of the punitive collective action against individuals these meetings involved a year after the Cultural Revolution had got underway, Dawson showed poor timing. But then that is how misconceptions as profound as his are exposed by reality. There is an uncanny parallel between his mishap with the truth and the hasty emendation by the Stalin sympathizers Sydney and Beatrice Webb of their book *Soviet Russia: A New Civilization?* It was published in the mid-Thirties and, like Dawson, his soul-mates the Webbs were caught out by events. Just as the authors decided to drop the question mark for the second edition, the Moscow show trials opened, in which numerous Party and military leaders were tortured into making grotesque public confessions before being shot.

The Webbs made things worse by hastily adding a postscript to their book by a Western lawyer defending the Moscow trials. Like Dawson on China he took the line that Soviet procedures were morally superior to those of the West. Purblind Westerners underestimated 'the therapeutic value of group activity' in China, in the Professor's view, and unlike us the Russians, the lawyer claimed, did not go through the farce of a pointless courtroom defence, in which guilty men wasted everyone's time by claiming to be innocent, but encouraged them to make a clean breast of their crimes. Far from being an indictment of the Soviet system, the Moscow trials showed it to be more honest than our own.

*

Professor Dawson was doubtless a humane man, with a great respect for China. Though not, it seems, for the Chinese as individuals. In this he was not alone. As the quotation at the head of this chapter from the nineteenth century French writer Paul Claudel shows, a tendency to see Chinese people in the mass, and to deny them the personhood we so jealously claim for ourselves, has long been characteristic of the Western approach. To this day an unwritten assumption remains that the Chinese, unlike others, are a species of collective human being. It surfaces casually, recently in the response to the remarkable 2007 exhibition of some of the recently discovered terracotta figures from the tomb of China's first Emperor Qin Shi Huangdi. Many critics marvelled at the fact that the soldiers or horsemen or musicians had individualized expressions, as though it would have been more fitting, given that they were Chinese, if they had anonymous, standardized faces.

Dawson seems to share this view where political and social freedoms are concerned. Personal rights he would have indignantly reasserted had his Government denied him the right to speak his mind on China are implicitly swept aside when it comes to the Chinese themselves. This insouciant view of the rights of others is no monopoly of left-wingers of his generation. It would have appalled Professor Dawson to hear it, but his underlying attitude would be shared by many a contemporary Western businessman eager to make a killing in the country.

I have met many businessmen over the years, some of them knowledgeable about China and respectful of individuals, though most of them prone to deal with the Chinese solely in quantitative terms: how many people, how much profit. What attracts the average businessman to China today is its huge market. Political reform interests him or her less, except if it concerns freedom to own property or the updating of commercial law. Then he is all for progress. On human rights he will have less urgent convictions. You can argue that campaigning for individual rights in a foreign country is not a businessman's job. A professor of Chinese, on the other hand, surely has an interest in promoting intellectual freedom amongst the objects of his study. Some might say a duty. Though not Professor Dawson, it appears, or the many who thought like him.

What it comes down to is this. Whether the Chinese are seen in the West as promising material for ideological experimentation, as in the professor's view, or as a promising source of profits, makes no difference. Either way the Chinese are not to be encouraged to behave as the individuals they ultimately are. Instead they are perceived as passive instruments to whom things are done, by colonisers, by dictators, by Western political theorists, or by investors.

In implicitly denying the Chinese the right to be a person in the full sense, the Marxist and the businessman are at one. The Marxist exults in the pressures of the community that force the individual to conform. Our businessman, for his part, shrugs off the notion that the Chinese deserve democracy as much as anyone else (I have heard them do it), on the grounds that they are a different race for whom personal choice means little - which happily predisposes them to eat junk food in McDonalds or wear identical jeans. In each case, it should be noted, a collectivized China is used to serve a Western purpose, whether the reveries of intellectuals, or fatter profits.

However camouflaged by high-toned academic theory or by the

salesman's low appeal to economic imperatives, this reluctance to treat the Chinese as real people has undertones of the bar-room kind. *They all look and behave alike* is the thought most likely to find space in the bar-fly mind, a state of affairs which, if only it could be brought about, would delight the socialist collectivist as much as the consumer-chasing manufacturer and salesman. Reasons for the lenient attitude shown by so many in the West towards Mao's 'abattoir of a state' include sheer indolence and a kind of patronizing sentimentalism, but there is something harsher.

By way of excuse for the fatal attraction of Chinese communism for intellectuals of Dawson's generation much is written about their generous hearts and good intentions. But there was a darker side. The assumption that Chinese lives and Chinese suffering weighed less in the balance than that of Europeans was crucial in condoning experiments which would have been unthinkable in the West. Behind their failure to question what life was like for ordinary people in communist China lurks a quasi-racist reflex. Implicitly (though never of course openly) the China in which the deaths of tens of millions was (and sometimes is) defended on the grounds that sacrifice was inevitable in the cause of the socialist future, is seen as a country of clones with a dispensable surplus of population.

In an ant-like society (*Life just doesn't mean the same there, does it?* the subconscious thinking goes), what does it matter if some get trodden on? In a worthy cause, naturally. Dawson may not have known it at the time, but it was during the Great Leap Forward, when he was in China, that Mao toyed with the idea of abolishing people's names and identifying them by numbers.

Dawson implies that the collective spirit instilled in the Chinese by centuries of cooperative agricultural practice (why only China?) makes them congenitally superior to selfish Westerners. Self-abasement before less evolved societies can be a form of condescension, but that aside we must doubt his sincerity. Did he believe that in our societies too all classes and conditions should submit to the inquisition of the masses? I don't think so.

He would have relished a hands-on criticism session in his Oxford quad conducted by the college cooks and bedders as much as the

Western businessman would enjoy working a robotic twelve hour day, seven day week in one of his textile or computer investments in China. And just as the professor celebrated in the safety of his study the therapeutic value of being mentally beaten up, so the Western man of commerce today downs his cocktails in a swanky Shanghai bar, marveling at the phenomenal Chinese work ethic and sense of social discipline.

In his book Dawson chides America for its 'obsession with the idea of freedom'. Personal rights he sees as an encumbrance we are guilty of foisting on China, a Western intrusion into its culture. Both Mao and the present Chinese administration would agree. So might the various American software companies who decided to cooperate with the Chinese Communist Party to suppress the right to access sensitive links on the web, such as 'democracy' or 'Tiananmen Square'. Though their motives are different, 'objectively', as Marxists of Dawson's generation liked to say, both the leftist professor and the capitalist corporation can be accessories to the denial of the Chinese personality and of Chinese freedoms.

*

It is poignant to think of our mild-mannered, crossword-setting don in any sense conniving, however unconsciously, in one of the greatest evils of the twenty-first century. Yet that is what he and others like him did, even if they have largely escaped criticism. The final section of Dawson's book brought no outcry at the time, and none since. Although it appeared in May 1967, the main review in the *Times Literary Supplement* (unsigned, in the fashion of the time) said nothing about the contrast between Dawson's agreeably cooperative China and the bloodier, irrational one in the news.

Failure to hold sinologists and other champions of Mao to account, or to discuss how intelligent people could have been so deluded, is another aspect of the China differential. Should you opine on events in France or America you are expected to make some sort of sense, and if you are a distinguished specialist who talks or writes moral nonsense in the end someone will reprove you for it. On China you can say pretty much anything, and as we have seen, people do.

When it comes to facing up to the past the contrast with the Soviet Union is telling. With some gallant exceptions the threshold of tolerance of Soviet atrocities in Russia by the Western intelligentsia of the day was notoriously high. In China it was higher, even though the toll of Mao's victims was roughly treble that of Lenin and Stalin put together, his personality cult more extravagant, and his suppression of human freedom more ruthless and efficient.

Apologists for Soviet Russia have frequently been exposed to ignominy by later generations, and those like Professor Eric Hobsbawm, who decline to recant their Stalinist past, invite revulsion. Holocaust deniers and the vindicators of Hitler face similar distaste and condemnation. Yet China specialists who remained silent or found ways to justify policies that led to the death of millions are rarely invited to perform a little self-criticism themselves. And when the extent of their intellectual collaboration with Maoist atrocities renders criticism inescapable, all we hear is that people like Raymond Dawson were merely dreamers and idealists. Fashioning one's dreams from the living flesh of others is not ideal behaviour, one might have thought, especially in Oxford professors.

*

And still today we have our dreamers and idealists. A few years ago I watched a TV discussion on BBC *Newsnight Review* of a book that was making waves on China. It was *Mao, The Unknown Story,* the steely biography of the Chairman by Jung Chang and Jon Halliday. A remarkable team, they had devoted ten years to unearthing the truth. Jung Chang, though a British citizen now, was brought up in China: as recounted in *Wild Swans* she had lived through the Cultural Revolution. And in a book relying heavily on newly accessible Soviet records about China, Halliday was a Russian speaker.

Selected to discuss the book were a gallery director, a journalist best known for her campaign to legalize cannabis, and a popular sentimental novelist. In the discussion none suggested that a reappraisal of Western attitudes to the Chairman would be in order in the light of the book's revelations. The gallery director sniffed that he found the whole thing rather negative. Mao was responsible for the largest man-made slaughter in the history of humanity, and our arts man, reflecting the fads about China common in his milieu, found this truthful account of his actions rather negative.

The journalist was more positive about the book, while simultaneously recalling, fondly and with no sense of remorse, the time when she and her friends were Maoists to a woman. I no longer recall the novelist's contribution, which was confused to the point of incoherence. I doubt whether any of them had read the eight hundred pages of the book, but one wonders what effect their opinions had on the viewers. After listening to them it is hard to imagine anyone wanting to read something so downbeat, or that risked making people of their generation feel bad about their rosy, iconoclastic youth.

The Western response to the most important book on modern China to have appeared in decades is a study in itself. Many reviews gave it its due, as the most forceful and well-researched record of the Chairman's cruelty and cynicism ever written. A significant number, however, including a number of sinologists, were loath to part company with the Mao Zedong whose regime they had traditionally regarded as an awesome, if necessarily harsh, feat of socialist engineering.

For them (especially if they were Americans) the adversary had never really been the Chinese totalitarian regime at all, but US policy towards it. In many cases their professional lives had been devoted to writing books or giving seminars challenging Washington's view on China, usually in favour of a friendlier approach. Acceptance of revelations of Mao's atrocities ran the risk of letting former American administrations off the hook by justifying retrospectively their hostility to the regime. What mattered was less the facts about China than parochial political concerns.

In these institutionally sinophile circles (liking China is fine, providing it does not undermine the critical faculty) such domestic or foreign policy excesses as the Chinese communists are admitted to have committed tend to be seen as the result of American policy failings. Had America engaged more positively with communist China from the beginning, I have heard it argued, for example by extending financial aid after the 1949 revolution, she would not have had to drive her people so hard in economic construction, and fewer would have starved or perished. Had America not cold-shouldered the new regime and given it the respect it deserved, others have stated, maybe it would not have gone to war in Korea. Then there is the question of the wisdom of America's military guarantees to Taiwan. Whatever the point under discussion, for such scholars the onus of the various disasters that afflicted China under Mao was invariably on the West.

The cruelest thing you can do to Anglo-American Puritans is to rob them of their sense of guilt, and that has been one effect of the book by Jung Chang. Not a few China experts responded with scarcely suppressed fury. Of course there were the usual debates about judgments and sources, but the onslaught went further than that, and a group of American academics went to the extent of setting up a website devoted to tearing the book apart. Fortunately there were exceptions, notably in the case of the China specialist Jonathan Mirsky, a former Asian editor of *The Times*. Such honesty was rare.

By concentrating on the deaths and suffering Mao had brought about, it was said, the authors were being one-sided. What about the improvements in health, schooling and housing? And surely Mao deserved praise for uniting his country? There are answers. One of the reasons the book dwells on Mao's atrocities is the damning new material the authors unearthed over a long period. Another is that it was time to reconfigure the Chairman's image after so many decades when the bloodiest aspects of his regime had been underplayed. And most importantly, many of the 'positive' aspects of Maoist China do not stand scrutiny for long when seen alongside the worst.

Medical advances that took place have been frequently oversold, and could have been achieved by a non-totalitarian government. Improvements must also be measured against the deaths caused by policies which brought about widespread malnutrition, disease and starvation. During the Great Leap Forward, according to a report to the Party Secretary Hu Yaobang twenty years later, an estimated 40 million Chinese died. How do medical advances, such as they were, look when set against that figure?

As regards education, large numbers of children went to school in communist China who would not have been educated before. But were an obscurantist dictatorship and the primitive cult of Mao necessary for that? Advances in literacy were not matched by the availability of reading matter, and the Chairman's thoughts increasingly comprised much of what there was to be learned in schools. Any discussion of improvements in education relative to what had gone before must be seen in the context of a suppression of intellectual freedom unparalleled in history, except perhaps during the reign of the first Chinese emperor Qin Shi Huangdi, burner of books and murderer of 460 scholars who were buried alive on his orders. Mao himself is said to have joked about their similarities in a private meeting in 1958, when the intellectuals had been effectively silenced after misinterpreting the 1956 campaign to 'Let a Hundred Flowers Bloom', fatally in many cases, as an invitation to criticize the CCP: 'He [the First Emperor] buried 460 scholars alive. We have surpassed him a hundredfold.'[2]

Another side of life in communist China that has been much lauded was the relative absence of thieves, drunkenness and loutishness. It is true that crime and disorder in Mao's China was low. Travellers returned with Marie-Antoinettish accounts of a poor but honest people, where modesty was the keynote of women's clothes, you could walk the streets in safety at midnight, and hotel maids would chase you down the stairs to return a broken comb or worn-out toothbrush deliberately abandoned. And it was true. Social discipline of every kind was far higher than in the West, but was bought at a cost of the denial of personal freedom at any level of life and of arbitrary and draconian punishments.

Double-think in this area has become part of the fellow-traveling tradition. When robust right-wingers propose that what we need in Britain (or America) is more law and order they will be pounced on for giving the police too many powers and ignoring our human rights. This may be a legitimate view - though not when it comes from people who were lyrical in their praise of the absence of crime and disorder in Maoist China, a country where human rights, as we understand them, were non-existent.

For all our current pessimism about the way the human species is going, there remains an assumption that, when it comes to the twentieth century's most pitiless despotisms, the world has learned its lessons. After the horror of fascism people give a wide berth to anything smacking of racist theories, and think twice before placating, in Chamberlain fashion, totalitarian regimes bent on aggression. After the ravages of communism only soft-living sophomores are attracted by the notion that ends justify means, however savage, or that human lives are mere eggs to be broken by Marxist dictators to make a better omelette. All this is progress of a kind. Where China is concerned however many have learned nothing, and there remains a stubborn (if often tacit) belief that human sacrifice under Mao was vindicated by results.

Again we see the China differential. Few would any longer seek to excuse the horrors of Stalin's Russia by reference to the increased output of engineers or the growth of steel production under his Five Year Plans. The same is true of Nazi Germany. Like Mao, Hitler was a mesmeric figure who enjoyed the devotion of a majority of his people, and whose advent to power in the destitute early Thirties was a boon for the German working man. The jobless rate declined dramatically, and incomes rose. Holidays also doubled—on that score the German worker was the best treated in world—and idealistic young people participated in all sorts of socialistic, state-sponsored programmes to improve their health and physique.

Yet no-one sees the Führer's economic successes as in any sense legitimizing the Nazi dictatorship, and they get short shrift in books about him. No serious historian would state that in arriving at a judgement on Hitler due account should be taken of his contributions to social welfare, or that his guilt for mass slaughter must be seen in the context of his housing record or health education successes. Like Jung Chang and Jon Halliday on Mao, biographers of the Führer tend for excellent reasons to focus on the negative. The comparison is crude, yet it is worth recalling that the total number of soldiers and civilians who died from all causes in Hitler's European war was some fifty million. In China Mao was responsible for the deaths of almost one and a half times that number.

Even the BBC were reluctant to admit the importance of the book by Jung Chang. For several weeks after its appearance the Corporation's Chinese language service made no mention of it, still less sought to interview the authors. Only when an item noting this censorship by silence appeared in the press was Jung Chang offered an interview. She accepted on condition that there would be no cuts in her broadcast, as had happened to her on the BBC before. No doubt the editors feared that her readiness to speak the truth about Mao would be found 'provocative' or 'offensive' by the Chinese authorities.

Banning the book makes good sense for the Chinese Communists themselves, who have their own mythology to preserve. The official CCP computation of the Chairman's merits and errors, as we have seen, is that he was 70 per cent right and 30 per cent mistaken, the seventy million deaths he brought about presumably featuring in the minority percentage of failings. In years to come, as the truth seeps out and the Chinese become less ready to accept sanitized accounts of their past, this calculus could be inflected in a less positive direction, and Jung Chang's book seems likely to play a historic role in the process of de-mystification.

Its suppression in China will slow but cannot permanently impede the truth. Despite the best efforts of its rulers the China of today is porous. Many Chinese now travel abroad, and chief among those who do are cadres and officials, a lot of them more sophisticated than in the past. The self-censorship of the old days, when disciplined communists wouldn't read controversial material even if given the chance to do so, is fading, and the Chinese translation of the book will be procured and read and passed from hand to hand by influential people.

Modern China being the manically entrepreneurial country it is, where demand exists someone will supply it. Thirty years ago it is unthinkable that a banned book would be brought out and sold in a pirated edition, let alone one denouncing the Chairman as a bloody dictator, but that is what is happening. Copies have been advertised on Chinese websites before the authorities caught on and closed them down. In seeking to suppress the book both China and the BBC are fighting a losing battle.

A full-scale relaxation of official attitudes will take time. When I tried out the Chinese reaction to the book on my last visit the response was as expected. After affecting not to have heard of it, a middle-aged academic and former communist official I spoke to told me somewhat brusquely that there was no interest in the book in China, a lie so splendidly surreal that for a moment I felt a pang of nostalgia for the old days: if it's banned, how can there be much interest? Even younger Chinese can display a sensitivity that confirms the book's potential power. Unconsciously echoing the older academic, an intelligent, thirty year old, modern-minded editor I had lunch with told me that no one would want to read a book so full of lies. As he spoke he had the grace to look shifty; I assumed that, as someone who traveled abroad, he had read it.

For now the Jung Chang biography will remain underground, an unexploded bomb, off limits for 95 per cent of the population. It is true that a fair percentage of these, especially in the countryside, remain nostalgic for the Mao era, and would be scandalized by what they read. They no longer starve but life is hard, especially where health and education are poor, and they find themselves at the mercy of unscrupulous entrepreneurs and officials. Yet the persistence of the Mao myth simply postpones the inevitable, and the longer the delay the greater the impact will be. When the time is ripe China will have its 1956—the year Stalin was denounced by Khrushchev—and when it does the fallout could be worse than in Russia.

Khrushchev's speech came only three years after Stalin died in 1953, and Mao has further to fall than the Georgian dictator. However much the Russians respected him for defending their homeland in war, historically he was a lesser figure than Mao. Stalin was not the originator of the revolution: that was Lenin. Nor was he seen as the unifier of the nation. Mao was a national as well as an ideological figure, the incarnation of China, its founder, guiding spirit and chief executive all in one. Only when his reputation is officially revised downwards will the historical falsity amidst which the Chinese continue to live their lives fall away.

NOTES

Preface

[1] William Hazlitt, Essays.
[2] Modern China by Graham Hutchings, Penguin Books, 2000
[3] See Golden Mangoes: The Life Cycle of a Cultural Revolution Symbol by Alfreda Murck, Research Fellow at the Palace Museum, Beijing.

Chapter 1

[1] John Pomfret, Chinese Lessons, reviewed Times Literary Supplement, 20 April 2007.
[2] Quoted in Red Dust, Ma Jian.
[3] See Guy Sorman, L'année du coq: chinois et rebelles, Fayard 2006.
[4] Montesquieu, De l'esprit des lois, book V chapter 2.
[5] New York Review of Books, 17 January 2008.
[6] Mao, The Unknown Story, by Jung Chang and Jon Halliday, Jonathan Cape, 2003.
[7] Jean-Luc Domenach, La Chine m'inquiète, Perrin, 2008.
[8] World Bank Quarterly Survey November, 2007.

Chapter 2

[1] David Hockney and Stephen Spender, China Diary, Thames and Hudson, 1982.
[2] Sir Robert Hart, These From the Land of Sinim, Chapman and Hall, 1901.
[3] Alberto Moravia, The Red Book and the Great Wall, Secker & Warburg 1968.
[4] Bernard-Henri Lévy, Sartre, The Philosopher of the Twentieth Century, Polity 2003.
[5] La Chine, Sera-t-elle Notre Cauchemar (China, Our Nightmare?) Editions Mille et Une Nuits 2005.
[6] An enlightening report on this subject appeared in the French newspaper Libération on 26 August 2007.
[7] My account of the dispute over the translation of yi and subsequent passages draw on Lydia H. Liu's The Clash of Empires: The Invention of China in Modern World Making, Harvard University Press, 2004.

Chapter 3

[1] Introduction to Imperial China: China Readings, edited by Franz Schurmann and Orville Schell, Random House 1967.
[2] See Roderick MacFarquhar, New York Review of Books, 28 June 2007.
[3] Partners in Power: Nixon and Kissinger by Robert Dallek, HarperCollins 2007.
[4] Introduction to Imperial China: China Readings, edited by Franz Schurmann and Orville Schell, Random House, 1967.
[5] Peter C. Perdue, review in H-World, August 2000, of The Great Divergence: China, Europe, and the Making of the Modern World Economy, Princeton University Press.
[6] See Breaking Open Japan: Commodore Perry, Lord Abe, and American Imperialism in 1853, by George Feifer, Smithsonian/Collins, 2007.
[7] See Giovanni Arrighi, Adam Smith in Beijing: Lineages of the Twenty First Century, Verso 2007.
[8] A.V.Lukin, Medved Nabludayet Za Drakonom (The Bear Watches the Dragon, China's Image in Russia from 17-21 Century) ACT, Moscow, 2007.
[9] Chetire Tisyatch Kilometrov Problem (Four Thousand Kilometres of Problems), by Akihero Ivasita. Moscow, AST, 2006.
[10] SSSR-KNR: Ot Konfrontatsii K Partnerstvu (USSR-CPR: From Confrontation to Partnership), Y.S. Peskov, Institute of Far Eastern Studies, Russian Academy of Sciences 2007.
[11] I.A. Malevich Vnimaniye, Kitai. Attention—China, Minsk-Moscow, Harvest, AST 2001
[12] Speech at the Royal Society, 29 October 2007.
[13] Professor A.D. Voskresenskovo.
[14] Zhongguo Keyi Shuobu (China Can Always Say No), Beijing 1996.
[15] A.V. Lukin: Medved Nabludayet Za Drakonom (The Bear Watches the Dragon, China's Image in Russia from 17-21

Century), ACT, Moscow 2007.

16 Andrei Piontkovsky, *At The Edge of the Middle Kingdom, Moscow Times,* August 15, 2005.

17 Putnam Weale, *Manchu and Muscovite,* Macmillan 1907.

Chapter 4

1 Guy Sorman, *L'Année du Coq: Chinois et Rebelles,* Fayard 2006.

2 For an excellent survey see Edward Lucas, *The New Cold War: The Future of Russia and the Threat to the West,* Palgrave Macmillan 2008.

3 *The Times,* 15 September, 2007.

4 *Sunday Times,* 24 June, 2007.

5 See his article in the *Times Literary Supplement,*1 June 2007.

6 *The Tiananmen Papers,* compiled by Zhang Liang and edited by Andrew J. Nathan and Perry Link, Little Brown 2001.

7 Zhao Ziyang, *Captive Conversations,* by Zong Feng-ming.

8 Jonathan Fenby, *The Penguin History of Modern China,* Allen Lane 2008.

9 Vladimir Milov, *New York Review of Books,* 15 May 2008.

10 Will Hutton, *The Writing on the Wall,* Little, Brown 2007.

11 Ross Terrill, *The New Chinese Empire, And What it Means for the United States,* Basic Books 2003

12 *Democracy's Good Name,* by Michael Mandelbaum, Public Affairs 2007.

13 I am indebted for these quotations to Guy Sorman's accounts of his meetings with dissidents in *L'année du Coq: Chinois et Rebelles, Fayard 2006.*

14 *Aujourd'hui la Chine,* 22 January 2008.

15 See Pankaj Mishra, *Times Literary Supplement,* 11 January 2008.

16 I am indebted for these details to Abel Segrétin for his study on this subject in the French daily *Libération.*

17 *The Times,* 7 November 2007.

Chapter 5

1 Interview in *The Art Newspaper,* March 2008

2 Guardian Unlimited, blog of 16 February 2007, *Don't believe the Hype about Chinese Art.*

3 Interview in *The Art Newspaper,* March 2008.

4 Oswald Spengler, *The Decline of the West.*

5 See *Le Monde* 30 December, 2007

6 Jennifer Wallace, *Times Literary Supplement,* 18 April 2008

Chapter 6

1 Tsungli Yamen (Foreign Ministry) circular issued in 1875.

2 *The Making of Chinese Foreign and Security Policy in the Era of Reform, 1978-2000,* Edited by David Lampton, Stanford University Press 2001.

3 Jean-Luc Domenach, *La Chine m'inquiète,* Perrin 2008.

4 Ibid.

5 Oswald Spengler, *Man and Technics,* 1927.

6 *Les Echos* (French economic newspaper), 14 January 2008.

7 See for example David C. Kang, *China Rising: Peace, Power and Order in East Asia,* University of Colombia Press 2008.

8 *Foreign Affairs,* January/February 2007.

9 'How We Would Fight China', *Atlantic Monthly,* June 2005.

10 'China: Containment Won't Work', *Washington Post ,* 13 June 2005.

Postscript

1 *The Chinese Chameleon, An Analysis of European Conceptions of Chinese Civilization,* by Raymond Dawson, Oxford University Press 1967

2 Kenneth Lieberthal, *Governing China: From Revolution Through Reform,* Norton 1995..